Series Editors:
Alan Ware (University of Oxford) and
Vincent Hoffmann-Martinot (Sciences Po Bordeaux)

parties and elections in new european democracies

Richard Rose and Neil Munro
University of Aberdeen

First published by the ECPR Press in 2009

The ECPR Press is the publishing imprint of the European Consortium for Political Research (ECPR), a scholarly association, which supports and encourages the training, research and cross-national cooperation of political scientists in institutions throughout Europe and beyond. The ECPR's Central Services are located at the University of Essex, Wivenhoe Park, Colchester, CO4 3SQ, UK

Book design by Richard Rose

British Library Cataloguing in Publication Data
A catalogue record for this book is available from the British Library

ISBN13 978-0-9558203-2-8

To all those who waited patiently for free elections,
To those who fought for them, and
To those who have fought in free elections

Other titles published by the ECPR Press

Identity, Competition and Electoral Availability: The stabilisation of European electorates 1885–1985
Stefano Bartolini and Peter Mair

People, States and Fear: An agenda for international security studies in the post-Cold War era
Barry Buzan

Elite and Specialized Interviewing
Lewis A. Dexter

System and Process in International Politics
Morton A. Kaplan

Democracy
Jack Lively

Individualism
Steven Lukes

Political Elites
Geraint Parry

Parties and Party Systems: A framework for analysis
Giovanni Sartori

The Return of the State of War: A theoretical analysis of Operation Iraqi Freedom
Dario Battistella

Gender and the Vote in Britain: Beyond the gender gap?
Rosie Campbell

Paying for Democracy: Political finance and state funding for parties
Kevin Casas-Zamora

The Politics of Income Taxation: A comparative analysis
Steffen Ganghof

Joining Political Organisations: Institutions, mobilisation and participation in western democracies
Laura Morales

Citizenship: The history of an idea
Paul Magnette

Representing Women? Female legislators in West European parliaments
Mercedes Mateo Diaz

Deliberation Behind Closed Doors: Transparency and lobbying in the European Union
Daniel Naurin

Globalisation: An overview
Danilo Zolo

CONTENTS

TABLES AND FIGURES

Preface

UNDERSTANDING ELECTIONS

Free elections blow away the pretensions of dictators to speak for everyone; this was spectacularly demonstrated after the fall of the Berlin Wall in November 1989. The elections held in Communist party-states were elections without choice. Officially reported turnout was virtually 100 per cent and more than 99 per cent of the electorate was counted as having voted as the ruling party demanded. Free elections since then have shown that the results of Communist ballots were too good to be true. Instead of unanimity, citizens in post-Communist countries register big differences about who should govern.

The purpose of this book is to examine the results of free elections held since 1990 in the ten new democracies that have become members of the European Union – Bulgaria, the Czech Republic, Slovakia, Estonia, Hungary, Latvia, Lithuania, Poland, Romania, and Slovenia – plus Russia, which influenced their politics in Communist times.

The outcome of an election is a function of laws that determine how votes are cast and converted into seats in parliament; the parties supplied by political elites; and how voters respond to the choices they are offered. While specialists address each issue separately, knowledge of all three elements must be combined to understand electoral competition. Part One provides an overview of electoral competition and comparative analyses of the workings of election systems as outlined in the supply-and-demand model set out in Chapter 1.

Political elites in new regimes have an urgent need to elect a parliament. However, this could happen only after the adoption of an electoral system. Everywhere some form of proportional representation was chosen, rejecting the Anglo-American first-past-the-post system in whole or in part. Free elections offered electors not only a choice of parties but also the choice of whether or not to vote. Chapter 2 compares electoral systems and their effects on the turnout of voters and the proportionality of results.

The West European assumption that political parties reflect established institutions of civil society does not fit Central and Eastern Europe, for these institutions were purged and replaced by puppets of the Communist party-state. Given this legacy, at the first free elections political elites organized parties without knowing how much or how little support they could rely on. Many parties have failed to win any seats in parliament and disappeared; some have merged or split; and new parties have come forward. Chapter 3 shows the fragmenting effects of the entry and exit of parties competing along different political, economic, and social lines.

The Communist practice of telling subjects what to think and do has left a legacy of distrust in politicians and parties. In consequence, most electors in new European democracies do not identify with a political party. Opinion polls find that the 'don't knows' are usually the biggest group in the electorate. Yet most citizens do have political values and outlooks that parties could in theory represent. Drawing on New Europe Barometer survey data, Chapter 4 identifies how distrustful electors differ in their values or remain uncommitted to any kind of distinctive political outlook.

Notwithstanding difficulties, free elections are now an established part of the political process throughout new European democracies. Political elites depend on popular support to gain office and governments are often turned out of office by voters. However, a high level of party competition has not led to the institutionalization of a party system in which voters are offered a choice of the same parties at one election after another. Instead, as Chapter 5 shows, there is a floating system of parties, as political elites frequently disband, merge, or create parties. In response to a rapid turnover in the supply of parties, electors are forced to become floating voters. The resulting electoral volatility is far greater than in established democracies and voters face difficulties in holding governors accountable.

The countries covered in Part Two were chosen on political and geographical criteria. Politically, ten have introduced free elections since 1990 and have had their democratic credentials endorsed by the European Union. The Russian Federation is included because it shows that there is nothing inevitable about the democratization of post-Communist regimes. Whereas the first Russian elections were competitive and showed that the Kremlin could not control Duma voting, elections with "too many" choices have been replaced by a system with a hegemonic United Russia party controlled by Vladimir Putin. The record of the majority of successor states of the Soviet Union is one of unfair and often unfree elections (www.freedomhouse.org; www.osce.org/odihr).

A common set of topics is covered in each country chapter. During the twentieth century all these lands have experienced the radical transformation of their boundaries, upheavals in political regimes, and forced movements of population. In view of the great disjunction between past and present and the prevalence of unfree and unfair elections from the end of the Second World War to 1990, the historical experience of national elections is summarized briefly. The electoral system adopted for the first free election is presented in detail, along with subsequent amendments. The references in each chapter are to articles, books, and web sites with specialist information on each country.

The list of parties identifies all associations that have gained one per cent or more of the popular vote or at least two parliamentary seats in any election. In 11 countries a total of 335 parties meet these criteria. Where there is political interest in ethnic, green, or other parties that do not meet these criteria, their results are included too. Parties that have never received one per cent of the vote are grouped together as 'others'. This avoids treating all parties as equal when the electorate patently does not do so. For example, in the 1991 Bulgarian election, 26 parties had less than one per cent of the vote. The Christian Radical Democratic Party took the booby prize with only five votes.

The name of each party is given in the national language as well as in English to facilitate tracing information in primary sources and identifying party acronyms. Since splits, mergers, and electoral alliances have been frequent, factual information is given, tracking the careers of parties (for further details, see Bugajski, 2002; Day, 2005; Banks, et al., 2007). The numbering of parties makes it easy to link information in the party list with entries in the results tables.

Results are reported for all elections of the principal chamber of the national parliament and popular elections of presidents up to 1 March 2009. Chapters have four two-page tables that give the absolute number and percentage of votes and seats won by each party. Wherever possible, votes and seats have been taken from reports of the government agency responsible for electoral administration. We have edited these figures as necessary to maintain consistency and clarity. For referendums, see Auer and Bützer, 2001.

The authors published an earlier version of this work in 2003 with CQ Press, Washington, DC, under the title *Elections and Parties in New European Democracies.* All the comparative chapters in Part One have been substantially revised and in country chapters both the election results and text have been updated. The European focus of the book makes it more appropriate to publish this book under the imprint of the European Consortium for Political Research. As one of the Consortium's founders, the first-named author particularly welcomes the expansion since then of the ECPR and of European democracies.

Producing a book about elections across half a continent has been possible only with the assistance of organizations and individuals in more than a dozen countries. We wish to thank all the officials of national election institutions for publishing detailed information promptly in print and on the World Wide Web and for responding to questions that arose as we edited official statistics for publication. Useful comments on national chapters in Part Two have been provided by Daunis Auers, University of Latvia; Dennis Deletant, University College London; Krzysztof Jasiewicz, Washington and Lee University; Algis Krupavicius, University of Kaunas; Vladimir Krivy, Slovak Academy of Sciences; Maria Spirova, Leiden University; Rein Taagepera, University of California at Irvine and University of Tartu; Gabor Tóka, Central European University, Budapest; and Stephen White, University of Glasgow. The chapter on Russian elections was made possible with the support of British Economic & Social Council grant RES 062 23 0341 and it also contributed to the analysis in Part One. Karen Anderson Howes has shown exceptional skill in copy-editing a manuscript with references in thirteen different languages.

RICHARD ROSE *NEIL MUNRO*
University of Aberdeen

PART ONE
THE FRAMEWORK OF COMPETITION

1

ELITE SUPPLY AND MASS RESPONSE: AN INTERACTIVE MODEL

Election outcomes reflect both supply and demand. Political elites supply the rules by which an election is held and parties qualify for the ballot. After the fall of the Berlin Wall in 1989 elites took decisions in conditions of great uncertainty about what people wanted, because Communist repression had led to a dissociation between public opinion – that is, what the party allowed to be expressed in public – and the private opinions of individuals (Havel, 1985; Shlapentokh, 1989). There was no time to find out what would be the best way to win votes and seats in parliament. The overriding priority was to hold elections in order to replace discredited Communist officials with popularly elected governors.

While elites propose the choice of parties, voters dispose of their fate. Many theories of democratization go further: they assume that popular values and national political culture will determine what happens to a new regime. Russell Dalton (2000: 934) postulates, 'Citizen attitudes and behaviours will be prime factors in determining how and whether democratization processes continue.' From that perspective, political elites must supply parties that reflect popular demands, or risk electoral failure and the failure of the new regime as well.

To concentrate solely on elites or on voters misses the crucial point: the outcome of democratic elections is an interactive process. Political elites are oligopolists, restricting the supply of parties that appear on the ballot. Competition for votes tests which parties secure the most votes. Concurrently, voters accumulate knowledge about parties from what they do in and out of office. They can decide to vote by rewarding a party that comes closest to their own views, even if it is only a second-best choice or a lesser evil, or they can withdraw their vote from a party that does not live up to their expectations. In the course of time, this trial-and-error process can lead to a democratic equilibrium in which the parties that elites supply become institutionalized as a party system and voters identify with parties suited to their preferences. In the older democracies, it took generations to establish such an equilibrium. However, the shift from Communist party-states to regimes with free elections occurred in a matter of months.

Democratization Backwards – and in a Hurry

Free elections are a necessary but not sufficient condition for the creation of a completely democratic state; it must govern by the rule of law too (Rose, 2009). The rule of law is necessary for political elites to organize opposition parties, for elections to be free and fair, and for an elected government to be accountable to parliament and the electorate. Definitions of democracy that treat elections as a sufficient condition of democracy presuppose a rule-of-law state. However, introducing elections where the rule of law is weak or absent is democratization backwards (Rose and Shin, 2001).

States with the longest record of democratic elections institutionalized the rule of law centuries before granting every adult the right to vote. In England the principle of the king being subject to the law was established in the seventeenth century. So too was the principle of the monarch being accountable to Parliament. Gradually, the law recognized the right of individuals to organize civil society institutions. By the middle of the nineteenth century the government of Britain was accountable to Parliament, even though three-quarters of adults did not have the right to vote and membership in its upper chamber, the House of Lords, was hereditary. Concurrently, Prussia developed a *Rechtsstaat*, a bureaucratic form of government based on the impersonal rule of law. However, the government was accountable to the king and not to the Prussian electorate. In continental Europe elections were often held, but the suffrage was very restricted and so too were the powers of elected representatives (E. Anderson and P. Anderson, 1967). To describe nineteenth-century monarchies of Sweden or Germany as pre-democratic is to project contemporary values backwards into the distant past. Where the rule of law prevailed but elections were undemocratic, the government was a constitutional oligarchy.

After the First World War both old and new states of Europe introduced elections with universal suffrage (Bartolini, 2000). In a minority of countries, this completed an uninterrupted transition from constitutional oligarchy to a democratic rule-of-law state. However, throughout most of Europe fledgling electoral democracies broke down and undemocratic successors took over (Linz and Stepan, 1978). Breakdowns occurred not only in Balkan states, where the rule of law was historically weak, but also in Germany, Austria, Italy, and Spain. Following the Second World War countries such as Germany and Austria, where the foundations of a rule-of-law state had been laid before the rise of Hitler and Mussolini, re-introduced free elections and are now established democratic states. In the 1970s Spain and Portugal re-introduced free elections and have become established democracies too.

Until 1990 the tradition of countries that were incorporated into the Communist bloc was that of a sequence of undemocratic political regimes. Before the First World War Central and Eastern European territories were governed by multi-national empires: the Prussian Empire in Berlin; the Habsburg Empire with bases in Vienna and Budapest; the Russian Empire in St Petersburg; and the Ottoman Empire in Constantinople. The extent to which these empires governed by the rule of law varied greatly. Elections – if held at all – were not based on the principle of one person, one vote, one value; they were based on estates of the realm representing hereditary nobles, landed interests, the clergy, and prosperous urban merchants. Estates were given similar numbers of representatives in the national parliament and an estate with only a small percentage of the population could outvote representatives of a majority of the population (Seymour and Frary, 1918). In Russia, tsarist absolutism frustrated attempts at introducing meaningful elections (Emmons, 1983).

For many nationalities the political goal was to achieve an independent nation-state rather than to create a democratic multi-national state. The 1919 Versailles Peace Treaty sought to apply the principle of national self-determination by creating successor states from defeated multi-national empires. However, most were mixed in their ethnic composition; for example, a third of the population of what was then Poland was either German or Jewish. New regimes held one or another form of election, but by the 1930s undemocratic forces were in control. Parliaments and parties could be intimidated or suspended and, if elections were held, they were unfair or unfree. Rulers of nationalist and authoritarian regimes were more concerned with enhancing their power than institutionalizing the rule of law. Democratic Czechoslovakia was the chief exception to these generalizations.

The Nazi–Soviet Pact of August 1939, the Second World War, the Holocaust, the forced movement of populations, and changes of state boundaries created a great break with the past, even where countries retained the same name. By 1945 Soviet troops had advanced as far west as Prague. By 1948 one-party Communist regimes were common throughout Central and Eastern Europe, non-Communist politicians were purged, and institutions of civil society suppressed. The Communist Party supplied a definition of what the people wanted and, if there were still signs of popular dissatisfaction then, as Bertolt Brecht put it, the government could 'dissolve the people and elect another'.

Communist regimes held elections that were neither free nor fair (Pravda, 1978; Furtak, 1990). Differences between countries were minor: for example, whether the Communist Party was the sole party or controlled a bloc in which nominally different parties were Communist fronts. Voting against the official candidate could not be done secretly; it was a public act that invited reprisal by the authorities. Staying away from the polling station was ineffectual, for election officials padded turnout figures to make it appear that the total population supported the party-state. In the extreme case of the Soviet Union, the official result of the 1984 election reported a turnout of 99.99 per cent and credited Communist-endorsed candidates with 99.95 per cent of the vote (White, Rose, and McAllister, 1997: Table 1.3).

Mikhail Gorbachev's policy of *glasnost* (openness) and *perestroika* (restructuring) undermined the authority of the Communist party-state in its heartland, the Soviet Union. When elections were held in which unofficial candidates could challenge party candidates, Boris Yeltsin became the popularly elected president of the Russian Republic. In other republics Communists used elections to go into business for themselves, claiming independence for historic nations such as Armenia and for ethnically mixed republics in Central Asia. From Belarus to Central Asia, a majority of the successor states of the former Soviet Union have become independent but not democratic. Leaders of many post-Soviet regimes are not failing to democratize; instead, they are succeeding in their goal of establishing undemocratic regimes (cf. Fish, 2005).

In Central and Eastern Europe, public demonstrations demanded fundamental changes in the one-party state. In Poland a semi-free election was held in June 1989. The fall of the Berlin Wall in November 1989 signalled that Soviet troops would no longer shoot to kill. In Estonia, Latvia, and Lithuania, which had been forcibly incorporated as republics of the Soviet Union during the Second World War, multi-candidate elections produced pro-independence majorities for assemblies that now represented the Baltic peoples. In Slovenia a similar process led to its peaceful secession from the Federal Republic of Yugoslavia. Of the 11 countries covered in this volume, Romania was exceptional in its change of regime being accompanied by violent conflicts in which thousands were killed. By June 1990 every country in the region had held an election offering a choice between candidates for and against a Communist party-state.

The political revulsion against the Communist party-state produced a treble transformation (Rose, 2009). Everywhere new political regimes replaced the old; some form of market economy replaced a command economy in which bureaucratic decisions determined supply and demand; and there was a collapse of a social structure based on party cards. The boundaries of 7 of the 11 countries examined here were radically altered – and the first free elections were sometimes part of the process of breaking the boundaries of states.

Multi-party elections were new events for both political elites and voters. Even in Czechoslovakia and Hungary, where relatively free elections had been held immediately after the Second World War, only voters over the age of 65 could have participated. The introduction of electoral contests has aptly been described as 'democracy from scratch' (Fish, 1995). By contrast, the median voter in the first free election held in Germany after the Second World War had also voted in the last election of the democratic Weimar Republic.

Today, ten countries of Central and Eastern Europe (CEE) have had their status as established democracies recognized by becoming members of the European Union (Figure 1.1). The speed with which countries have turned from being dominated by Moscow to being a partner in a league of democratic states rejects theories claiming that democratization is 'a slow process measured in generations' (Dahl, 1971: 47). The rapid tempo with which countries changed from being Communist party-states to new European democracies is consistent with European precedents. Three of the six governments that participated in founding the precursor of the European Union in 1957 had only re-introduced free elections after the Second World War.

Figure 1.1 FROM FIRST FREE ELECTION TO EUROPEAN UNION ENTRY

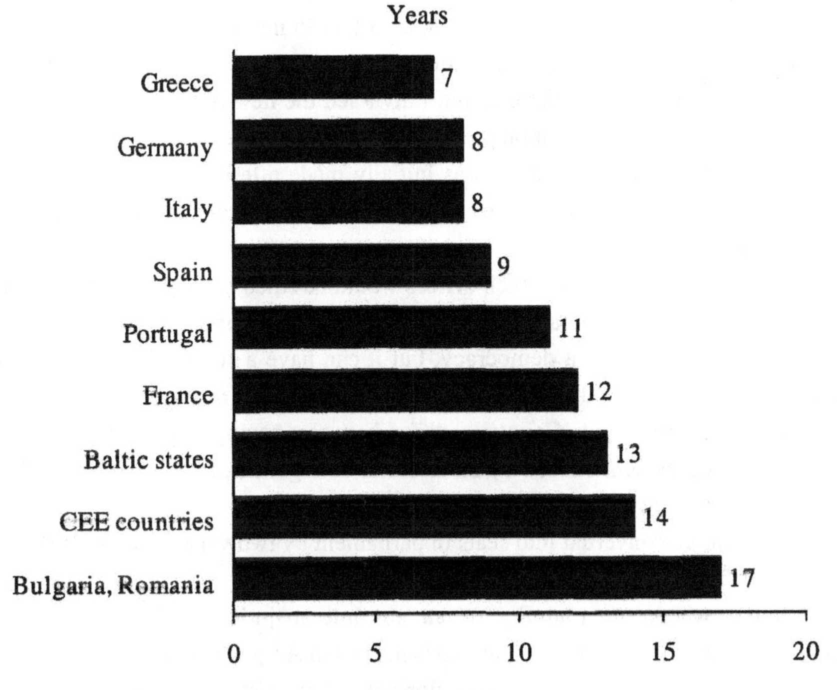

Mediterranean dictatorships were admitted to the EU less than a decade after holding free elections. The new democracies of Central and Eastern Europe have required 13 to 17 years to be accepted as EU members (Rose, 2008). Many problems of governance remain, such as reducing corruption. However, these challenges face older member-states such as Italy and Greece as well.

Understanding Election Outcomes

Differences between electoral systems in established democracies demonstrate that there is more than one way to conduct a democratic election (Rose, 2000; Blais and Massicotte, 1997). In each country, custom and habit encourage rules chosen in the past to be maintained from one election to the next. However, in the founding election of a new regime, election rules could not be taken for granted.

Since elections held in the old regime were discredited, political elites had substantial discretion in deciding the rules of the *electoral system* that would identify winners and losers at the first free election. There was overwhelming agreement that every citizen age 18 or above should have the right to vote. However, in Estonia and Latvia there were contentious debates about who qualified for citizenship. Soviet annexation of the Baltic states resulted in a post-1945 immigration of Russians and the subsequent Russification of education, employment, and government. The size of the Russian minority in Estonia and Latvia led the new regimes there to make citizenship initially contingent on pre-1940 citizenship in the family. Knowledge of the Estonian or Latvian language was initially made a test for Russian-speaking immigrants wanting to become citizens and vote in national elections (see Chapters 10 and 12).

Elites also had to decide which offices would be filled by popular election. An elected assembly, whether called a parliament or congress, or by another name, is a defining characteristic of a democracy, but it can have a single chamber or two. Every country established a parliament and made the prime minister depend on the confidence of parliament. Countries differ between having a popularly elected president or a president chosen by an electoral college; Estonia and Slovakia first adopted one method and then the other.

Votes can be converted into seats in parliament by two very different electoral formulas, a first-past-the-post (FPTP) rule that awards a seat to the candidate with the most votes, whether a plurality or an absolute majority, or by proportional representation (PR). The former method is normal in Anglo-American democracies and it was also normal in the unfree elections of Communist party-states. In Western Europe proportional representation is the norm; seats are allocated in parliament to reflect each party's share of the popular vote. Every country included in this book elects all or some of its members of parliament by proportional representation.

The *supply of parties* reflects both the electoral system and decisions by political elites. Proportional representation makes it necessary for parties to be organized, because seats are distributed according to the share of the vote that parties receive. By contrast, the election of members of parliament by first-past-the-post rules does not require parties, for the winner is the individual candidate with the most votes. Candidates in single-member districts can run as independents or form a local group that does not compete as a party nationwide. The mixed electoral system formerly in use in the Russian Duma illustrates how party systems differ with electoral systems. All the proportional representation seats in the Duma were awarded to parties, whereas in contests held by first-past-the-post the party (*sic*) winning the most seats was not a party but a collection of independents (see Chapter 17).

If the rules of the electoral system were all-important, then elections under similar rules would produce similar outcomes. Since election rules change very little from one election to the next, we would expect different elections in the same country to produce similar results, However, no law requires a party to persist in contesting elections and in new democracies political elites have frequently exercised their right not to do so. As the result of splits, mergers, and the creation and the termination of parties, there has been a turnover of large parties as well as small parties that win few votes. This produces a floating supply of parties. In Romania, for example, the party winning the most votes in three of its six parliamentary elections has only fought a single election. Furthermore, in the first round of four presidential elections Ion Iliescu has each time come first and each time fought under a different party label.

The *demands of electors* can be expressed only in response to the menu of parties supplied by elites. The intensive politicization of society under Communist regimes forced people to think about politics. Most Central and East Europeans had formed a political outlook under the old regime; typically, it was in opposition to Communist doctrines. The party-state took care that private opinions could not be expressed publicly; it controlled the media and prevented the organization of competing parties. The best-known opposition group, Solidarity in Poland, was not a party but a mass movement of protest against the Communist party-state and it broke up soon after free elections were introduced. When founding elections were called, competing party leaders had no time to conduct public opinion research to learn what electors wanted them to represent. On election day both political elites and voters were flying blind.

The first decision electors must make is whether to vote or abstain. The intense and intrusive efforts of Communist regimes to indoctrinate their subjects created a reaction against participation in politics. Yet disaffection from the old regime was an incentive to vote, since people now had the opportunity to express their own views rather than simply doing as they were told. A majority of electors have usually turned out to vote.

A change of regimes left many citizens with a clear idea of a party they would not vote for (Rose and Mishler, 1998). However, this was not enough to determine which party to vote for. When every party was new, electors could not rely on past experience. Proportional representation made it necessary for voters to endorse a party because seats in parliament were rewarded on the basis of each party's share of the vote. In most countries, the ballot restricted the choice of voters to placing a mark beside a party list or in a few cases endorsing a candidate and a list. In the four founding elections with mixed PR and FPTP systems, casting a second vote for an individual candidate was also necessary.

The choice of voters has remained difficult because of a floating supply of parties. People are forced to become floating voters when the party they endorsed at the previous election fails to appear at the following election. From one election to the next the appearance of new parties presents voters with decisions about whether to vote for them on the basis of their promises for the future or to favour a persisting party on the basis of its past record. The only way in which an elector can be sure of being consistent is to abstain at every election.

The *outcome of an election* reflects the interaction among the rules of the electoral system, the supply of parties, and the response of voters. Figure 1.2 shows the sequence linking these influences. In mathematical terms, a simple identity can describe an election outcome as a function of the rules of the electoral system (R), the supply of parties (P), and the response of voters (V):

$$\textit{Election outcome} = f(R)\,(P)\,(V)$$

Focusing on a single element in an election, such as the preferences of voters, risks arriving at a misleading conclusion because it ignores the fact that the same behaviour can produce different outcomes, depending on the supply of parties and the rules of the electoral system. In a two-party system, a voter who wants to turn the government out of office is compelled to vote for a single opposition party, but in a six-party system voters have a multiplicity of ways in which they can vote. A first-past-the-post electoral system can manufacture an absolute majority in parliament for a party with two-fifths or less of the popular vote and give no seats to a party with the support of five or ten per cent of the electorate nationwide. However, in a

Figure 1.2 INTERACTIVE MODEL OF ELECTION OUTCOMES

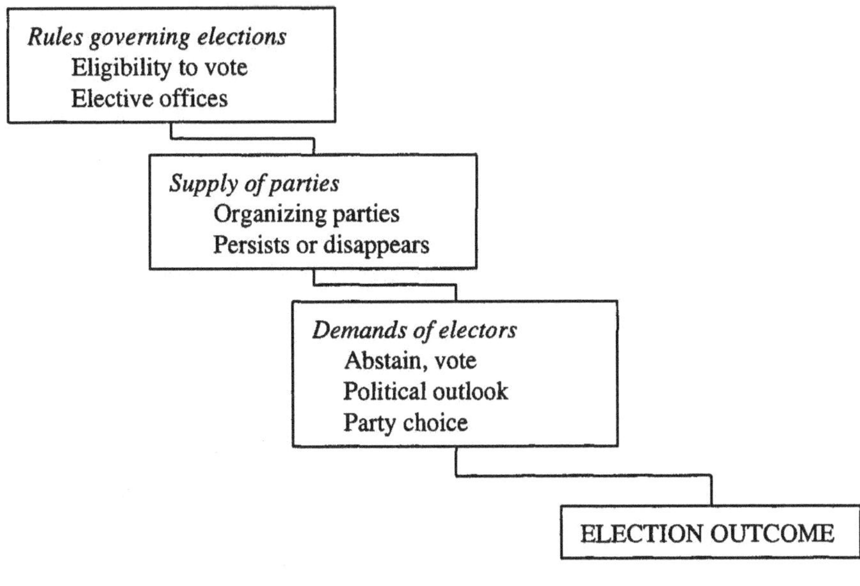

proportional representation contest, no party is likely to win an absolute majority of seats and a party with five or ten per cent of the vote can win enough seats to participate in a coalition government.

The multiple influences determining election rules, the supply of parties, and responses of voters make the outcome of an election contingent, which is as it should be in a democracy committed to free and fair competition. While the legacy of a one-party state is common to all new democracies of Central and Eastern Europe, there are significant differences between countries in each of the elements influencing an outcome. In the chapters that follow we systematically review similarities and differences in the determinants of electoral outcomes in the ten new European democracies and in the Russian Federation. This is followed by chapters reporting for each country the rules of the electoral system, parties competing in at least one election and the resulting distribution of votes and seats.

2

ELECTORAL SYSTEMS COMPARED

Since the electoral system decides who wins and who loses, in a new democracy the system must be accepted as fair by both winners and losers (C. Anderson, et al., 2005). In the final stage of Communist regimes, election laws in one-party states such as Russia were adapted to permit multi-candidate elections in which challengers to the official candidates sometimes won many votes, but such events were ad hoc and transitional.

The rules for the first post-Communist elections were negotiated around a table by politicians representing diverse positions. In some countries politicians of the disappearing old order, anxious to maintain their political careers in the successor system, participated extensively (Ishiyama, 1997: 101f.). Organizers of mass street demonstrations in autumn 1989 and dissidents who had remained outside the old regime's inner circle also took part. All the participants in transitional round tables had one thing in common: none could be confident of how many votes they and their allies would gain. In the absence of clear-cut evidence about how the electorate would divide, elites made decisions without knowing what would turn out to be in their interest and what would not.

An electoral system requires many decisions. The first section of this chapter details the electoral systems adopted to choose members of parliament (MPs). Since an elected president is not necessary in a democracy, the different methods adopted to fill the office of head of state are then described. Decisions taken in a hurry have long-term consequences. Thus, the chapter concludes by analyzing the effect of choices of electoral systems on the turnout of voters and on the extent to which the distribution of votes and seats is more or less proportional.

Electing Representatives

For an election to be fair, the rules for conducting it should be decided in advance, so that once ballots are cast the party in power cannot change rules in its own interest. While many technical points are of limited significance, decisions about elective offices and about the formula for converting votes into seats are of fundamental political importance.

The first decision is whether a parliament should have one or two chambers. Six countries – Bulgaria, Estonia, Hungary, Latvia, Lithuania, and Slovakia – have a single-chamber parliament. Where there is a second chamber, it is usually chosen on a basis different from the representative chamber so that it cannot claim equal popular legitimacy. The 81 members of the Czech Senate are elected for six-year terms from single-member districts by an absolute majority; one-third of the seats are up for election every two years. The Polish Senate consists of 100 members representing 40 districts and elected by a simple plurality. In Slovenia the second chamber includes 18 members chosen by electoral colleges of employers, employees, the self-employed, and non-commercial corporatist organizations, and 22 members directly elected for five-year terms in single-member districts. Romania is exceptional in electing its Senate at the same time and by the same method of proportional representation as that used for its Chamber of Deputies. In Russia the Council of the Federation consists of two representatives of the country's 83 constituent administrative regions, one chosen by the governor and one by its legislative assembly.

The number of MPs should be enough to represent constituents, organize opposition to well-briefed government ministers, staff parliamentary committees, and satisfy the ambitions of politicians. The median parliament has 200 members; the range is from 90 in Slovenia to 460 in Poland (see Table 2.1). There is a positive correlation between the number of MPs and the size of the national electorate (r: 0.67). The ratio of electors to MPs is as low as one to 8,884 in Estonia and rises to one Duma member for every 242,546 registered electors in Russia. In all countries the ratio of electors to MPs is much lower than for the United States House of Representatives.

The method of electing MPs involves a strategic choice about how a government is to be constituted as well as how electors are to be represented. Proportional representation tends to increase the number of parties winning seats, thus reducing the likelihood of any one party having a majority of seats in parliament. Therefore, the government must either be a coalition or hold office without a parliamentary majority. This creates a more substantial check on executive power than does a government chosen by a first-past-the-post electoral system. An FPTP system usually manufactures an absolute parliamentary majority for a single party that wins a plurality but not a majority of the popular vote. In secure democracies such as Britain, politicians are prepared to give all the power to an executive with a plurality of the vote. In new democracies, a higher priority is given to preventing the emergence of an all-powerful executive.

Table 2.1 CHARACTERISTICS OF ELECTORAL SYSTEMS

	Seats	Districts	Electors	Seat allocation		% PR	
	N	N (seats[1])	per MP	Regional	National	thresh.	Ballot
Bulgaria	240	31 (4–14)	28,004	—	d'Hondt	4	List
Czech R.	200	14 (5–25)	41,667	d'Hondt	—	5[2]	List[3]
Estonia	101	12 (6–13)	8,884	Hare	d'Hondt	5	Ind'l
Latvia	100	5 (14–28)	14,480	Ste-Lag.	—	5	List[3]
Poland	460	41 (7–19)	66,555	d'Hondt	—	5[4]	Ind'l
Romania	334	43 (4–28)	55,282	Hare	d'Hondt	5[5]	Ind'l
Russia	450	1	242,546	—	Hare	7	List
Slovakia	150	1	28,483	—	Hag-Bis.	5[6]	List[3]
Slovenia	90[7]	8 (11)	18,849	Droop	d'Hondt	4	Ind'l
Lithuania SMD	71	71	37,973	FPTP	—	—	Ind'l
national	70	1	38,516	—	Hare	5[8]	List
Hungary SMD	176	176	45,717	2 ballot[9]	—	—	Ind'l
region	146	20 (4–28)	55,110	Hag-Bis.	—	5[10]	List
national	64	1	125,721	—	d'Hondt[11]	5	n.a.

Source: For each country the latest election as reported in this book.

1 Range from fewest to most seats in a district.

2 For alliances of two parties, 10 percent; three parties, 15 percent; four or more parties, 20 percent.

3 Electors can also cast preferential votes for individual candidates on the list.

4 For electoral alliances, 8 percent. No threshold for ethnic minority parties.

5 For alliances of two parties, 8 percent; three parties, 9 percent; and four or more parties, 10 percent; threshold waived for minority parties.

6 For alliances of two or three parties, 7 percent; four or more, 10 percent.

7 Includes one seat each for Hungarian and Italian minorities.

8 For electoral alliances of two or more parties, 7 percent.

9 Three leading candidates are eligible to contest the second round, and the outcome is decided by plurality.

10 For alliances of two parties, 10 percent; three or more parties, 15 percent.

11 Allocation based on votes wasted in single-member districts and regions.

Proportional representation. In every post-Communist country PR was adopted, thus encouraging a multiplicity of voices in parliament and making the prime minister dependent on the support of a coalition of parties. In a new regime, PR was attractive to politicians uncertain whether they would come first or second in a first-past-the-post ballot. The endorsement of PR in principle left politicians with a series of specific choices between alternative ways of implementing many details that are an integral part of allocating seats by proportional representation (Cox, 2000).

Proportional representation requires multi-member districts. Its logic implies that the country as a whole should be one district. However, this would eliminate any territorial link between MPs and voters. Four countries, Bulgaria, Lithuania, Russia, and Slovakia, allocate all their PR seats at the national level. Most countries have multi-member districts with boundaries that match those of large cities, counties, or regions with which voters can identify.

Given differences in the population of regions, within a country the number of MPs elected from a district varies substantially. In Romania the least populous district returns four MPs while Bucharest returns 28. The fewer the seats in a multi-member district, the larger the proportion of the vote that a party must win in order to gain a seat there; the greater the number of seats in a district, the more proportional the distribution of seats is likely to be. For example, in a three-member district a party must win more than one-quarter of the vote to be sure of gaining a seat, whereas in an eight-member district just over one-ninth of the vote should be sufficient to gain a seat. To encourage turnout, in Bulgaria and the Czech Republic the number of seats allocated to each district is determined after the election according to its share of the total valid vote.

Since differences in the number of MPs returned by multi-member districts can result in deviations from strict proportionality, compensation can be achieved by creating a national pool of votes to award seats to parties that have failed to benefit proportionally in districts. National-level pools of seats operate in Estonia, Hungary, Romania, and Slovenia.

If seats were distributed in exact proportion to each party's share of the vote, in a parliament with 200 seats a party could win a seat with as little as 0.5 per cent of the national vote. To reduce the proliferation of parties with very few seats, PR systems normally set a threshold, the percentage share of the vote that a party must reach in order to share in the distribution of seats. In the absence of a threshold, 29 parties won at least one seat in the Polish *Sejm* in 1991. When a five per cent threshold was introduced for the 1994 election, only seven Polish parties won seats. The threshold is now five per cent in eight countries, four per cent in Slovenia and Bulgaria, and seven per cent in Russia. It is lowered for parties representing ethnic groups constituting only a small percentage of the electorate in Romania, Poland, and Slovenia. To discourage small parties from forming ad hoc electoral alliances to raise their combined vote above the threshold, six countries have a higher threshold for such blocs. In the Czech Republic the threshold for a two-party alliance is as high as 10 per cent; for a three-party bloc it is 15 per cent; and for a four-party alliance, 20 per cent.

Allocating seats in a multi-member district requires a quota to divide each party's total vote in order to determine how many seats it should get. The largest-remainder system consistently uses the same divisor when allocating seats. By contrast, the highest-average method increases the divisor for a party every time it gains a seat. Within each category, there are differences in how the quota is calculated.

One or another form of the largest-remainder method is used in seven countries. The Hare quota is the simplest; it is calculated by dividing the total number of valid votes in a district by the number of its seats. Initially, parties are awarded seats for each full quota of votes they have won. After this is done, some seats remain unallocated and each party normally has a remainder of votes, that is, less than a full quota. The parties with the largest remainders are allocated seats in order of the size of their remainder. This method is used at one or another tier of distributing seats in Estonia, Lithuania, Romania, and Russia. The Hagenbach-Bischoff largest-remainder method calculates a quota by dividing the total vote by the number of seats plus one. This marginally lowers the number of votes required to win a seat. It is used in Hungary and Slovakia. Sometimes it is referred to as the Droop method. While the two are very similar, the Droop system adds one vote to the quota calculated by the Hagenbach-Bischoff method in order to eliminate the theoretical possibility of a tie. It is used at the regional level in Slovenia.

In the highest-average method the divisor differs between parties; it increases after every round in which a party is awarded a seat. In the d'Hondt version, the divisor increases by one for each seat awarded. In the Sainte-Laguë version each time a seat is awarded to a party its divisor is increased by two, thus going from 1 to 3, 5, 7, and so on. This reduces the average of the largest party faster and makes it easier for parties to win seats at an earlier stage, an important point in a multi-member district with few seats. Differences in methods of calculating quotas can alter the PR distribution of seats, but only to a limited extent.

The choice of individuals receiving seats depends on the *form of ballot.* In a closed-list ballot, voters determine how many seats a party wins, but each party determines who represents it by ranking its candidates on the ballot in the order in which they are to be allocated seats. If, for example, a party qualifies for two seats, the top two names on its list become MPs; if more seats are awarded, then the third and subsequent names enter parliament. In practice, names low on a party's list have virtually no chance of gaining a seat. The closed-list system is the sole or primary method used in most countries. However, a person must vote for one candidate on a party's list in Estonia, Poland, Romania, and Slovenia. In a system with a preferential ballot, the vote gained by all candidates of a party is totalled to determines its number of seats, and the allocation of seats to individuals depends on the vote each has gained. In the Czech Republic, Slovakia, and Latvia, voters may endorse a candidate on the party list but are not required to do so. If no choice is made, the voter is presumed to have endorsed the party's ranking.

Mixing proportional representation and first-past-the-post systems. Although American advisors were ubiquitous and Britain a familiar example of parliamentary democracy, no Central or East European country adopted the first-past-the-post system as it is used in Anglo-American democracies. However, mixed electoral systems in which some members of parliament are chosen in single-member districts and some by PR from multi-member districts are in place in Hungary and Lithuania (Massicotte and Blais, 2000; Shugart and Wattenberg, 2001). In Hungary 176 seats are elected by FPTP and 210 by PR. If no candidate secures an absolute majority in a district, a second-round vote is held in which the top three candidates compete and the seat is awarded to the candidate with a plurality of votes. In Lithuania 71 seats are elected by FPTP in single-member districts and 70 by PR. A plurality of votes is now sufficient to win FPTP seats, but in the first two Lithuanian elections an absolute majority was required, and second-round contests were frequent.

Mixed systems differ in the extent to which they are designed to compensate for the disproportional effect of first-past-the-post outcomes. When the two systems operate independently of each other, as in Lithuania, the allocation of PR seats is unaffected by disproportional outcomes in first-past-the-post seats. In Hungary there is a degree of compensation, because the distribution of PR seats at the national level takes into account votes that did not gain seats for parties in single-member districts or the regional PR allocation. However, the Hungarian system is not intended to be fully compensatory, as is the case in Germany (Nohlen, 2000).

The outcome of a proportional representation election does not identify a single winner, because it is very rare for one party to win half the votes or seats, and the leading party can have less than a third or a quarter of the vote. Parties can be classified as having done better, worse, or the same as before by comparing their current election result with the previous election. However, a PR election outcome does identify some parties as unambiguous losers, those that fail to reach the threshold for gaining seats.

In a parliament in which no party has a majority of seats, there is more than one way to create a governing coalition. The election outcome decides how many seats each party can offer in the bargaining that leads to the formation of a coalition government. At the next election some coalition parties are likely to see their vote increase while other partners see their vote fall (Rose and Mackie, 1983).

Choosing a president. Every country needs a head of state to represent it formally; it can be a hereditary monarch, a president chosen by an electoral college, or a popularly elected president. The experience of dictatorship between the two world wars and in the Communist era effectively eliminated monarchical government from the region.

There is no agreement among political scientists about whether a democracy is better governed by a president with substantial statutory powers or a figurehead president (cf. Linz and Valenzuela, 1994; Mainwaring and Shugart, 1997). Globally, two-fifths of democratic regimes have an elected president and so do almost two-thirds of undemocratic regimes (Golder, 2005).

The argument for the popular election of a president is the same as the argument against: it concentrates more power in the hands of one individual. Of the countries reviewed here, the Russian president has had the broadest powers. The Russian constitution was drafted by the Kremlin after Boris Yeltsin emerged triumphant in a shoot-out with the Russian parliament in October 1993. However, a succession of presidents from Yeltsin to Vladimir Putin to Dmitry Medvedev demonstrate that the role of a president can vary with an incumbent's political standing.

To maintain the strongest safeguard against a president challenging an elected parliament, three countries have consistently chosen their president by an electoral college of MPs. In Latvia a simple majority in a secret vote of parliament chooses a president for a four-year term. In the Czech Republic a majority vote in a joint session of both houses of parliament chooses a head of state for a five-year term. In Hungary Communists favoured a directly elected president in the belief their leader could win and for the same reason anti-Communists opposed this. In a July 1990 referendum on directly electing the president, opponents defeated the proposal by boycotting the election, thus nullifying the pro-presidency vote of the 14 per cent who did cast a ballot (O'Neil, 1997: 208). The president of Hungary is chosen for a five-year term and requires support by a two-thirds' majority of parliament in a first- or second-round secret ballot. If a third ballot is required, it is a run-off between the top two second-round candidates.

Two countries have switched between methods of choosing a president. In Estonia the constitution specified the indirect election of the president but in 1992 a popular vote was held under terms of a special act. Since no candidate secured the absolute majority required for victory, parliament chose between the top two candidates and endorsed the candidate coming second in the popular vote. Since then the Estonian parliament has been empowered to select the president (see Chapter 10). Initially, the Slovak parliament selected the president by a three-fifths' parliamentary majority. However, in March 1998 no candidate received this many votes. After a change of government in the September 1998 election, the constitution was amended to introduce the direct election of the president by an absolute majority, with a second round run-off ballot if necessary (Malová and Učeň, 2000: 512–13).

In the seven countries that now directly elect a president, procedures are very similar. The winner requires an absolute majority of votes. If no candidate gains a majority in the first ballot, a second-round run-off is held between the top two candidates. In the interim Romanian presidential election of 1990, and the two most recent Russian elections, the winner's first-round total has been much higher than that of winners in American presidential landslides. In 19 of 23 presidential elections, the leading candidate has been forced into a second-round ballot in which defeat is a real threat. In Lithuania Valdas Adamkus finished second in the first round in 1997, yet won in the second round, while in 2002 he led in the first round but lost in the second-round run-off.

To win the presidency with an absolute majority of the vote, the support of a single party is insufficient. In the six new European democracies electing a president, the largest party's vote at the latest election averaged 31 per cent. To win a presidential election, a candidate needs support from people who favour different parties or none. In Slovenia Milan Kučan, running as an independent, twice won more than half the vote in the first-round presidential ballot. Loose links between independent presidential candidates and parties encourage fragmentation of the party system (Filippov, et al., 1999).

Effects of Electoral Systems

Since both election outcomes and rules of electoral systems vary, political scientists have developed theories to predict the effects of electoral systems on election outcomes (see, e.g., Taagepera and Shugart, 1989; Cox, 1997; Norris, 2003). However, differences in principle are more likely to produce differences in degree rather than kind, for there are limits to which rules can control the outcome of free and fair elections since voters and elites can switch between parties even when laws remain constant. Statistical analysis identifies the degree to which electoral systems have an effect.

Turnout. In new European democracies election laws are designed to encourage turnout. Elections are always held on weekends, when most electors have more free time, rather than on a normal working day, as is the case in the United States and Britain. In seven countries, voting is on a Sunday; in Latvia and Slovakia on a Saturday; and in the Czech Republic on Friday and Saturday. In Bulgaria an election cannot be held on a working day: four elections have been held on Sunday and two on Saturday.

In new European democracies turnout has averaged 68.2 per cent since 1990. Turnout differs between countries. In Slovakia's six elections, an average of 77.3 per cent of the electorate has voted and in the Czech Republic 75.9 per cent. At the other extreme, turnout has averaged only 47.3 per cent in Poland. However, it is misleading to ascribe variations in turnout to unique national characteristics, because turnout varies greatly within each country too. There is a difference of 47 percentage points between turnout at the 1990 election in Romania and the 2008 parliamentary election, and a difference of almost 38 percentage points between the abnormally high turnout at the first Czech election in 1990 and the election of 2002.

Turnout in the 15 older European Union countries has tended to be higher than in new EU members, averaging 77.4 per cent since 1990. There are substantial variations in turnout between Belgium, with a mean of 92.4 per cent, and France, where it averages 64.4 per cent in elections to the national assembly. In old EU countries turnout is higher where there is proportional representation, where elections are held on a rest day, and where there is a tradition of compulsory voting (Rose, 2003: Table 4). However, these influences cannot account for variations in turnout in new EU countries, since none of these conditions varies between the ten countries.

Four variables together account for 31.6 per cent of the variance in turnout in 56 elections in new EU countries since 1990 (Table 2.2). A higher threshold for winning PR seats, and thus an increased likelihood of wasting votes, lowers turnout. Attitudes towards parties have a significant effect on turnout too. A higher level of distrust in parties tends to depress turnout while the perceived level of government corruption, as measured by the Transparency International index (www.transparency.org) significantly boosts turnout, as some voters appear stimulated to vote in hopes of

Table 2.2 INFLUENCES ON TURNOUT

Variance accounted for: R^2 31.6%

	b	s.e.	Beta
Height of PR threshold	–4.60	1.11	–.49***
Distrust of parties in electorate	–.53	.21	–.31*
Perception of corruption	3.74	1.50	.29*
Percent of electorate with a political outlook	.33	.14	.28*
Number of parties with 1% vote	–.37	.57	–.08

*** significant at .001, * .05 level

Sources: Turnout in 56 national elections in 10 new EU democracies, as reported in Chapters 6–16. Electors distrusting parties, see Table 4.1; percentage with political outlook, see Table 4.2. Corruption: Transparency International index reversed.

turning a corrupt government out of office. The higher the percentage of a country's electorate that identifies with a political outlook such as the market or social democracy, the higher the turnout. The one influence tested that lacks any significant influence is the number of parties participating in elections.

Proportionality. No electoral system can produce an election outcome that is 100 per cent proportional. While votes can be calculated to one-hundredth of a percentage point, seats must be allocated in whole numbers. The use of thresholds to qualify for seats demonstrates that no new democracy electoral system is intended to be 100 per cent proportional. Thresholds of up to five per cent or higher prevent the smallest parties from winning any seats, and larger parties can win more than their strict arithmetic share of seats.

The degree of proportionality can be calculated by an index that sums the absolute value of the difference between each party's share of the vote and its share of seats; divides that sum by two; and subtracts it from 100. The index gives equal weight to over- and under-representation. The greater the overall match between shares of votes and seats, the closer the index is to 100; where proportionality is less, the index number falls.

Elections in new EU democracies are substantially but not completely proportional: the Index of Proportionality averages 87 per cent (Table 2.3). It is as high as 92 per cent in Slovenia, where the threshold to qualify for seats has been three per cent and is now four per cent. The Index is lowest in Lithuania, averaging

Table 2.3 PROPORTIONALITY BETWEEN VOTES AND SEATS

Election:	1st	2nd	3rd	4th	5th	6th	Mean
			Index of Proportionality: %				
Slovenia	94	85	91	97	90	94	92
Estonia	82	88	90	93	94	—	90
Romania	97	84	85	82	92	95	89
Latvia	89	87	89	84	89	—	88
Bulgaria	97	75	85	92	86	91	88
New EU mean	88	78	86	90	88	—	87
Czech R.	81	81	89	89	87	90	86
Hungary	78	79	86	88	94	—	85
Slovakia	92	76	87	94	82	76	85
Poland	87	62	82	91	87	92	84
Lithuania	86	67	78	91	79	—	80
Russia	87	51	83	72	93	—	77

Note: Index calculated for PR seats only, except in Hungary, where it is based on all seats.

80 per cent. The Index tends to fluctuate more between elections within a country than between CEE countries. In six Polish elections proportionality has veered between 62 and 92 per cent. In elections for the Russian Duma proportionality in nominally PR seats has ranged from 51 to 93 per cent.

Proportionality in new European Union democracies tends to be a little lower than in older EU countries using PR but higher than in established democracies with FPTP elections. In the old EU countries electing MPs by some form of PR, the Index of Proportionality averaged 91 per cent between 1990 and 2008; this is four percentage points higher than in CEE countries. However, in democracies with the first-past-the-post system, proportionality is much lower than in CEE countries. Between 1990 and the end of 2008 in France the Index of Proportionality averaged 72 per cent, and in Britain, 80 per cent. In both countries, proportionality on average is less than in PR elections in nine new EU member-states.

Two influences account for half the variation in the proportionality of election outcomes in new EU democracies (Table 2.4). The tendency of PR elections to encourage more parties to contest elections actually reduces proportionality, for the more parties contesting elections the greater the number of parties that fail to clear the PR threshold to qualify for seats, thus increasing wasted votes and giving a disproportionate number of seats to parties that do clear the threshold. Relatedly, a higher threshold to qualify for seats also tends to reduce proportionality. After controlling for these influences, the choice of a highest-average or largest-remainder method of allocating seats has no significant influence on the proportionality of an outcome. Nor is there any significant tendency for the size of the vote for the largest party to influence the overall proportionality of an election outcome.

While many features of election laws vary between countries, the only feature that is significant for both turnout and proportionality is the threshold to qualify for seats. A higher threshold tends to depress both turnout and proportionality. The

Table 2.4 INFLUENCES ON PROPORTIONALITY

Variance accounted for: R^2 48.9%

	b	s.e.	Beta
Number of parties with 1% vote	–1.76	.25	–.72***
Height of PR threshold	–1.81	.48	–.38***
Highest average PR system	–.93	1.36	–.07
Vote share of largest party	–.04	.07	–.05

*** significant at .001 level

Note: Proportionality in 56 national elections in ten new EU countries, as reported in Table 2.3.

threshold is determined by laws written by political elites. However, even though election laws usually remain the same, within a given set of laws there remain substantial variations in election outcomes because of the behaviour of elites in supplying parties and the response of voters.

3

PARTIES WITHOUT CIVIL SOCIETY

Theories of the formation of democratic parties presuppose the existence of civil society, that is, social, economic, and cultural organizations that represent group interests independently of the state. In nineteenth-century Europe, even though parties in the modern sense did not exist, competing interests could be advanced through such institutions. Parliaments did not represent individuals but estates of the realm. Members were chosen by a very small fraction of the populace to represent the nobility, clergy, landed interests, and leaders of urban communities (Koenigsberger, 1971; Myers, 1975). This created undemocratic but representative institutions that pressed demands on monarchs. Unlike latter-day totalitarian rulers, monarchs were unable to suppress all critics completely (Daalder, 1995).

The history of democratization in Western Europe reflects civil society demands to expand representation and the response of elites wanting to maintain their power. Institutions promoted the organization of political parties along major cleavages between church and state, city dwellers and agrarian interests, factory owners and industrial workers, and linguistic and ethnic groups. Political socialization through church schools, trade unions, and ethnic associations led people without the right to vote to develop loyalties to political parties. Many European socialist parties were organized before most working-class adults had the right to vote. Parents often passed these loyalties to their children and the identification of party and family created stable ties between individual electors and parties. Parties founded when the franchise was expanded early in the twentieth century were, to a surprising degree, able to 'freeze' support for half a century or more (Lipset and Rokkan, 1967: 50; Bartolini and Mair, 1990; Karvonen and Kuhnle, 2001).

However, in post-Communist countries party formation commenced without civil society institutions. Soviet troops advancing across Central and Eastern Europe were accompanied by political commissars. Non-Communist political leaders from the pre-war era were threatened with exile, deportation, imprisonment, or worse. Popular front governments with Communists in key positions were established and non-Communists were quickly eliminated by show trials and even executions (Crampton, 1994: Chapter 13). For example, in Bulgaria Nikola Petkov, leader of the main party opposing the new regime, was arrested in 1947, charged with treason, and hanged. In Czechoslovakia the Communist take-over was sealed in 1948 when Foreign Minister Jan Masaryk was found dead after being taken into custody. Communist regimes poisoned the idea of an independent civil society, since trade unions, the media, cultural associations, and universities were under the control of the party-state rather than enjoying the political independence of their Western counterparts.

The Soviet repudiation of Stalinism was not the end of the one-party state; it marked a shift to post-totalitarian rule by a single party. Relaxation of totalitarian controls could not replace purged institutions. The degree of control over organized political dissent varied greatly from Romania, where Nicolae Ceauşescu maintained a personalistic form of totalitarian rule, to Hungary, where multi-candidate but not multi-party elections were initially tried in 1983. Politically committed individuals who had what Germans call *zivil courage* criticized government, but they did so as individuals or members of small groups such as Charter 77 in Czechoslovakia. Except for in Poland, individual dissidents were not able to organize mass movements challenging the party-state. When activities appeared to do so, Communist authorities cracked down hard, as in the Soviet-led invasion of Czechoslovakia in 1968 and the declaration of martial law in Poland in 1981.

Success destroyed the unity of opponents of the old regime. As long as a Soviet-sponsored party-state was in existence, anti-Communist movements faced a common enemy. The collapse of the Soviet empire achieved the negative goal of destroying the party-state. However, there was an institutional vacuum due to the lack of organizations to replace discredited institutions of the old regime.

The need for free elections forced national elites to organize political parties. However, many dissidents associated party politics with Communist-style repression, hypocrisy, and corruption. In the words of Václav Havel, leader of the Czech dissidents, 'Parties are for [Communist] party members; the Civic Forum is for all' (Olson, 1993: 642). Yet activists had to form political parties if they wanted to participate in the new regime. As subsequent pages show, dozens of new parties were formed with a great variety of appeals and labels. However, many parties disappeared quickly too, as "political hitchhikers" moved around in search of a vehicle to advance themselves. Fragmented party systems are today the norm.

A Big Supply of Parties

When an election is called in an established democracy, the supply of parties is not in doubt: the parties nominating candidates are the same as before. In such circumstances, politically ambitious individuals do not need to form a party to go into politics; they join a party created long before they were old enough to vote. To enter parliament, budding politicians seek a favourable place on their party's PR list. Nomination goes to those who have shown commitment to the party, its institutions, and its leaders. National leaders have normally been in the same party throughout their political career.

In post-Communist countries, the supply of parties was problematic. Even where there had been competitive elections as a prelude to the collapse of the old regime, candidates had usually made their political careers within the Communist Party. The partially free Polish election of June 1989 was exceptional because voters were offered a clear choice between Communist and anti-Communist candidates.

The adoption of proportional representation made it mandatory for parties to be listed on the ballot. Before this could happen, political elites had to create organizations that would be legally recognized as parties by the national election authority; recruit candidates for their party list; file nomination papers; conduct a nationwide election campaign; and raise money to pay for these activities. All this had to be done under great pressure from the electoral calendar. Almost every party contesting the first election was created just a few months or even a few weeks before the election was called.

Easy entry to the ballot. The rules laid down for the registration of parties made it easy to qualify for a place on the ballot; this gave voters a choice between dozens of parties. For example, in Romania the period between the adoption of an election law in March 1990 and the first parliamentary election was less than ten weeks. Nonetheless, more than 60 parties nominated lists of candidates. However, 51 parties having an average vote of one-seventh of one per cent failed to win seats.

In some countries the first multi-party election was not called until a parliament had been in operation for a year or more. This not only gave governors time to draft electoral laws but also gave diverse groups time to develop a party organization. The consequence was the proliferation of hopeless parties. In the October 1991 Polish election, 111 parties filed a list of candidates in at least one multi-member district, 42 in at least two districts, and 27 registered candidates for the national list. However, only 29 parties won seats in the *Sejm* (Szczerbiak, 2001). In Russia prior to the announcement of the December 1993 Duma election, there were 130 proto-parties registered with the Ministry of Justice. Of these, 35 secured approval from election authorities for their proposed candidates, 21 submitted nomination papers, 13 had their papers accepted for the list ballot, and 8 won list seats.

Counting parties. The larger the number of parties on the ballot, the smaller the average share of the vote for each. However, it is unrealistic to treat all parties as if they were average in importance when voters conspicuously do not do so. Since most voters will neither know nor care about some parties, we count parties as part of a system of electoral competition if they receive at least one per cent of the national vote in at least one election or have won at least two seats, a requirement that means they are not a one-man or one-woman band.

In new European democracies competitive elections are very much multi-party events (Figure 3.1). In Lithuania 37 different parties have contested at least one election and in nine out of ten new European democracies at least 26 parties have

Figure 3.1 NUMBER OF PARTIES BY COUNTRY SINCE 1990

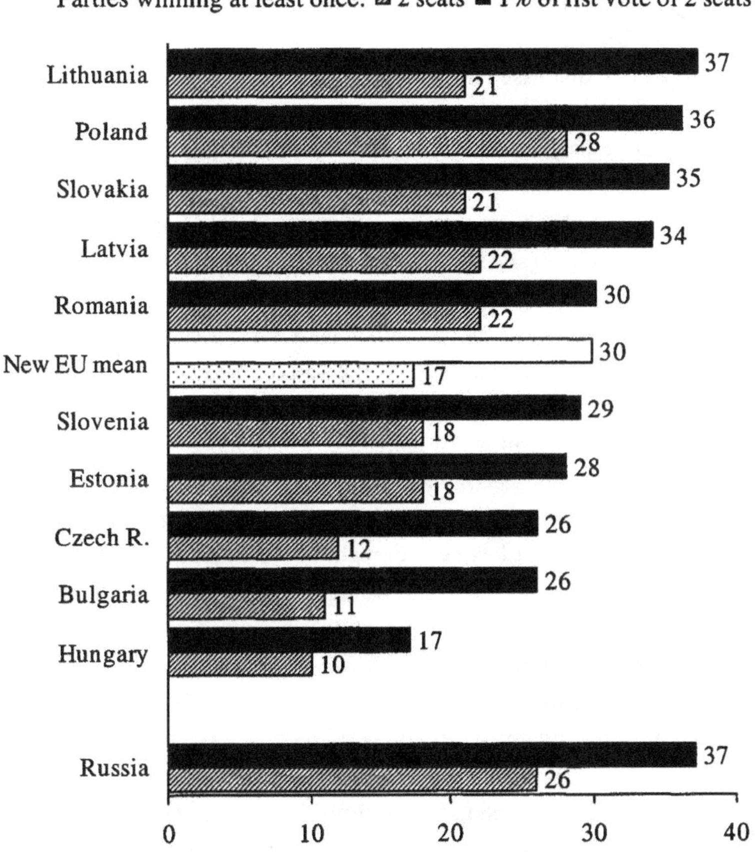

Source: Calculated from national chapters in Part Two.

done so. In the same period only four parties have won at least one per cent of the American presidential vote, in Britain only seven parties have done so, and in proportional representation Sweden nine parties have gained one per cent or more of the vote.

Counting names on the ballot actually understates the number of parties participating in elections, because many names are convenient labels for electoral alliances created by parties hoping to increase their chances of clearing the PR threshold by forming an electoral bloc. In Poland the Solidarity Electoral Action banner was an umbrella label for 35 nominal parties in 1997 and won the most seats. However, it was a very temporary electoral alliance and broke up before the next election. Such a lack of cohesion contrasts with the unity that dissident groups showed in opposition to Communist rule.

Without MPs the influence that a party can exert on government is minimal and its views can be dismissed as having been rejected by the electorate. Thus, a more stringent criterion for evaluating electoral competition is to count only parties winning seats in parliament. Proportional representation thresholds of up to five per cent and sometimes higher for alliances can consign parties to political limbo. For example, in the 1995 Duma election, Women of Russia won more than three million votes but failed to gain any Duma seats, and more than 31 million list votes were cast for parties that failed to win any seats.

Two-fifths of the parties that gain at least one per cent of the vote fail to win at least two seats in Parliament (Figure 3.1). The failure rate is highest in Bulgaria and the Czech Republic, where more than half of parties do not win as many as two seats at one election. By contrast, in Romania, where there was initially no minimum threshold to qualify for seats, almost three-quarters of parties winning at least one per cent of the vote have also won more than one seat. As long as Russian parties could win single-member districts even though they did not qualify for list seats, many parties could be represented in the Duma. However, after the abolition of single-member districts by President Putin, only four parties won Duma seats in the all-proportional representation ballot in 2007.

Because of the turn-over of parties from one election to the next, the number of parties contesting any given election is substantially less than the total number that have done so at least once since 1990. In the average election, 10 parties win at least one per cent of the vote and in Latvia upwards of 12 parties do so. In every new EU democracy, at least eight parties on average win one per cent of the vote or more at an election.

Ironically, the legacy of one-party rule is that party competition in new European democracies is now very fragmented. Not only do political elites supply parties in double-digit numbers but also voters disperse their choices widely. In new EU democracies, an average of 17 parties have won at least two seats in at least one election and at the average election six or seven parties win seats (Figure 3.2). In Poland as many as eight parties are represented on average and even more appeared in the Russian Duma when there were single-member districts.

Weighing parties. Parties must be weighed as well as counted; this is recognized in the commonplace but vague distinction between big and small parties. Winning half the seats in parliament qualifies a party as big, for it can thereby enjoy a majority

Figure 3.2 AVERAGE NUMBER OF PARTIES IN AN ELECTION

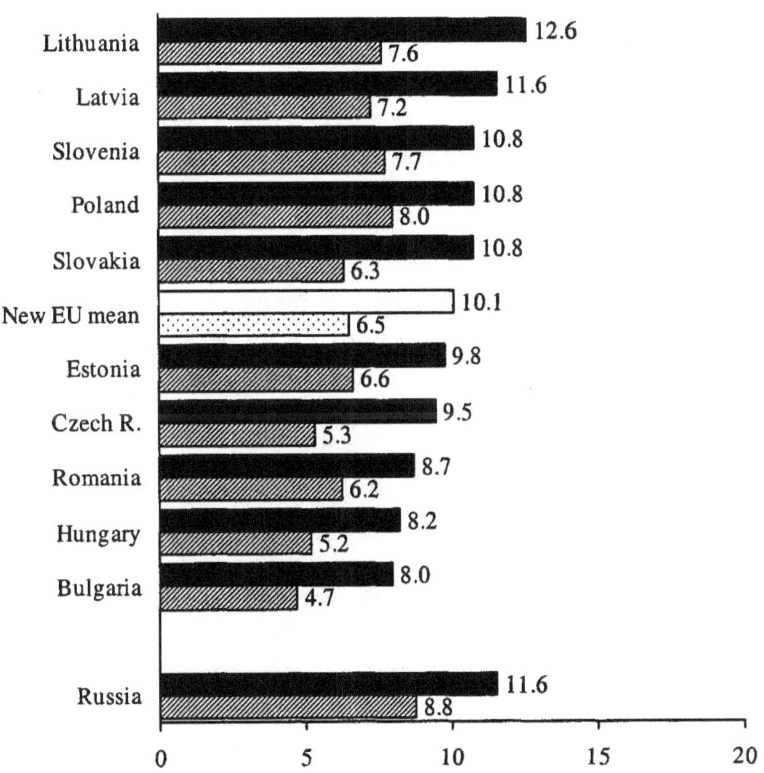

Source: Calculated from national chapters in Part Two.

for the life of a parliament. Moreover, if it consistently does so, then it is not just another competitor but the dominant party in the system. One-party dominant systems have lasted for decades in countries with competitive elections such as Italy, Japan, and Sweden (Pempel, 1990), and in big American cities such as Chicago.

No party is dominant in any of the new European democracies and the "biggest" party is small by the standards of first-past-the-post systems. The average vote for the largest party at a national election is 32.0 per cent. In Latvia the party coming first usually has barely one-fifth of the vote. In Poland the "largest" party in 1991 had only 12.3 per cent of the vote and only one other party secured as much as one-tenth of the vote. Proportional representation provides a bonus of seats for the party with the most votes as a byproduct of some parties failing to clear the electoral threshold. However, the bonus is limited (see Table 2.3). The leading party wins an average of 37.6 per cent of seats in parliament, 5.8 percentage points more than its share of the vote.

A single party usually wins a big share of the vote in Bulgaria and in Romania, but this is not a sign of one-party dominance, for in each country the biggest party tends to differ from one election to the next. In Bulgaria three different parties – the Socialists, the United Democratic Forces, and the National Movement Simeon II – have been the biggest party at least once. What appeared to be a nascent two-party system in Bulgaria broke up in 2001 when both the Socialist Party and the United Democratic Forces each won less than a fifth of the vote in competition with a new party led by King Simeon. The average vote for the leading party in Romania is distorted by the National Salvation Front claiming 66 per cent shortly after the execution of Nicolae Ceauşescu. However, in the following year the Front split and in five subsequent elections four different parties have come first, taking on average less than one-third of the vote.

There could be a semblance of two-party competition if the two largest parties won enough votes and seats so that one or the other could govern on its own or act as the dominant partner in a coalition government. Alternatively, voters could be offered a clear choice if, as in Sweden, one large party, the Social Democrats, were consistently challenged by a multi-party opposition bloc. In new EU countries this has not been the case. No two parties can claim the duopoly of the vote that Republicans and Democrats enjoy in the United States or the duopoly of power that the Labour and Conservative Parties have enjoyed in Britain. In six of the ten new European democracies, the biggest pair of parties on average fail to win as much as half the popular vote and the combined vote for the two largest parties averages 52.9 per cent.

Fragmentation increases the need for governing coalitions to include more parties. Even when the two largest parties together have a majority of seats in the parliament, if they are rivals neither will join in a coalition with the other. Thus, the leading party in a coalition will need several parties to form a majority government. A party does not need a lot of seats to be relevant in the post-election bargaining leading to the formation of a coalition government (Sartori, 1976). In Estonia, Latvia, and Slovenia, seat distribution is so fragmented that normally at least three parties are required to claim a majority in parliament – assuming that three largest parties are willing to combine. In negotiations for a coalition government, parties with an indeterminate political outlook are at an advantage, for they can find it easier to collaborate with other parties for the sake of gaining office in government.

Competition Along Multiple Dimensions

Within a party system, competition is defined by the number of dimensions on which parties differ (Sartori, 1976: 44; Mair, 2002). The simplest model is that of competition along a single dimension, for example, a left–right scale placing parties according to their position on issues of concern to specific socio-economic groups within the electorate. In Western Europe Communist parties have traditionally been classified along with socialist parties as parties of the left promoting radical change. However, in Central and Eastern Europe Communist parties sought to conserve the power of an undemocratic party-state. This point was recognized by the West German Social Democratic Party, which refused to collaborate with the East German Socialist Unity Party on the grounds that it was not democratic in either name or practice. Contrasting contexts raise doubts about generalizing left and right as symbols of wide-ranging political values.

In new democracies some parties have targeted their appeal to a well-defined segment of the electorate (cf. Kitschelt, 1995; Lawson, et al., 1999). While such exclusive appeals limit their potential support, as long as a party can gain five per cent of the vote, it will win PR seats in parliament. In the absence of civil society institutions mobilizing support from a target group, an alternative strategy is to make vague and inclusive claims to represent the public interest or promote the personality of a leader. Parties making such fuzzy-focus appeals can adopt names such as the party of democrats, the party of citizens, or simply the party of the people. Up to a point, both exclusive targeted appeals and inclusive fuzzy-focus images have been successful.

Classifying parties into cross-national political families is not straightforward (Mair and Mudde, 1998). Some parties are members of the five major party

Internationals – the Socialist International (www.socialistinternational.org); the Centrist Democrat International, formerly the Christian Democrat International (www.cdi-idc.com); the International Democratic Union (www.idu.org); the Liberal International (www.liberal-international.org); and the European Greens (www.europeangreens.org). However, many parties are not affiliated to any International. Among members of one or another International, some have failed to fight the most recent national election or win one per cent of the vote, and in some countries two competing parties belong to the same International. Moreover, networks such as the Liberal and Christian Democrat Internationals have very vague criteria for membership.

The outcome of an election is determined not so much by the appeals in party programmes read by a small minority of electors but by how voters perceive differences between parties. To ascertain this, the New Europe Barometer survey of the Centre for the Study of Public Policy asked respondents in nationwide samples in ten new democracies to select the two dimensions that best explained differences between parties in their country. Theoretical models of cleavages, plus evidence from election results, were used to formulate six different dimensions of competition. Each respondent was asked to choose one or two sets of political alternatives that best described differences between parties in their country.[1]

There was clear rejection of theories reducing party competition to a single dimension; only seven per cent see party competition in their country as involving such a choice. Three-quarters see their system as offering two different dimensions on which parties compete. This requires voters to decide which dimension is most important to them as well as which party they prefer. Only 18 per cent were unable to identify any basis for differentiating parties. In the following paragraphs the dimensions offered survey respondents are given in italics, followed by the percentage seeing each dimension as relevant.

Big personalities are the chief appeal of some parties, while others ask voters to support their political ideas (33 per cent). In the absence of civil society institutions to mobilize voters, politicians have incentives to create fuzzy-focus parties. Like an indeterminately shaped ink blot, such parties can adapt to different tastes in the electorate. The easiest way to do this is to emphasize the personality of the party leader, without any indication of the direction in which he or she will lead. A fuzzy-

---

[1] A total of 11,010 adults were interviewed face to face. The percentages that follow are based on averaging replies from all ten countries, weighting each equally. For full survey details, see Rose (2002).

focus party can also appeal on the grounds that it is more competent in governing or, if it is in opposition, on the grounds that it cannot be as incompetent as an unpopular government. References to ideas, political principles, and political ideologies are avoided. Many parties have appeared in new European democracies that cannot easily be placed in categories defined by the social structure of West European countries and this is even more true of governing coalitions of disparate parties. Hence, the dimension that NEB respondents most frequently cited as differentiating parties was that between parties of ideas and parties of personality.

Some parties believe the Communist regime did much more harm than good, while others want to preserve many of its achievements (30 per cent). A new democracy is vulnerable to attack from parties favouring the old regime. In states with new boundaries, returning to the old regime also implied giving up national independence. Communist parties could not advocate a return to the *status quo ante*, for party-states had depended heavily on the resources of the Soviet Union and it was no more. Most Communist politicians abandoned their old party name and re-packaged their organizational assets as a more or less democratic socialist party (Bozóki and Ishiyama, 2002; Waller, 1995). Only in the Russian Federation and the Czech Republic have Communists maintained a party identified with the previous regime and attracted many votes. Nonetheless, almost one-third of the electorate continues to see the evaluation of the old regime as a major political fault line.

Some parties want government to manage the economy, while others prefer the market (30 per cent). The implosion of the command economy has encouraged parties to articulate competing views about the role of the state and the market. These issues divide electorates along lines not dissimilar to opinion in Western Europe (Rose and Makkai, 1995). Social democratic parties have emphasized social protection policies, often with significant electoral success. In a number of countries these parties are headed by politicians who first made their name in a Communist regime. In the Czech Republic and Poland, outspoken advocates of pro-market principles have won electoral support. While parties have differed about the priorities of social protection and promoting the market, in office their actions often reflect economic exigencies and demands of coalition partners. Although economic issues are of continuing importance, contrary to left–right theories, in new European democracies two-thirds do not see economic issues as a major dividing line between parties.

Some parties represent big cities, while others defend rural and peripheral regions (19 per cent). Communist regimes industrialized rural areas by introducing collective farming, industry, and secondary education, and there was population movement to cities. While most countries have had one or more agrarian parties, they have been of little electoral significance or ceased to exist. Poland is unique in having agrarian parties winning significant shares of the vote. In the 2007 election the Polish Peasants' Party, allied with the Democratic Left in government, won 8.9 per cent of the vote. In the three Baltic states agrarian parties contest seats and usually win between six and nine per cent of the vote. In Hungary the Independent Party of Smallholders, a revival of a pre-war conservative party, sought restitution of nationalized land and participated in coalition governments before splits caused its disappearance from parliament. One-fifth of the electorate sees urban–rural differences as important in differentiating parties.

Some parties promote national traditions, while others emphasize integration in Europe (32 per cent). In Central and Eastern Europe the fall of a Communist regime was celebrated as regaining national independence from the dictates of Moscow. This was most strongly the case in the Baltic states, which had been forcibly incorporated into the Soviet Union. Post-1989 national pride has largely been expressed in democratic ways, in contrast with the undemocratic words and deeds of the region's inter-war nationalist parties. However, as national governments began negotiating membership in the European Union, this stirred up concerns about the potential risk posed to national identity, a concern found to some extent in older member-states too. A third of citizens see parties competing according to the priority given to promoting national traditions and integration in Europe.

Some parties represent ethnic minorities, while others oppose special policies for minorities (12 per cent). The forced movement of population during the Second World War and the break-up of multi-national states that occurred with the collapse of Communism have resulted in minority ethnic groups being a limited percentage of the electorate. The vote for parties claiming to represent ethnic minorities often falls short of the PR threshold to win seats, because many minorities are small and ethnic minorities often do not vote as a bloc. The Czech Republic and Hungary do not have any ethnic parties in parliament. In Poland, Slovenia, and Romania special rules have been introduced to allow a few minority representatives to sit in parliament since they lack the votes to clear the PR threshold. The Bulgarian constitution explicitly bars ethnic parties. In consequence, the Turkish minority has been mobilized to support the Movement for Rights and Freedoms, which has participated in coalition governments. Romania is an exception in that extreme nationalist parties have won more than one-eighth of the vote. Polarization between majority and minority ethnic parties has been avoided in Estonia and Latvia, because ignorance of the state's official language means that most Russian residents are not citizens and therefore cannot vote in national elections (Rose, Berglund, and Munro, 2006). In Lithuania, where language is not a requirement for citizenship, Russians and Poles usually support non-ethnic parties. Across the region as a whole, competition along ethnic lines appears important for one-eighth of voters, fewer than the proportion supporting anti-immigrant parties in France and in Austria.

After the end of the Second World War secularism spread throughout Europe and Communist party-states strictly limited the capacity of churches to become involved in public affairs. Poland was unique in having a church that retained the loyalty of most citizens. However, the end of Moscow's domination there meant that the Catholic Church no longer served as a unifying national institution. Whereas the Catholic Church sponsored pro-clerical parties in France and Italy after 1945, it has not done so in Central and Eastern Europe (Chan, 2000). Church abstention from party politics has also avoided counter-mobilization by anti-clerical parties. Since a NEB surveys showed that religion and church attendance have been of little political significance, it was not included as a dimension differentiating parties.

Ecology groups have organized green parties in old EU member-states, but their electoral success has usually been limited. After the Berlin Wall fell ecology groups sought to organize parties in Central and Eastern Europe. However, supporters have been unable to create durable green parties. In the most recent election in seven countries green parties did not appear on the ballot or failed to win one per cent of the vote. Latvia's Green and Farmers' Union was exceptional in winning 16.8 per cent of the vote in 2007.

Instead of a consensus about the primary dimension of political competition, voters see parties competing along half a dozen different dimensions. Fuzzy-focus personality parties are recognized as important along with parties emphasizing political ideas. Attitudes towards the old regime as against the new are a significant cleavage. The future is seen as dividing parties between those giving priority to integration in Europe and those placing national traditions first. While the shift from a state-controlled to a market economy has affected every voter, more than two-thirds do not see economic differences as a dominant difference between parties.

Even though people were asked to identify two important dimensions of party competition, none was viewed as of major importance by more than one-third of respondents. Moreover, in no country does half the electorate see any one dimension as dominant. In such circumstances, parties that stress different appeals are not so much competing with each other as talking past each other, while fuzzy-focus parties make vague appeals to everybody in general and nobody in particular.

4

VOTERS WITHOUT TRUST

In Communist times people learned to vote without thinking. Elections did not offer citizens a choice; they were intended to mobilize a unanimous show of support for the party of power. Instead of voting being a civic right, as in established democracies, it was one more demand imposed by governors. The consequence of intrusive mobilization of support was political privatization as people sought to insulate themselves from a distrusted party-state. If contacts with public officials were necessary, for example, to secure subsidized housing, individuals sought to exploit corrupt state institutions (Rose, 1999). Communist regimes gradually accepted the failure of their efforts to mobilize society, accepting the cynical formula of János Kádár, prime minister of Hungary, 'He who is not against us is with us.'

Communist party-states operated in accord with Leon Trotsky's dictum, 'Even if you are not interested in politics, politics is interested in you.' Given this early introduction to political participation, citizens in new democracies welcome the right *not* to take part in politics. New democracies not only provide elections with choice, but also recognize the right of citizens to enjoy freedom *from* the state (Berlin, 1958). When citizens are asked to compare their freedom today with that under the old regime, three-quarters or more of Central and East Europeans consistently report that they have more freedom from the state today than before (Rose, 2009a: Chapter 10). The great majority not only feel freer to say what they think but also to decide whether or not to take an interest in politics.

When an election is called, electors are cross-pressured. A big majority distrust political parties and the MPs who claim to represent them. Competition between more than half a dozen parties usually makes the don't knows the largest "party" in public opinion surveys. Yet over a lifetime of living under different regimes, most adults have developed political values and outlooks that are less subject to change than the parties on the ballot. An election challenges electors to match their political outlook with a party supplied by political elites or else abstain from voting.

Election results show how citizens respond to the choices that political elites supply, but leave open whether voters favour a party because they agree with it or because it is viewed as a lesser evil. To understand what is going on in the minds of electors, we need evidence from public opinion surveys. In this chapter we analyse data from New Europe Barometer surveys of the Centre for the Study of Public Policy. In October–November 2001 and again in the autumn and winter of 2004/2005, the New Europe Barometer (NEB) asked the same questions of representative nationwide samples in all ten countries that are now new EU democracies (Rose, 2002, 2005). The results show an apparent paradox: there is widespread distrust of parties yet a widespread readiness to vote.

A Legacy of Distrust

While competition between parties gives post-Communist voters a choice, it does not mean that the alternatives offered are deemed trustworthy. Since the fall of the Berlin Wall, new opportunities for corruption have emerged with the privatization of state assets and the creation of a few rich groups displaying wealth gained from shadowy sources. Altogether, 73 per cent of NEB respondents think that most or almost all public officials are corrupt.[1]

Distrust of political parties is very widespread. A decade and a half after the collapse of Communist regimes, only 10 per cent trust parties, 74 per cent show active distrust, and the remainder are neutral. In all new EU countries, an absolute majority distrusts parties and in Poland, Bulgaria, and Romania four-fifths or more are distrustful. So widespread is distrust that the chief difference in attitudes is not between those trusting and those distrusting parties, but between those who actively distrust parties and those who are sceptical, choosing a neutral midpoint on the trust scale (see Mishler and Rose, 2001). Distrust in political parties is part of a generalized distrust of political institutions. Trust in MPs is almost as low as in parties; only 14 per cent trust their elected representatives (Table 4.1).

A distrust of parties is not an absolute barrier to voting. In Schumpeter's (1952) theory of two-party competition, voters with a strong distrust of government can vote for the opposition as the lesser evil and, similarly, those fearful of the opposition party winning an election can vote to keep a distrusted government in office. In new EU democracies there is a basis for negative voting: 77 per cent of electors have no difficulty identifying at least one party that they would *never* vote

[1] In this chapter aggregate results of Barometer surveys are reported for the ten new European Union member-states. Percentages are calculated by pooling respondents and weighting each country's contribution to represent 1,000 respondents, approximately the number of respondents in each national survey. For further details of the New Europe Barometer, see www.abdn.ac.uk/cspp.

Table 4.1 DISTRUST IN PARTIES HIGH

Q. To what extent do you trust political parties to look after your interests? Please indicate your view on a scale with 1 showing no trust at all and 7 great trust.

	Trusts %	Sceptical %	Distrusts %
Poland	3	10	87
Bulgaria	6	10	84
Romania	9	11	80
Slovakia	10	14	76
Latvia	10	16	74
New EU mean	(10)	(16)	(74)
Estonia	7	20	73
Slovenia	10	19	71
Czech R.	15	15	70
Lithuania	10	21	69
Hungary	16	25	59
Russia	10	14	76

Trust: chooses points 5–7; sceptical, point 4; distrust, points 1–3.

Source: Centre for the Study of Public Policy, University of Aberdeen, New Europe Barometer survey, November–December 2004, total number of respondents: 10,392; New Russia Barometer XIV, January 2005, total respondents 2,107.

for (Rose and Mishler, 1998). This can be a major party closely associated with the old Communist regime, as in Hungary; an unsuccessful anti-Communist governing party, as in Poland; or a party representing an ethnic minority, such as the party favoured by ethnic Turks in Bulgaria or by Hungarians in Romania.

In Russia voters could register their rejection of all political parties when the ballot offered 'against all' as an option (McAllister and White, 2008). In single-member districts in the 1993 Duma election, the vote against all parties, 14.8 per cent, was greater than for any named party. In the three subsequent Duma elections, the vote against all remained high, 9.6 per cent, 11.6 per cent, and 12.9 per cent. When the Putin government changed election laws before the 2007 election, it also abolished the option of voting against all.

When an election is called, the first decision an individual must make is whether or not to vote. Notwithstanding widespread distrust of parties, a majority of electors do go to the polls (see Chapter 2). However, their choice is often transitory rather than expressing a long-standing commitment to a particular party. Between elections, when there is no immediate pressure to have a preference, people are often completely detached from parties and respond 'don't know' when asked their voting intention. Media reporting of polls tends to set aside these views in order to concentrate on identifying the party with a plurality of endorsement. Yet the don't knows can be the largest "party" in the electorate and those favouring the nominal leader can be the current choice of one-quarter or less of the electorate.

Barometer surveys conducted when an election is not imminent find that the largest group in new European democracies are electors without any party preference (Figure 4.1). In Russia and Slovenia an absolute majority express no party preference and more than one-third of the electorate declares no party preference in eight additional countries. Even in the Czech Republic, where those naming a party

Figure 4.1 NO PARTY THE MOST POPULAR CHOICE

Q. Please put a cross on the ballot by the name of the party you would vote for if an election were held this week.

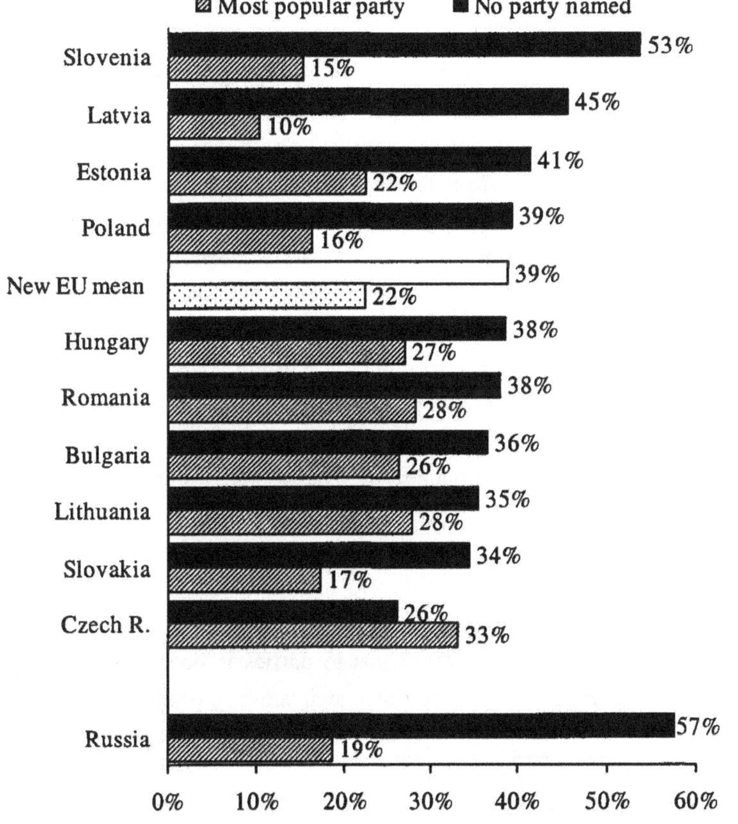

Source: As in Table 4.1.

outnumber unaligned electors, the leading party is endorsed by only one-third of the electorate.

Attempts to apply the American concept of party identification in new European democracies are inappropriate (cf. Dalton and Wattenberg, 2001; Miller and Niemi, 2002: 175f.). In the United States, where the concept was first developed (Campbell, et al., 1960), parties have great longevity. The Democratic and Republican Parties have each been in existence for more than 150 years; thus, voters can identify with the same party throughout their life and parents can pass their party identification on to their children. However, in a floating system of parties, the supply of parties changes from one election to the next; therefore, it is not possible to develop a long-term identification with a political party (see Chapter 5). This point was inadvertently demonstrated by a survey conducted in 1998, midway between two Russian elections (Miller and Klobucar, 2000). It asked about identification with 14 parties nominally active at the time. However, when the 1999 Duma election was held, nine of the parties named did not nominate candidates and most Russians voted for parties that were not in existence when the inter-election survey was undertaken. When asked about party identification in the 2004 New Europe Barometer survey, only 21 per cent identified with a party, half the proportion of those who said 'don't know' when asked how they would vote if an election were held that week and one-third the proportion likely to vote when an election was actually held.

Combining the responses that electors give to questions about trust in parties and party preferences divides new European electorates into four unequal groups. The largest group, 44 per cent, consists of distrusting citizens who nonetheless name a party they would vote for. The second largest group, 32 per cent, distrusts all parties and favours none. Sceptical voters, who give a neutral answer to a question about trust in parties, are 17 per cent of all respondents.[2] The civic ideal, voters who not only have a party preference but also trust parties, are the smallest group, only 7 per cent. In short, knowing how a person votes is not sufficient to understand how they actually view the party that gets their momentary support, if only as a lesser evil.

Political Values Without Parties

The limited attachment of citizens to parties is not proof of the absence of political values. It can also reflect a mismatch between what parties supply and what

---

[2] They sub-divide into 12 percent stating a party preference and 5 per cent without a preference. The 2 per cent who expressed trust in parties but had no preference are excluded from these calculations.

electors want. Political values express major normative principles that can be found in ideologies, albeit lacking the logical rigour and comprehensiveness of a fully developed ideology. Democratic values are consensual; however, the political values of voters identify differences that are the stuff of competitive party politics. Values provide principles relevant to many issues of public policy, such as support for markets, national traditions, or the environment. They indicate which side people take in disputes about public policy. When governors have important decisions to make, principles give grounds for choice between competing policies.

While party labels differ greatly between countries, symbolic terms associated with political values are common throughout Europe, such as left and right. However, citizens in post-Communist Europe do not see parties or themselves in such terms. In six new European democracies the European Social Survey has asked respondents to place themselves on an 11-point scale from 0 to 10; 0 means left, 10 means right, and 5 is both the arithmetic and psychological centre. In response, almost half reject taking a side. An average of 29 per cent place themselves at the centre of the scale, 5, and 20 per cent respond 'don't know'. In Slovenia and Estonia, the don't knows and centrists form a majority of the electorate and in the other four countries they are the largest single group.[3] After four generations of living in so-called Workers' Republics, only 22 per cent describe themselves as being more or less on the left, as against 29 per cent saying that they are more or less on the right.

Since political values are expressed by symbols rather than mathematical scales, the New Europe Barometer asks whether respondents favour any one of five different values. Three reflect economic concerns: the market, social democracy, and Communism. A fourth alternative, national traditions, evokes the politics of national defence. A green outlook has particular relevance in post-Communist countries because of the old regime's degradation of the environment. Respondents also have the choice of saying that they have other values or no political outlook.

Focussing on a multiplicity of values is consistent with the multi-party systems found in new democracies and how they are perceived by the electorate (Chapter 3). It also avoids the reductionist assumption that all values can be reduced to a single left/right dimension. The alternative to a Communist outlook is not necessarily commitment to the market. It can be identification with national traditions or green values. The placement of social democrats depends on which of the terms in its name

---

[3] These percentages pool results from the Czech Republic in the second-round European Social Survey of 2004, and from Estonia, Hungary, Poland, Slovakia, and Slovenia in the third round of the ESS survey, 2006–07.

is emphasized. If the underlying distinction is between freedom and the party-state, social democrats line up in defence of freedom with those favouring the market. However, if the underlying principle differentiates state as against market provision of welfare, then social democrats are closer to Communists.

In new European democracies, 69 per cent endorse one or another political outlook, while 31 per cent have none (Table 4.2). In five new EU countries and in Russia those without any political outlook are the largest group. In the extreme case of Poland, more than half are not committed to any political outlook, notwithstanding extensive political mobilization against the Communist regime. The lack of any outlook is what would be expected when voters do not trust a floating system of parties. It is also a caution against generalizing to the whole population of a country the views of civil society organizations.

The market and social democracy are the most commonly favoured outlooks; each is chosen by one-fifth of the electorate. However, nowhere do more than one-third endorse a market outlook and only in the Czech Republic are supporters of social democracy the most numerous. In Russia self-proclaimed social democrats are just nine per cent of the electorate. It would thus be misleading to describe the whole of the electorate as divided ideologically between pro-market and social democratic outlooks. In no country do these two outlooks dominate the electorate.

Table 4.2 POLITICAL OUTLOOKS OF THE ELECTORATE

Q. Which broad political outlook are you most inclined to favour?

	None	Market	Social dem.	Com.	Nat'l trad'n	Green	Other
Poland	51	8	18	4	9	5	5
Hungary	43	10	13	2	6	16	10
Bulgaria	41	20	19	10	2	4	4
Romania	38	24	23	4	6	4	1
Slovakia	36	13	25	10	8	5	3
New EU mean	(31)	(21)	(22)	(5)	(9)	(8)	(4)
Slovenia	25	30	21	1	6	12	5
Latvia	23	34	17	1	8	16	1
Lithuania	19	31	28	4	9	5	4
Estonia	19	22	22	2	17	13	5
Czech R.	13	23	32	7	14	6	5
Russia	41	17	9	16	5	6	6

Source: Centre for the Study of Public Policy, University of Aberdeen, New Europe Barometer survey, October–November 2001, total respondents: 11,010. New Russia Barometer XIV, January 2005, total respondents 2,107.

Cradle-to-grave indoctrination impressed Communist subjects, but not in the compliant manner that was sometimes assumed by Western observers. In new European democracies only five per cent describe their outlook as Communist and in four countries only one or two per cent do so. This is less than the nominal membership of national Communist parties twenty years ago. Many party members were not believers, but held a party card because it offered material advantages and required only ritual repetition of party slogans (Rose, 2009: Chapter 13). Russia is the exception, for there the Communist Party is identified with achievements of the Soviet Union. Almost one-sixth of Russians describe their values as Communist and a lineal heir of the Soviet-era party continues to contest elections. However, at the latest Duma election that party won less than one-eighth of the vote.

National traditions have limited salience, being the choice of nine per cent. Even in the Baltic countries, which gained freedom from Moscow by staging mass demonstrations demanding national independence, only a limited minority describes their political outlook as nationalist. Commitment to green values is limited to eight per cent, and it is below average in the industrialized Czech Republic and Poland. The capacity of electors to form values in the absence of political parties is illustrated by the above-average levels of green respondents in Hungary, Estonia, and Slovenia, where no green party has recently contested the election.

A question designed for application across many countries risks omitting values that could be important in a particular national context, for example, those of ethnic Turks in Bulgaria. Therefore, respondents were offered the option of other values, a category that people could relate to country-specific circumstances and to a value that lacked salience to parties. In the event, only four per cent named an outlook other than those offered in the NEB question.

Consistent with many analyses of political participation, a multinomial logit regression finds that people who are not inclined towards any political outlook are likely to be significantly less educated, older, and less positive about economic circumstances. The same is true of those who call themselves Communists, an indication that in new European democracies Communists are not energetic radicals believing in a new society but backward-facing citizens who have had difficulties adapting to political changes following the fall of the Berlin Wall. Those who are pro-market are significantly more educated.

The varied outlooks of voters are consistent with the varied choices offered by multi-party competition on multiple dimensions. For Western political scientists to regard multi-dimensional competition as abnormal shows a lack of awareness of Western history. Competition between a limited number of parties along a single left/right dimension has not been true of most European countries for most of their electoral history (Lipset and Rokkan, 1967; Rose, 1974). The importance of civil society institutions in mobilizing electoral support in established democracies implies that, where civil society institutions have been purged, there is no particular link between the parties that elites supply and voters, thus encouraging floating supply of parties and voters without trust.

5

COMPETITION WITHOUT INSTITUTIONALIZATION

A party system is completely institutionalized when there is a *stable equilibrium* between the parties supplied and the demands of voters. The same parties compete at successive elections and voters do not float between parties. If the supply of parties is stable but there is a substantial shift in votes, this is a *dynamic equilibrium*; voters signal to parties to change their ways in order to remain competitive. If the supply of parties changes substantially from one election to the next, there is a *structural disequilibrium*; the disappearance of old parties and the emergence of new ones disrupts competition and voters are forced to alter their behaviour.

Competitive elections are a necessary but not a sufficient condition for democratization; the extent to which a party system is institutionalized is important too (Lipset, 2000). The completion of democracy requires leaders to be accountable as well as elected. This requires an institutionalized party system, so that voters can hold the government of the day accountable by voting for or against the governing party or an opposition party. However, when there is the continuing entry and exit of parties from the ballot voters cannot hold governors accountable. The deficit in accountability is especially severe in new European democracies, because of the weakness of civil society institutions, the chief alternative means by which citizens can hold governors to account.

Institutionalization is a process; it takes time before competition arrives at a stable equilibrium. In a new democracy the first election occurs amidst turbulence and uncertainty. The results show which parties have best gauged popular demands and which have misjudged them. Politicians can then transfer their allegiance from hopeless parties to parties that win seats. The adaptation of political elites to election results can quickly lead to the supply of parties becoming steady from one election to the next. Voters offered the same alternatives can learn, by a process of trial and error, which party best represents their views. The outcome of learning by political elites and voters is a party system in a stable equilibrium.

Two decades have passed since the fall of the Berlin Wall made free elections possible in Central and Eastern Europe and countries have now held five or six free elections. The following pages test the extent to which a stable equilibrium has developed. The evidence shows that there is competition without institutionalization.

Institutionalization in Theory

In established democracies the institutionalization of party systems occurred very gradually and long ago. By contrast, electoral competition was introduced in Central and Eastern Europe by the abrupt collapse of a repressively stable equilibrium, the Communist party-state. Politicians who had made their career within the Communist Party were cut loose by events, while small groups of dissidents unexpectedly found themselves needing to organize electoral parties in order to maintain their political position. Instead of being compelled to endorse a one-party regime, citizens unexpectedly became free to vote for a party that actually represented their views – if only they could figure out which party that might be.

The party names that appeared on the ballot at the first post-Communist elections were not the labels of well-organized groups with strong roots in society. They were *proto-* or *pre-*parties with uncertain prospects of development. The greater the number of parties competing for votes, the greater the number of parties likely to fail to clear the PR threshold to qualify for seats in parliament. The results of the first free election created three categories of parties: those with enough votes to be confident of a significant position in parliament in future; parties that faced an uncertain electoral future because they had only just cleared the PR threshold; and parties falling well below the threshold and having no representatives in parliament.

Given a base-line distribution of votes and seats, four conditions must be met before a party system can arrive at a stable equilibrium. *Party systems will become institutionalized depending on the extent to which:*

♦*1. Election laws are stable.* Laws for the conduct of elections offer incentives and constraints to party elites. It follows that a change in election laws will influence elite decisions about whether to maintain, create, or abandon parties. A change in the law not only will affect how votes are cast but also may affect how electors choose between parties. If election laws are stable or are changed in only minor ways, this should increase the institutionalization of a party system.

♦*2. Elites have durable commitments to a party.* In theory, leaders of larger parties can consolidate existing support and use their parliamentary numbers to influence government policies in ways attracting more support. Leaders of parties with uncertain prospects of continuing to win seats can adapt tactics to their limited support or merge with other parties to form a bloc with greater influence. Politicians in parties going nowhere can abandon them in order to further their political career elsewhere. The consequence of a rational process of adaptation will be that the supply of parties rapidly stabilizes as the most successful parties offer incentives to aspiring politicians to join them rather than launch a new party.

♦3. *Voters have durable commitments to a party.* As the supply of parties stabilizes, the demands of voters should show greater consistency too. Socialization can create durable electoral commitments through 'a strengthening of ties between socio-demographic groups and political parties' (Wessels and Klingemann, 2006: 24). However, in post-Communist countries socio-economic commitments to parties have tended to be weak (McAllister and White, 2007: Table 3). If electors decide their choices by calculating the net present value of different parties, then current conditions such as the state of the economy or the personality of party leaders become important and produce temporary rather than durable commitments, as parties change leaders and economic conditions fluctuate.

♦4. *Learning occurs among elites and voters.* On the supply side, party politicians 'experiment and learn through repetition how to campaign effectively for votes. They also learn how to combine with and against each other' (Olson,1998: 433). Since the penalty for failing to learn is political marginalization or extinction, by the third election elites should be committed to a party on a long-term basis (Mainwaring and Zoco, 2007: 165f.). The first free election teaches voters which parties are important and which unimportant in parliament. Voters thus learn to avoid wasting votes on parties that cannot represent their views because they have no seats in parliament (Tavits and Annus, 2005; Duch and Palmer, 2002). The rotation of parties in and out of office enables voters to learn how competing parties perform in government. As parties establish a record in office or in opposition, voters can identify with the party that best matches their broad political outlook, thus creating a stable equilibrium of supply and demand.

A stable equilibrium is not static, for party leaders are under continuing pressure to respond to those they represent or risk losing votes. The electoral pendulum can swing back and forth while the parties between which voters oscillate remain the same. If established parties ignore popular demands, a new party can emerge to articulate these views. If a new party wins a significant share of votes, this will signal the need for institutionalized parties to adapt to crush a new competitor. This has been the recurrent pattern in American presidential elections. Since 1948 five different third-party presidential candidates have won a substantial share of the popular vote – Strom Thurmond, Henry Wallace, John Anderson, Ross Perot, and Ralph Nader – only to see their voters disappear as the Democratic and Republican Parties have adapted and restored the former equilibrium. In Britain there has been a dynamic equilibrium because of the failure of established parties to respond to competitors. In the decade after 1974 the two-party system of Conservative and Labour was challenged by the Liberal and Social Democratic Parties. The result has been the establishment in England of a new and stable three-party system of competition.

Stable Election Laws

When election laws were adopted, there was extreme uncertainty among political elites about how citizens would vote. Even if elites expected that voters would reject a party of Communists, there were no grounds for knowing which party or parties would win support. The first election produced many surprises. While a few party leaders were pleased with their success, many were shocked to learn that voters held them in much lower esteem than they held themselves.

The first election immediately created support for the new electoral system by giving hundreds of MPs an interest in maintaining the system that had brought them to parliament. Since then, there have been frequent changes in election outcomes, but new MPs are as ready as their predecessors to maintain the system by which they have won their seats. Coalition governments establish barriers to any one party changing election laws to their own benefit. Those with the biggest grievances – leaders of parties that fail to win any seats in parliament – are in the weakest position to achieve change. Hence, election laws enacted without knowing what their consequences would be have lasted with relatively few and minor amendments (cf. Bielasiak, 2002: 191ff.; Benoit, 2004).

The biggest change would be a shift from a proportional representation to a first-past-the-post system or vice versa. So great is the impact of such a change on the interest of parties that it very rarely occurs. Since 1990 nine new European democracies have consistently maintained their proportional representation or mixed electoral system. The sole exception is Bulgaria, which moved from a mixed to an exclusively PR system after its first election in 1990.

Limited rule changes have occurred within PR systems. The most noteworthy have involved raising the threshold of votes for electoral alliance of parties to win seats (for details, see chapters in Part Two). This has been justified as avoiding a parliament with "too many" parties, since it makes it more difficult for small parties to win a few seats in parliament by forming temporary alliances. For example, in Poland there was initially no threshold for a party to qualify for PR seats. However, after more than two dozen parties won at least one seat at the 1991 election, a five per cent threshold was introduced and the threshold for party alliances was set at eight per cent. The Czech Republic has raised the 5 per cent threshold for a single party to 10 per cent for an alliance of two parties, 15 per cent for three parties, and 20 per cent for four parties. In an attempt to increase the accountability of MPs to voters, before the 2008 election Romania changed from a PR list ballot to one requiring voters to cast a vote for an individual name on a party list rather than giving a blanket endorsement to all the candidates named there.

Russia is exceptional in switching from a mixed electoral system to an exclusively PR list system before the 2007 election. Concurrently, it raised the threshold to qualify for seats in the Duma from five to seven per cent. This was done to weaken opposition parties and benefit United Russia, the party created by Vladimir Putin to maintain his control of the Russian state. The strategy worked: in 2007 Putin's party won sufficient Duma seats to amend the constitution. In November 2008 a law increased the term of office for Russia's next president from four to six years and that of Duma members from four to five years (Rose and Mishler, 2009). In Ukraine a floating party system has made it difficult to establish an authoritarian regime, but conflicts between Ukrainian leaders have prevented the institutionalization of a democratic party system. In most successor states of the Soviet Union, leaders who initially seized power quickly changed electoral laws in order to institutionalize a system of unfair and unfree elections (see, e.g., Fish, 2005; Rose, Mishler, and Munro, 2006: Chapter 3).

The consistency with which election laws have been maintained in new European democracies shows the commitment of political elites to the rules of the electoral game. This is not proof that all contestants in national elections are convinced democrats, but that there is a consensus among elites that competitive elections are the only way to decide who is in office and who is not. However, agreement about the rules of game leaves open how elites play the game and whether they win or lose.

Floating Systems of Parties

Founding elections faced party leaders in new democracies with a far greater challenge than that of West European politicians after the Second World War, because the latter could fall back on party organizations created before military occupation and defeat. By contrast, in Central and Eastern Europe parties were eliminated by Stalinist measures. After the fall of the Berlin Wall in 1989, new parties had to be created. Yet they could be little more than networks of individuals that came together to fight a specific election and afterwards went separate ways.

Few parties show stamina. The minimum requirement for institutionalizing a party system is that parties persist from one election to the next. However, this has not happened. The destruction and creation of parties have produced floating systems of parties. In the average new European democracy, 30 parties have contested at least one election, but only two have fought every election (Figure 5.1). Of the remaining 28, a total of 22 have already disappeared while 6 have yet to confirm whether they are short-lived or long-lived. For example, none of the parties that competed in the first free election in Latvia in 1993 were still on the ballot at the 2007 election, while 34 parties had come, gone, or both come and gone.

Russia is exceptional in that four parties have contested every Duma election since the first. The two consistently winning seats – the Communist Party and Vladimir Zhirinovsky's Liberal Democratic Party – are hardly parties. Parties can persist at a very low level of support. For example, Yabloko has fought every Russian election but never secured more than 7.3 per cent of the list vote. The

Figure 5.1 FEW PARTIES SHOW STAMINA TO PERSIST SINCE 1990

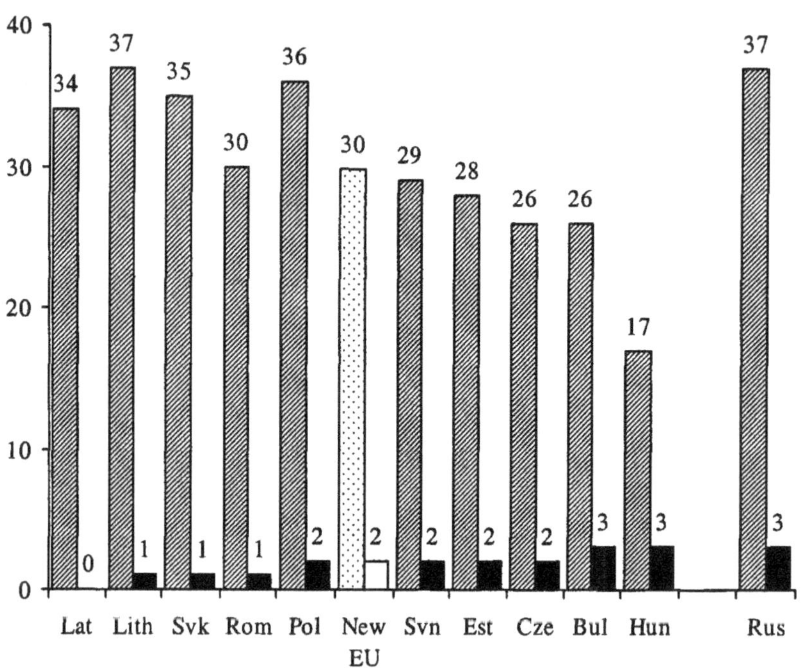

Source: Calculated from national chapters in Part Two.

turnover of parties is particularly striking, given state subsidies to political parties and additional resources available to parties in government (Lewis, 2000: 107ff.).

Volatility without learning. Given the uncertainties involved in founding new parties, theories of institutionalization predict that the large number of parties launched at the first election will be reduced at each successive election as party leaders respond to signals of support or rejection by the electorate (Kitschelt, 1995: 452). However, this has not happened.

In founding elections of new European democracies, an average of almost 12 parties won at least one per cent of the vote or two seats, and in Poland 29 parties did so. While an average of four parties disappeared from the ballot at the second election, seven new parties won some electoral support.[1] The third set of elections showed a trend in the opposite direction, as an average of seven parties dropped out of competition while five new parties successfully entered. In the fourth round, the number of parties dropping out, six, was greater than new parties entering, three. However, in the fifth set of elections, the number of new parties, three, averaged slightly less than the number of parties disappearing.

The extent of electoral volatility depends on the size of the vote for parties that exit or enter the system. The Index of Volatility sums the arithmetic change in the distribution of the vote between parties at a given pair of elections. The Index can be as low as 0 per cent if there is no change on either the demand or the supply side, to 200 per cent, if the turnover of parties on the supply side is total. Because it relies on the aggregate vote for each party, the Index actually understates the extent of change in individual electors, in so far as individuals switching in opposite directions tend to cancel out. Focussing on aggregate behaviour is consistent with the outlook of political elites; the number that matters most to a party is its total vote, because that determines how many seats it gets in parliament.[2]

Theories of institutionalization predict that volatility will initially be high, because parties cannot appeal to pre-existing loyalties. Between the first and second contests, the average Index of Volatility in new EU countries averaged 110 per cent.

---

[1] The average number of parties is rounded to the nearest whole number.

[2] Our Index differs from Pedersen (1979), because his divides the total change of votes by two, thus calculating a net swing. It produces a familiar 0 to 100 scale, but understates by half the actual amount of change. For example, an increase of 15 per cent in the vote for one party and a fall of 15 per cent for another is registered in our Index as 30 per cent, whereas the Pedersen Index shows a change of 15 per cent.

A major cause of high volatility was that after the defeat of their common enemy anti-Communist movements that had fought the founding election as a single party broke up. In the Czech Republic volatility of 138 per cent was largely due to the break-up of Civic Forum, which won 49 per cent of the vote in the first election. In Romania volatility of 170 per cent was principally due to the break-up of the anti-Ceauşescu National Salvation Front, which won 66 per cent of the vote in the founding election.

If a big initial shift in votes is the price that party politicians pay to learn which parties attract voters, the Index of Volatility should subsequently fall. However, this has not happened. Instead of moving towards a stable equilibrium, the opposite has happened. In six of ten countries the Index of Volatility actually rose between the second and third elections; it averaged 111 per cent. Between the third and fourth elections, average volatility rose by 9 percentage points compared to the previous pair of elections. The average Index of Volatility between the fourth and fifth election was 14 points lower than in the previous pair of elections, but was still 101 per cent.

In every post-Communist country the Index of Volatility between the first and most recent election is at least 100 per cent (Figure 5.2). In Latvia all the votes have shifted between parties and in Slovenia, Lithuania, and Poland more than nine in ten votes have shifted. Altogether, volatility averages 166 per cent. High volatility in the Czech and Slovak Republics cannot be explained away by the break-up of Czechoslovakia, for in Poland and Romania, where the state has remained intact, volatility has been higher still. Notwithstanding the turnover of Russian parties, volatility there has actually been below the new EU average. While electoral volatility has been least high in Bulgaria, 111 per cent, only 3 of its 26 parties have fought all its elections.

Volatility in supply more important. Electoral volatility reflects the combined effect of supply and demand. Supply-side volatility is structural: parties disappearing force their former supporters to behave differently at the next election and votes attracted by new parties reduce the vote share of parties that had previously been on the ballot. However, when voters change their minds about the appeal of parties that remain on the ballot from one election to the next, this produces demand-side volatility. In order to determine which is more important, the Index can be disaggregated to show the amount of change due to alterations in the supply of parties or in the demands of voters.

In every new European democracy the supply-side actions of political elites are

Figure 5.2 VOLATILITY OF VOTE: FOUNDING AND LATEST ELECTIONS

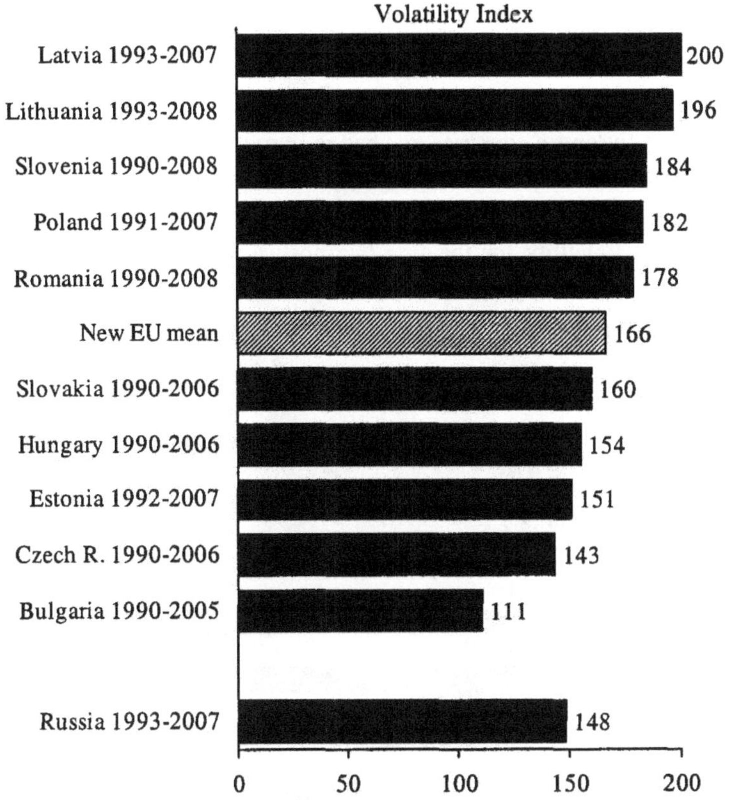

Volatility Index

	Volatility Index
Latvia 1993-2007	200
Lithuania 1993-2008	196
Slovenia 1990-2008	184
Poland 1991-2007	182
Romania 1990-2008	178
New EU mean	166
Slovakia 1990-2006	160
Hungary 1990-2006	154
Estonia 1992-2007	151
Czech R. 1990-2006	143
Bulgaria 1990-2005	111
Russia 1993-2007	148

0 50 100 150 200

Index of Volatility: sum of the arithmetic change in each party's percentage share of the list vote between a pair of elections.

Source: Calculated from national chapters in Part Two.

the primary cause of electoral volatility between the first and the most recent election. Of the total volatility, more than five-sixths has been due to the actions of party elites creating, abandoning, or merging parties. The impact has been greatest in Latvia, Lithuania, and Poland, where changes in the supply of parties have almost completely transformed the party system. In all but two countries supply-side changes have accounted for more than 100 points of the change registered by the Volatility Index (Figure 5.3).

In principle, a rise in demand-side volatility would be a sign of a dynamic equilibrium replacing the structural disequilibrium caused by floating supply of parties. However, in the most recent pair of elections in each new European democracy, supply-side influences remain the dominant cause of volatility. The entry and exit of parties account for an average of 59 points of change in the Index of Volatility, as against demand-side shifts between existing parties contributing 36 points to the Index.

Initial volatility was much higher in Central and Eastern Europe in the 1990s than in West European countries that had re-introduced competitive elections after 1945 (Turner, 1993). Notwithstanding 12 years of Nazi domination in Germany and 7 in Austria, parties with origins in the late nineteenth century re-emerged. In Austria the Index of Volatility for the first two postwar elections was 24 per cent; in

Figure 5.3 SUPPLY-SIDE ACTIONS CHIEF CAUSE OF VOLATILITY

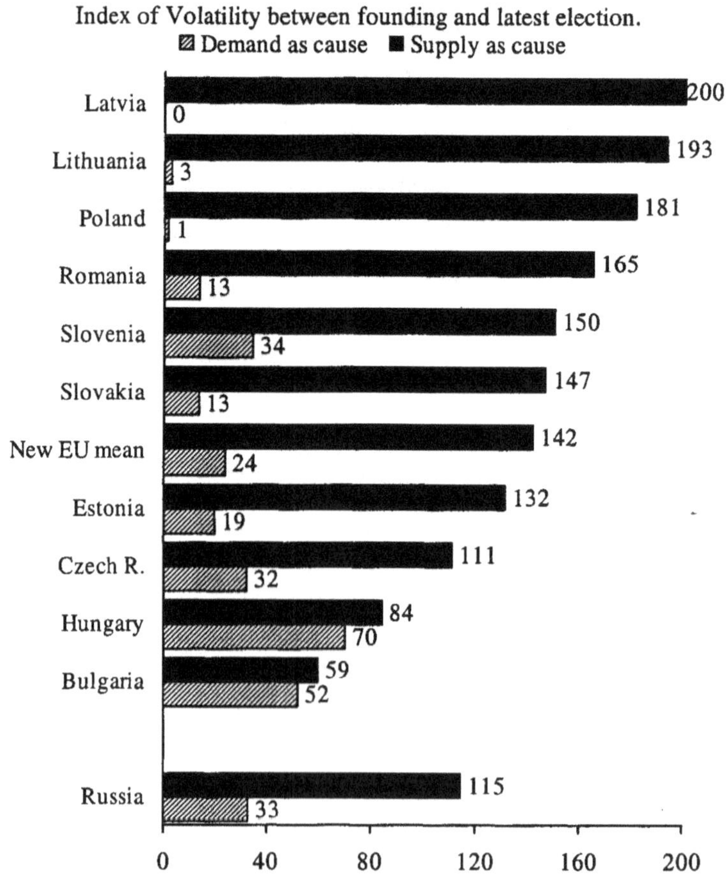

Source: Calculated from national chapters in Part Two.

Germany it was 52 per cent; and in post-fascist Italy 46 per cent. In the first pair of free elections in Spain and Portugal in the 1970s, the Index of Volatility was 25 per cent, less than one-quarter that of the average new European democracy in the early 1990s.

For a generation after the Second World War, party systems of Western Europe combined consistency in the supply of parties and stability in the response of voters (Rose and Urwin, 1970). Since then, that stability has been under pressure on the demand side, as greater prosperity, education, secularization, and new life-styles have weakened established loyalties of voters. More open-minded voters are readier to re-evaluate family loyalties and float between parties on the basis of priorities given to particular issues or short-term events (Dalton, 2008). Concurrently, well-publicized scandals involving prime ministers and presidents have encouraged distrust of politicians and party politics (Pharr and Putnam, 2000).

Party leaders in Western Europe have responded to changes in the electorate by sticking with their party organization while adapting what they supply. Their characteristic strategy is to become a catch-all party making fuzzy-focus appeals that draw temporary support from variegated sections of the electorate (Kirchheimer, 1966; Koole, 1996). A catch-all party can avoid taking sides on issues, claiming it is best able to achieve consensual goals such as prosperity and peace. It can also promote personalities rather than policies and values. However, personalities such as Ronald Reagan and Gerhard Schröder did not become national leaders by founding their own party or running as independents. Instead, each first joined a political party founded in the previous century and sought its nomination for the highest office in the land as a necessary condition of winning office.

Although volatility has risen in Western Europe, it remains far less than in post-Communist party systems (cf. Caramani, 2006). Between 1990 and the most recent national election, the Index of Volatility in the 15 older European Union countries has averaged 61 points, less than two-fifths the Index in new European countries. Moreover, in 14 of these 15 countries the Index of Volatility has been below the new Europe average. In the Federal Republic of Germany, notwithstanding the collapse of the one-party East German state, volatility was only 32 per cent, due to West German parties instantly supplying parties that won the bulk of the vote in East as well as West Germany (Rose and Haerpfer, 1997). The dynamic of party competition in Western Europe is much more affected by changes in electoral demands than by changes in the supply of parties.

Of the four conditions necessary to institutionalize a party system, only one has been met in new European democracies: election laws have been stable. However, within these stable rules of the game, political elites have repeatedly disrupted party competition by creating, abandoning, splitting, or merging parties, thus creating floating party systems. In so far as learning has occurred among elites, it has taken the form of "party hopping" rather than the development of a long-term commitment to one party. In consequence, electorates consist of floating voters whose distrust of parties is compounded by their inability to hold political elites accountable.

Institutionalizing an Incomplete Democracy

Entry to the European Union marked the end of the transition of ten Central and East European countries from the backward-facing status of a post-Communist regime to being a new European democracy. As the experience of Soviet successor states demonstrates, this accomplishment was by no means certain in the aftermath of the fall of the Berlin Wall.

Over two decades new democracies have held free and fair elections in which many parties compete and the results demonstrate the most basic feature of democracy: the movement of parties in and out of office. Citizens can and do use their vote to turn the governing parties out of office. Moreover, the division of votes among many parties prevents anything like the development of a hegemonic party system such as existed in Sweden in the heyday of the Social Democrats or even the long periods in office of the British Conservative and Labour Parties. Coalitions form and break up, and politicians find themselves in and out of office with chastening speed.

Public opinion surveys find that, even though citizens distrust parties, there is widespread support for the principle of free elections. Even more important, there is widespread endorsement of the conduct of elections. In reply to a question in the 2004 New Europe Barometer, 76 per cent of citizens across new EU member-states described elections as completely or substantially fair; the percentage doing so was as high as 90 per cent in the Czech Republic.

In new EU member-states, democracy is strongly endorsed as an ideal. When the 2004 New Europe Barometer asked people where they would like their political system to be on a scale ranging from complete democracy to complete dictatorship, 86 per cent endorsed democracy as an ideal, 5 per cent endorsed a dictatorship, and 9 per cent were neutral (Rose, 2009a: 164ff.). The only difference between countries was in the extent to which citizens were positive. In Hungary as many as 93 per cent favoured democracy as an ideal and in Bulgaria, where support was least high, 77 per cent nonetheless favoured it. Moreover, the meaning given to democracy is that common to most European countries: freedom from the state to say and do what you like, a chance to choose representatives through elections, and the social benefits of a welfare state (Simon, 1998).

However, new EU democracies have yet to supply the institutions that their citizens want. While giving three cheers for democracy as an ideal, citizens are barely willing to give two cheers for the way their political system operates today. When asked to rate it, an average of 53 per cent see it as democratic, 24 per cent are neutral, and 23 per cent see it as to some extent resembling a dictatorship.

The substantial gap between the ideal and the reality of the political system does not mean that democratic institutions are threatened with repudiation. Even though citizens are often very critical, there is no expectation of reverting to the inter-war practice of getting rid of elections and parliament. When the 2004 New Europe Barometer asked whether people think parliament could be closed down and parties abolished, only 2 per cent believed it likely and another 11 per cent thought it might happen. Notwithstanding having spent most of their lives under unrepresentative regimes, 87 per cent of new EU citizens find it inconceivable that they could now be governed without a freely elected parliament. The only difference between countries was in the size of the majority seeing elections and parliament as here to stay. It is as high as 97 per cent in Hungary and even where it is least high more than four-fifths regard their political system as proof against repudiation (Table 5.1). Not only is there widespread confidence that parliament will not be overthrown, but also the proportion thinking it possible has fallen substantially since 1991. At that time, the first New Europe Barometer survey found that in Poland as many as 53 per cent thought their parliament might be suspended.

Preferences for change differ from expectations, because the minority who would like to get rid of parliament is larger than those thinking it possible. When people are asked whether they would approve if political elites closed down parliament and abolished parties, 73 per cent disapprove. The proportion expressing a preference for getting rid of parliament is as low as 12 per cent in Hungary and as high as 37 per cent in Bulgaria (Table 5.1).

Combining answers to questions about the likelihood and the desirability of the suspension of parliament emphasizes that representative institutions are strongly rooted, even if some citizens view them as unsatisfactory. Across new democracies of Europe, 70 per cent are confident democrats. They do not think that parliamentary elections could be abolished and would not approve if it happened. An additional four per cent are anxious democrats; they would disapprove of an end to parliament but are worried that it could happen. The minority who would like to get rid of

Table 5.1 GETTING RID OF ELECTIONS UNLIKELY

Q. Some people think this country would be better governed if parliament were closed down and all parties were abolished.

a) How likely do you think this is to happen in the next few years?

b) If parliament were closed down and parties abolished, would you approve or disapprove?

	Likely	Not likely	Disapprove	Approve
	%	%	%	%
Hungary	3	97	88	12
Romania	15	85	78	22
Estonia	13	87	77	23
Lithuania	9	91	77	23
Slovenia	14	86	76	24
New EU mean	(13)	(87)	(73)	(27)
Slovakia	16	84	73	27
Latvia	19	81	67	33
Poland	19	81	66	34
Czech R	10	90	66	34
Bulgaria	13	87	63	37

Source: Centre for the Study of Public Policy, University of Aberdeen, New Europe Barometer survey, November–December 2004, total number of respondents: 10,392.

parliament are divided. The larger group, 17 per cent, are dejected authoritarians. They would like to see representative institutions abolished but do not think it could happen. Hopeful authoritarians who think parliamentary elections could be abolished and would approve if it happened are only 9 per cent.

Elections and party competition have broad support, if only as a lesser evil by comparison with undemocratic alternatives (see Rose, 2009: Chapter 17). In every country today, most of those who would like to see parliament abolished are dejected authoritarians who do not think it could happen. Any demagogue declaring that parliament and elections should be got rid of would not only face strong resistance from a big majority of citizens but also face doubts from nominal supporters who do not believe that this could be done.

While the institutions of new European democracies appear secure, they are incomplete. The consolidation of a completely democratic regime requires something more than a population committed to democracy as an ideal and to free elections. It also requires a government that is accountable to the electorate and this is lacking. When parties disappear from the ballot, electors are deprived of the chance to pass judgement on the party they voted for at the last election. When new parties appear, they cannot be assessed on their record because they have none. Free elections give voters the opportunity to turn rascals out of office. However, in a floating system of parties this may only lead to a rotation of rascals. Full accountability requires an institutionalized rather than a floating party system.

REFERENCES

Anderson, Christopher J., A. Blais, S. Bowler, T. Donovan, and O. Listhaug, 2005. *Losers' Consent: Elections and Democratic Legitimacy*. Oxford: Oxford University Press.

Anderson, Eugene N., and Pauline R. Anderson, 1967. *Political Institutions and Social Change in Continental Europe in the Nineteenth Century*. Berkeley: University of California Press.

Auer, Andreas, and Michael Bützer, eds., 2001. *Direct Democracy: The Eastern and Central European Experience*. Aldershot: Ashgate.

Banks, Arthur S., Thomas C. Muller, and W. R. Overstreet, eds., 2007. *Political Handbook of the World 2007*. Washington, DC: CQ Press.

Bartolini, Stefano, 2000. "Franchise Expansion". In Rose, 2000, 117–30.

Bartolini, Stefano, and Peter Mair, 1990. *Identity, Competition and Electoral Availability: The Stabilisation of European Electorates, 1885–1985*. Cambridge: Cambridge University Press.

Benoit, Kenneth, 2004. "Models of Electoral System Change", *Electoral Studies* 23, 3, 363–84.

Berlin, Isaiah, 1958. *Two Concepts of Liberty: An Inaugural Lecture*. Oxford: Clarendon Press.

Bielasiak, Jack, 2002. "The Institutionalization of Electoral and Party Systems in Postcommunist States", *Comparative Politics* 34, 2, 189–210.

Blais, André, and Louis Massicotte, 1997. "Electoral Formulas: A Macroscopic Perspective", *European Journal of Political Research* 32, 107–29.

Bozóki, András, and John T. Ishiyama, eds., 2002. *The Communist Successor Parties of Central and Eastern Europe*. Armonk, NY: M. E. Sharpe.

Bugajski, Janusz, 2002. *Political Parties of Eastern Europe: A Guide to Politics in the Post-Communist Era*. Armonk, NY: M. E. Sharpe.

Campbell, Angus, P. E. Converse, W. E. Miller, and D. E. Stokes, 1960. *The American Voter*. New York: John Wiley.

Caramani, Daniele, 2006. "Is There a European Electorate and What Does It Look Like? Evidence from Electoral Volatility Measures 1976–2004", *West European Politics* 29, 1, 1–27.

Chan, Kenneth K., 2000. "The Religious Base of Politics in Post-Communist Poland: A Case of Bounded Secularisation". In D. Broughton and H. ten Napel, eds., *Religion and Mass Electoral Behaviour in Europe*. London: Routledge, 176–97.

Cox, Gary W., 1997. *Making Votes Count: Strategic Coordination in the World's Electoral Systems*. New York: Cambridge University Press.

———, 2000. "Proportional Representation". In Rose, 2000, 227–38.

Crampton, R. J., 1994. *Eastern Europe in the Twentieth Century*. London: Routledge.

Daalder, Hans, 1995. "Paths Toward State Formation in Europe". In H. E. Chehabi and Alfred Stepan, eds., *Politics, Society and Democracy: Comparative Studies in Honor of Juan J. Linz*. Boulder: Westview Press, 113–30.

Dahl, Robert A., 1971. *Polyarchy: Participation and Opposition*. New Haven: Yale University Press.

Dalton, Russell J., 2000. "Citizen Attitudes and Political Behavior", *Comparative Political Studies* 33, 6–7, 912–40.

———, 2008. *Citizen Politics*. Washington, DC: Congressional Quarterly Press, 5th edition.

Dalton, Russell, and Martin Wattenberg, eds., 2001. *Parties Without Partisans: Political Change in Advanced Industrial Democracies*. Oxford: Oxford University Press.

Day, Alan J., ed., 2005. *Political Parties of the World*. London: John Harper, 6th edition.

Duch, Raymond M., and Harvey D. Palmer, 2002. "Strategic Voting in Post-Communist Democracy?", *British Journal of Political Science* 32, 1, 63–91.

Emmons, Terence, 1983. *The Formation of Political Parties and the First National Elections in Russia*. Cambridge, MA: Harvard University Press.

Filippov, Mikhail G., Peter C. Ordeshook, and Olga V. Shvetsova, 1999. "Party Fragmentation and Presidential Elections in Post-Communist Countries", *Constitutional Political Economy* 10, 1, 3–26.

Fish, M. Steven, 1995. *Democracy from Scratch: Opposition and Regime in the New Russian Revolution*. Princeton: Princeton University Press.

———, 2005. *Democracy Derailed in Russia: The Failure of Open Politics*. New York: Cambridge University Press.

Furtak, Robert K., ed., 1990. *Elections in Socialist States*. New York: Harvester Wheatsheaf, 20–52.

Golder, Matt, 2005. "Democratic Electoral Systems around the World, 1946–2000", *Electoral Studies* 24, 103–21.

Havel, Václav, 1985. *The Power of the Powerless: Citizens Against the State in Central Eastern Europe*. London: Hutchinson.

Ishiyama, John T., 1997. "Transitional Electoral Systems in Post-Communist Eastern

Europe", *Political Science Quarterly* 112, 1, 95–115.

Karvonen, Lauri, and Stein Kuhnle, eds., 2001. *Party Systems and Voter Alignments Revisited.* London: Routledge.

Kirchheimer, Otto, 1966. "The Transformation of the West European Party System". In J. LaPalombara and M. Wiener, eds., *Political Parties and Political Development.* Princeton: Princeton University Press, 177–200.

Kitschelt, Herbert, 1995. "Formation of Party Cleavages in Post-Communist Democracies: Theoretical Propositions", *Party Politics* 1, 4, 447–72.

Koenigsberger, Hans G., 1971. *Estates and Revolutions: Essays in Early Modern European History.* Ithaca: Cornell University Press.

Kohler, Ulrich, and Richard Rose, 2008. "Election Outcomes and Maximizing Turnout". Berlin: *WZB Discussion Papers* SP 1 2008-203.

Koole, Ruud, 1996. "Cadres, Catchall or Cartel?", *Party Politics* 4, 507–23.

Lawson, Kay, Andrea Römmele, and G. Karasimeonov, eds., 1999. *Cleavages, Parties and Voters: Studies from Bulgaria, the Czech Republic, Hungary, Poland and Romania.* Westport, CT: Praeger.

Le Duc, L., R. G. Niemi, and P. Norris, eds., 2002. *Comparing Democracies* 2. London: Sage Publications.

Lewis, Paul G., 2000. *Political Parties in Post-Communist Eastern Europe.* London: Routledge.

Linz, Juan J., and Alfred Stepan, eds., 1978. *The Breakdown of Democratic Regimes.* Baltimore: Johns Hopkins University Press.

Linz, Juan J., and Arturo Valenzuela, eds., 1994. *The Failure of Presidential Democracy: Comparative Perspectives.* Baltimore: Johns Hopkins University Press.

Lipset, S. M., 2000. "The Indispensability of Political Parties", *Journal of Democracy* 11, 1, 48–55.

Lipset, S. M., and Stein Rokkan, eds., 1967. *Party Systems and Voter Alignments.* New York: Free Press.

McAllister, Ian, and Stephen White, 2007. "Political Parties and Democratic Consolidation in Post-Communist Societies", *Party Politics* 13, 2, 197–216.

———, 2008. "Voting against All in Post-Communist Russia", *Europe-Asia Studies* 60, 1, 67–87.

Mainwaring, Scott, and Matthew Soberg Shugart, eds., 1997. *Presidentialism and Democracy in Latin America.* New York: Cambridge University Press.

Mainwaring, Scott, and Edurne Zoco, 2007. "Political Sequences and the Stabilization of Interparty Competition", *Party Politics* 13, 2, 155–78.

Mair, Peter, 2002. "Comparing Party Systems". In Le Duc, et al., 2002, 88–107.

Mair, Peter, and Cas Mudde, 1998. "The Party Family and Its Study", *Annual Review of Political Science* 1, 211–29.

Malová, Darina, and Peter Učeň, 2000. "Slovakia", *European Journal of Political Research* 38, 3–4, 511–16.

Massicotte, Louis, and André Blais, 2000. "Mixed Electoral Systems". In Rose, 2000, 165–71.

Miller, A. H., and T. F. Klobucar, 2000. "The Development of Party Identification in Post-Soviet Societies", *American Journal of Political Science* 44, 4, 667–85.

Miller, William L., and Richard G. Niemi, 2002. "Voting: Choice, Conditioning and Constraint". In Le Duc, et al., 2002, 169–88.

Mishler, William, and Richard Rose, 2001. "What Are the Origins of Political Trust?", *Comparative Political Studies* 34, 1, 30–62.

Myers, Alec R., 1975. *Parliaments and Estates in Europe to 1789*. London: Thames and Hudson.

Nohlen, Dieter, 2000. "Additional Member System". In Rose, 2000, 4–6.

Norris, Pippa, 2003. *Electoral Engineering: Voting Rules and Political Behavior*. New York: Cambridge University Press.

Olson, David M., 1993. "Political Parties and Party Systems in Regime Transformation: Inner Transition in the New Democracies of Central Europe", *American Review of Politics* 13 (Winter), 619–58.

———, 1998b. "Party Formation and Party System Consolidation in the New Democracies of Central Europe", *Political Studies* 46, 3, 432–64.

O'Neil, Patrick H., 1997. "Hungary: Political Transition and Executive Conflict". In Ray Taras, ed., *Postcommunist Presidents*. New York: Cambridge University Press, 195–224.

Pedersen, Mogens, 1979. "The Dynamics of European Party Systems: Changing Patterns of Electoral Volatility", *European Journal of Political Research* 7, 1, 1–26.

Pempel, T. J., 1990. *Uncommon Democracies: The One-Party Dominant Regimes*. Ithaca: Cornell University Press.

Pharr, Susan J., and Robert D. Putnam, eds., 2000. *Disaffected Democracies: What's Troubling the Trilateral Countries?* Princeton: Princeton University Press.

Pravda, Alex, 1978. "Elections in Communist Party States". In Guy Hermet, Alain Rouquié and R. Rose, eds. *Elections Without Choice*. London: Macmillan, 169–95.

Rose, Richard, ed., 1974. *Electoral Behavior*. New York: Free Press.

———, 1999. "Getting Things Done in an Anti-Modern Society: Social Capital

Networks in Russia". In Partha Dasgupta and Ismail Serageldin, eds., *Social Capital*. Washington, DC: World Bank, 147–71.

———, ed., 2000. *The International Encyclopedia of Elections*. Washington, DC: CQ Press.

———, 2002. *A Bottom Up Evaluation of Enlargement Countries: New Europe Barometer I*. Glasgow: CSPP Studies in Public Policy No. 364.

———, 2003. "Voter Turnout in Western Europe". In *The Western European Experience of Elections*. Stockholm: International IDEA, 17-24.

———, 2005. *Insiders and Outsiders: New Europe Barometer 2004*. Glasgow Centre for the Study of Public Policy SPP 404.

———, 2008. "Evaluating Democratic Governance", *Democratization* 15, 2, 251–71.

———, 2009. "Democratic and Undemocratic States". In C. W. Haerpfer, P. Bernhagen, R. Inglehart, and C. Welzel, eds., *Democratization*. Oxford: Oxford University Press, 10–23.

———, 2009a. *Understanding Post-Communist Transformation: A Bottom Up Approach*. London and New York: Routledge.

Rose, Richard, Sten Berglund, and Neil Munro, 2006. "Baltic Identities and Interests in a European Setting". In John McGarry and Michael Keating, eds., *European Integration and the Minorities Question*. London: Routledge, 308–28.

Rose, Richard, and Christian Haerpfer, 1997. "The Impact of a Ready-Made State", *German Politics* 6, 1, 100–21.

Rose, Richard, and Thomas T. Mackie, 1983. "Incumbency in Government: Liability or Asset?" In H. Daalder and P. Mair, eds., *West European Party Systems*. London: Sage Publications, 115–37.

Rose, Richard, and Toni Makkai, 1995. "Consensus or Dissensus in Welfare Values in Post-Communist Societies?", *European Journal of Political Research* 28, 203–24.

Rose, Richard, and William Mishler, 1998. "Negative and Positive Partisanship in Post-Communist Countries", *Electoral Studies* 17, 2, 217–34.

———, 2009. "A Supply–Demand Model of Party System Institutionalization: The Russian Case", *Party Politics*, in press.

Rose, Richard, William Mishler, and Neil Munro, 2006. *Russia Transformed: Developing Popular Support for a New Regime*. New York: Cambridge University Press.

Rose, Richard, and Doh Chull Shin, 2001. "Democratization Backwards: The Problem of Third-Wave Democracies", *British Journal of Political Science* 31, 2,

331–54.

Rose, Richard, and Derek W. Urwin, 1970. "Persistence and Change in Western Party Systems", *Political Studies* 18, 3, 287–319.

Sartori, Giovanni, 1976. *Parties and Party Systems: A Framework for Analysis.* Cambridge: Cambridge University Press.

Schumpeter, Joseph A., 1952. *Capitalism, Socialism and Democracy.* London: George Allen & Unwin, 4th edition.

Seymour, Charles H., and Donald Paige Frary, eds., 1918. *How the World Votes: The Story of Democratic Development in Elections.* Springfield, MA: C. A. Nichols.

Shlapentokh, Vladimir, 1989. *Public and Private Life of the Soviet People.* New York: Oxford University Press.

Shugart, Matthew Soberg, and Martin P. Wattenberg, eds., 2001. *Mixed Member Electoral Systems: The Best of Both Worlds?* Oxford: Oxford University Press.

Simon, Janos, 1998. "Popular Conceptions of Democracy in Postcommunist Europe". In S. H. Barnes and J. Simon, eds., *The Postcommunist Citizen.* Budapest: Erasmus Foundation and Institute for Political Science, Hungarian Academy of Sciences, 79–116.

Szczerbiak, Aleks, 2001. *Poles Together? Emergence and Development of Political Parties in Post-Communist Poland.* Budapest: Central European University Press.

Taagepera, R., and M. S. Shugart, 1989. *Seats and Votes: The Effects and Determinants of Electoral Systems.* New Haven: Yale University Press.

Tavits, Margit, and Taavo Annus, 2005. "Learning to Make Votes Count: The Role of Democratic Experience", *Electoral Studies*, 25, 2, 72–90.

Turner, Arthur W., 1993. "Postauthoritarian Elections: Testing Expectations About 'First' Elections", *Comparative Political Studies* 26, 3, 330–49.

Waller, Michael, 1995. "Adaptation of the Former Communist Parties of East-Central Europe: A Case of Social Democratization?", *Party Politics* 1, 4, 473–90.

Wessels, Bernhard, and Klingemann, Hans-Dieter, 2006. "Parties and Voters – Representative Consolidation in Central and Eastern Europe?", *International Journal of Sociology* 36, 2, 11–44.

White, Stephen, Richard Rose, and Ian McAllister, 1997. *How Russia Votes.* Chatham, NJ: Chatham House.

PART TWO
NATIONAL ELECTION RESULTS

CONVENTIONS IN REPORTING RESULTS

1. Electorate. The number of persons eligible to vote, as reported in official national statistics.

2. Invalid votes. Where official statistics do not report this, the number is arrived at by subtracting valid votes from the total number of ballots returned.

3. Turnout. The total number of valid and invalid votes as a percentage of the registered electorate.

4. Parties. Tables list parties that have contested at least one parliamentary election in their own name and gained at least 1.0 percent of the vote or at least two seats. Smaller but politically noteworthy parties are also listed. The Others category aggregates support for parties receiving less than 1.0 percent of the vote and the total vote for independents.

5. Non-contested election. A long dash (—) means the party did not contest an election.

6. Electoral alliances. An electoral alliance is formed when two or more parties use a common name on the ballot and official statistics report their total vote under that name. When parties which have never contested an election on their own or won more than 1.0 percent of the vote join an electoral alliance with a party which has previously done so, the alliance vote is assigned to the pre-existing party. When two or more parties that have won more than 1.0 percent of the vote on their own join together to fight an election, we treat this alliance as a new party. When two or more parties campaign under a common name but official results are reported separately for each, results are presented separately for each party.

7. Rounding. Percentages are given to the nearest tenth of a percent, and 0.05 percent is rounded up to 0.1 percent.

6

BULGARIA

In 1878 Bulgaria achieved autonomy as a principality within the Ottoman Empire, and in 1879 the Turnovo constitution proclaimed adult male suffrage. However, after a brief period of competition, elections were managed by the government. In 1908 Bulgaria became totally independent, and competition between political groups increased. Proportional representation was first introduced in 1910 and was generally in use from 1912 to 1934. The Agrarian People's Union, founded in 1899, won an absolute majority of votes in 1921, but its government was overthrown by a coup two years later and the prime minister was assassinated. Opposition parties won the 1931 election and the Bulgarian Communist Party began to show signs of gaining strength. In 1934 a military coup occurred and a dictatorship was imposed. During the Second World War Bulgaria sided with Nazi Germany, and a number of leading Bulgarian Communists took refuge in the Soviet Union (Kostadinova, 1995).

With the entry of the Soviet army into Bulgaria in September 1944, the Communist-dominated Fatherland Front formed a provisional government under the leadership of Kimon Georgiev; and it controlled the Ministry of the Interior, which organized elections. In the ballot of 18 November 1945 the Fatherland Front was awarded 86 per cent of the vote. In a referendum on 8 September 1946, 96 per cent of the votes favoured abolishing the monarchy, and the child king, Simeon II, was exiled. In the election to the Grand National Assembly of 27 October 1946, notwithstanding substantial government intimidation, the opposition parties won 29 per cent of the vote and 99 of the 465 seats. Immediately following the 1947 peace treaty securing international recognition of the Bulgarian government, Nikola Petkov, the leader of the Agrarians, the chief opposition party, was arrested, charged with treason, and hanged.

Unfree elections became the norm. There were nominally two parties, the Agrarians and the Communists, which were joined in the Fatherland Front. National Assembly elections were held in single-member districts; there was only one candidate allowed per district, a candidate favoured by the Front. The constitution adopted in 1971 created an elected presidency. All presidents were elected without competition (Schultze, 1969: 140ff.; Bell, 1997: 354ff.).

In November 1989 street demonstrations in Sofia led by Ecoglasnost and other groups later forming the Union of Democratic Forces led to the legalization of opposition political parties. Early in 1990 the governing party changed its name to the Bulgarian Socialist Party and round-table talks began. The Socialist Party wanted all MPs elected by first-past-the-post system, assuming it would benefit most as the best organized party. Opposition parties wanted proportional representation. A mixed system was agreed with 200 deputies elected by PR according to the d'Hondt formula and 200 in single-member districts. In the PR ballot, there was a four per cent threshold to qualify for seats, which were allocated to candidates by their ranking on a party list. Multi-member PR districts were created corresponding to local government boundaries; the number of seats assigned to a district varied with its population. In the single-member districts, if no candidate secured an absolute majority in the first round, the top two candidates contested a second round; the result was valid only if at least half the registered electorate voted. Parties with ethnic or religious goals could not nominate candidates, a move intended to prevent an ethnic Turkish party.

The first free post-Communist election to a Grand National Assembly (*Veliko Narodno Sobranie*) was held in June 1990. The Assembly was charged with preparing a constitution in a maximum of 18 months. Of its 400 seats, 200 were elected by first-past-the-post voting in single-member districts. The Bulgarian Socialist Party won 75 SMD seats and the Union of Democratic Forces (UDF) 32. Where no candidate won an absolute majority, the two top candidates faced each other in a run-off. In the second round, the UDF formed alliances and gained 37 SMD seats; the Socialists took 39. Forty different political associations contested the PR ballot but only four parties cleared the four per cent threshold (Ashley, 1990: 314ff.). After initial refusal by the electoral registration office, ethnic Turks succeeded in having the Movement for Rights and Freedoms recognized as a civil rights organization; it won both PR and single-member seats.

In July 1991, the Grand National Assembly adopted a new constitution making the National Assembly (*Narodno Sobranie*) the sole chamber of parliament. The new Assembly has 240 members elected for a maximum term of four years by the list form of proportional representation. A party must gain at least four per cent of the national vote to qualify for the allocation of seats by the d'Hondt quota. There are 31 districts having 4 to 14 seats. Exceptionally, an independent candidate may be awarded a seat by winning votes equal to the district vote quota. Elections are held on a non-working day.

The electorate consists of all citizens age 18 and over, except for persons serving in prison or otherwise under a legal disability. Any Bulgarian age 21 or older can be a candidate for the National Assembly, provided that he or she does not hold the citizenship of another country (Karasimeonov, 1997).

The constitution authorizes the direct election of a president for a five-year term. If no candidate achieves an absolute majority on the first ballot on a turnout of more than 50 per cent, the two leading candidates face each other in a run-off election. A minimum turnout is not required in the second round. To be nominated, a candidate must be at least 40 years old, and have resided in the country for the previous five years. A president is limited to two terms of office.

One major party, the Union of Democratic Forces, has always been a shifting coalition of groups and the Bulgarian Socialist Party has increasingly become so (Spirova, 2005, 2007). In April 2001 the former king, now known as Simeon Sakskoburggotski, returned from Spain and organized a new political movement which won the most votes and seats at the 2001 Assembly election. The king could not be a member of the National Assembly because of his dual nationality. However, as his party held half the seats in the Assembly, it could nominate and confirm him as prime minister.

To reduce the number of small parties (80 were registered in 2004), before the 2005 election a new law required parties to have signatures from at least 5,000 persons to be registered. In addition, a party had to post a deposit of 20,000 Bulgarian leva (or 40,000 leva for alliances and 5,000 leva for independents); it was returned if the party secured more than one per cent of the vote.

DATES OF ELECTIONS

President	*Narodno Sobranie* (parliament)
12, 19 January 1992	10, 17 June 1990
27 October, 27 November 1996	13 October 1991
11, 18 November 2001	18 December 1994
22, 29 October 2006	19 April 1997
	17 June 2001
	25 June 2005

REFERENCES

Ashley, Stephen, 1990. "Bulgaria", *Electoral Studies* 9, 4, 312–18.

Bell, John D., 1997. "Democratization and Political Participation in 'Post-Communist' Bulgaria". In K. Dawisha and B. Parrott, eds., *Politics, Power and the Struggle for Democracy in South-East Europe.* Baltimore: Johns Hopkins University Press, 353–402.

Central Electoral Commission, 1991. *Biuletin za rezultatite ot izborite za narodni predstaviteli, provedeni na 13 oktomvri 1991 g.*, November.

————, 2002. "2001 Parliamentary Elections, Nationwide Results", http://193.109.54.11/Final2001/res/2001/kpe00.htm, and "2001 Presidential Elections Round I", http://193.109.54.11/Demetra/tur1/6maine-k.htm.

————, 2005. "Parlamentarni izbori, 2005, okonchatelni rezultati za stranata", http://www.2005izbori.org/results/index.html.

————, 2006. "Izbori, 2006, okonchatelni rezultati za stranata", http://www.izbori2006.org/results_2.

Karasimeonov, Georgi, ed., 1997. *The 1990 Election to the Bulgarian Grand National Assembly and the 1991 Election to the Bulgarian National Assembly.* Berlin: Edition Sigma.

Kostadinova, Tatiana, 1995. *Bulgaria, 1879–1946: The Challenge of Choice.* New York: Columbia University Press.

Koulishev, Luben, 1991. Secretary General of the *Veliko Narodno Sobranie* of Bulgaria. Communication, 1 July.

Mathematical Collective 'Elections', Institute of Mathematics, Bulgarian Academy of Sciences, 2001. "Izbori", http://www.math.bas.bg/izbori/.

Schultze, R. O., 1969. "Bulgarien". In D. Sternberger and B. Vogel, eds., *Die Wahl der Parlamente und anderer Staatsorgane: ein Handbuch*, I:i, *Europa.* Berlin: Walter de Gruyter, 123–52.

Spirova, Maria, 2005. "Political Parties in Bulgaria: Organizational Trends in Comparative Perspective", *Party Politics* 11, 5, 601–22.

————, 2007. *Political Parties in Post-Communist Societies: Formation, Persistence and Change.* New York: Palgrave Macmillan.

Todorov, Antonii, 2002. Unofficial Central Electoral Commission single-member district figures. Communication, 22 August.

Todorov, Antonii, et al., 1997. *Balgarski izbori 1990–96: rezultati, analizi, tendentsii.* Sofia: Izdatelstvo Demokratichni Traditsii–Demetra.

Table 6.1 BULGARIAN POLITICAL PARTIES

1 *Bulgarian Socialist Party* (Balgarska Sotsialisticheska Partiya, BSP). Formerly Bulgarian Communist Party. Changed name early in 1990. Since 1991 has contested each election as dominant partner in alliances including: in 1991: Fatherland Party of Labour; in 1994: Bulgarian Agrarian National Union 'Aleksandr Stamboliiskii', Political Club Ecoglasnost; 1997: Political Club Ecoglasnost; 2001: a total of 19 groups including United Bloc of Labour, Communist Party of Bulgaria (KPB), Citizens' Union Roma, a splinter of Bulgarian Social Democratic Party, and

Movement for Social Humanism; 2005: eight groups: Party of Bulgarian Social Democrats, Political Movement Social Democrats, Movement for Social Humanism, Citizens' Union Roma, Communist Party of Bulgaria, BANU–Aleksandr Stamboliiskii, and Green Party. 1990–

2 *United Democratic Forces UtDF* (Obedineni Demokratichni Sili, ODS). An alliance opposed to BSP. Union of Democratic Forces or UDF (Sayuz na Demokratichni Sili, SDS) was formed in December 1989 by ten political groups. Splits in 1991 gave rise to UDF–Centre and UDF–Liberal. In summer 1996, UDF joined with People's Union and Movement for Rights and Freedoms as United Democratic Forces (UtDF) in a primary to nominate a joint candidate, Petar Stoyanov, for the presidential election. In 1997 UtDF included Democratic Party (itself a splinter of original UDF), the principal part of Bulgarian Social Democratic Party, Bulgarian Social Democratic Union, and Christian Democratic Movement. Movement for Rights and Freedoms refused to join. In 2005, alliance included UDF, Democratic Party, BANU–United, St George's Day, and Movement for an Equal Public Model. 1990–

3 *Bulgarian Agrarian National Union, BANU* (Balgarski Zemdelski Naroden Sayuz, BZNS). Descended from leading pre-war agrarian party. After 1990 split into several successor groups each claiming the BANU name. Main body contested 1991 election as BANU–United (BZNS–Edinen). 1990–91

4 *Movement for Rights and Freedoms, MRF* (Dvizhenie za Prava i Svobodi, DPS). Represents Turkish minority. Contested 1997 election in alliance with Green Party, BANU–Nikola Petkov, and Kingdom of Bulgaria Confederation. In 2001contested in alliance with Liberal Union and Euroroma. 1990–

5 *Bulgarian Agrarian National Union–Nikola Petkov* (Balgarski Zemdelski Naroden Sayuz–Nikola Petkov, BZNS–NP). BANU break-away named for agrarian leader executed by Communists in 1947. Split after 1991, one faction joining UDF and another People's Union. 1991

6 *Union of Democratic Forces–Centre, UDF–C* (Sayuz na Demokratichni Sili–Zentar, SDS–Z). Splinter of UDF, led by Social Democratic Party. 1991

7 *Union of Democratic Forces–Liberal, UDF–L* (Sayuz na Demokratichni Sili–Liberal, SDS–L). Splinter of UDF, led by Green Party. 1991

8 *Kingdom of Bulgaria Confederation* (Tsarstvo Balgariya Federatsiya). Monarchist party founded in 1990. 1991–94

9 *Bulgarian Business Bloc* (Balgarski Biznes Blok, BBB). Led by George Ganchev, three times presidential candidate. 1991–2001

10 *Bulgarian Communist Party* (Balgarska Kommunisticheska Partiya, BKP).

Marxist splinter of pre-1989 Communist Party. 1991–97

11 *People's Union* (Naroden Sayuz). Alliance with a splinter of BANU–Nikola Petkov led by Anastasia Dimitrova-Moser with Democratic Party. 1994

12 *Democratic Alternative for the Republic* (Demokraticheska Alternativa za Republika, DAR). Alliance of BSDP and Green Party. 1994

13 *New Choice* (Novy Izbor, NI). Dissident UDF group that backed 1992 Lyuben Berov government. 1994

14 *Patriotic Union* (Patriotichen Sayuz, PS). Alliance including elements of UDF–L and Fatherland Party of Labour. 1994

15 *Euroleft Coalition* (Koalitsiya Evrolevitsa, EL). Pro-European Union alliance including a splinter from BSP. 1997–2001

16 *Union for the King* (Obedinenie za Tsarya, OTs). 1997

17 *National Movement Simeon II* (Natsionalno Dvizhenie Simeon Vtori, NDSV). Founded before 2001 election by former king Simeon II, who became prime minister (2001–05). 2001–

18 *Simeon II Coalition* (Koalitsiya Simeon II, KSII). Identifies with former king but not his party. Originally an anti-corruption movement. Qualified for ballot by including two minor parties already registered to contest election. 2001

19 *National Union for Tsar Simeon II* (Natsionalno Obedinenie za Tsar Simeon II, NOTsSII). Splinter group opposing NDSV, but supporting king. 2001

20 *St George's Day–Internal Macedonian Revolutionary Organization, IMRO* (Georgevden–Vnatreshno Makedonska Revoliutsionerna Organizatsiya, VMRO). Formally recognizes independence of Macedonia but has the name of Bulgarian irredentist organization founded in 1893. 2001

21 *Attack Coalition* (Koalitsiya Ataka). Nationalist, anti-establishment party founded by TV talk show host Volen Sidorov. 2005–

22 *Democrats for Strong Bulgaria* (Demokrati za Silna Balgariya, DSB). UDF splinter led by former prime minister (1997–2001) Ivan Kostov. 2005–

23 *Bulgarian National Union* (Balgarski Naroden Sayuz, BNS). Allies Union of Free Democrats, Bulgarian Agrarian National Union, and IMRO. 2005–

24 *New Time* (Novoto Vreme). Youth-oriented NDSV splinter. 2005–

25 *Coalition of the Rose* (Koalitsiya na Rozata). Comprises Bulgarian Social Democracy, which includes remnants of Euroleft Coalition, National Movement of Rights and Freedoms, and United Bloc of Labour. 2005

26 *Euroroma* (Evroroma). Party seeking to represent Roma. 2005–

Table 6.2a PRESIDENTIAL VOTE: 12, 19 January 1992

	1st Round	%	2nd Round	%
Electorate	6,817,914		6,859,349	
Valid Votes	5,091,127	74.7	5,181,881	75.5
Invalid Votes	48,713	0.7	24,388	0.4
Total Votes	5,139,840	75.4	5,206,269	75.9
Zhelyu Zhelev, UDF	2,273,541	44.7	2,738,446	52.8
Velko Valkanov, BSP	1,549,970	30.4	2,443,435	47.2
George Ganchev, BBB	854,108	16.8	—	—
Blagovest Sendov, Independent	113,897	2.2	—	—
Slavomir Tsankov	50,247	1.0	—	—
Dimitar Popov	32,606	0.6	—	—
Andon Donchev, Independent	31,798	0.6	—	—
Asen Stoykov, BKP	29,646	0.6	—	—
Petar Gogov	21,302	0.4	—	—
Ivan Georgiev, BNRP[1]	19,495	0.4	—	—
Siyka Georgieva	17,150	0.3	—	—
Petar Georgiev, Independent	14,023	0.3	—	—
Kiril Borisov	11,227	0.2	—	—
Yolo Denev	10,769	0.2	—	—
Krum Krumov-Kumanov	10,266	0.2	—	—
Ivan Ivanov	10,099	0.2	—	—
Stoyan Tsankov	9,888	0.2	—	—
Dimitar Dimitrov	8,620	0.2	—	—
Dimitar Markovski	8,360	0.2	—	—
Pravdolyub Kozhuharov	7,808	0.2	—	—
Todor Pashaliyski	6,307	0.1	—	—
Kuzman Kuzmanov	0	0	—	—

Source: Mathematical Collective 'Elections', 2001.

[1] Bulgarian National Radical Party (*Balgarska Natsionalna Radikalna Partiya*).

Table 6.2b PRESIDENTIAL VOTE: 27 October, 27 November 1996

	1st Round	%	2nd Round	%
Electorate	6,837,737		6,832,197	
Valid Votes	4,288,500	62.9	4,189,759	61.3
Invalid Votes	28,907	0.4	11,561	0.2
Total Votes	4,317,407	63.3	4,201,320	61.5
Petar Stoyanov, UDF	1,889,825	44.1	2,502,517	59.7
Ivan Marazov, BSP	1,158,204	27.0	1,687,242	40.3
George Ganchev, BBB	937,686	21.9	—	—
Alexandar Tomov, Euroleft	135,571	3.2	—	—
Christo Boichev, Independent	57,668	1.3	—	—
Vera Ilieva, BKP	34,004	0.8	—	—
Slavomir Tsankov	22,724	0.5	—	—
Ivan Stoyanov	14,659	0.3	—	—
Mincho Minchev, OPT[1]	13,567	0.3	—	—
Mitko Dimitrov	7,793	0.2	—	—
Lyubomir Stefanov	6,056	0.1	—	—
Dimitar Markovski	5,823	0.1	—	—
Iiyan Nikolov	4,920	0.1	—	—

Source: Mathematical Collective 'Elections', 2001.

[1] Fatherland Party of Labour (*Otechestvena Partiya na Truda*).

Table 6.2c PRESIDENTIAL VOTE: 11, 18 November 2001

	1st Round	%	2nd Round	%
Electorate	6,847,422		6,889,638	
Valid Votes	2,837,701	41.4	3,775,119	54.8
Invalid Votes	12,589	0.2	8,917	0.1
Total Votes	2,850,290	41.6	3,784,036	54.9
Georgi Parvanov, BSP	1,032,665	36.4	2,043,443	54.1
Petar Stoyanov,[1] Independent	991,680	34.9	1,731,676	45.9
Bogomil Bonev,[2] Civic Party	546,801	19.3	—	—
Reneta Indzhova,[3] Democratic Alliance	139,680	4.9	—	—
George Ganchev, BBB	95,481	3.4	—	—
Petar Beron,[4] Union Bulgaria	31,394	1.1	—	—

Source: Central Electoral Commission, 2002.

[1] Backed by the UDF and NDSV.

[2] Minister, 1997–99 UDF government. Then founded Civic Party, which did not contest the 2001 Assembly election.

[3] Interim prime minister, October 1994–January 1995.

[4] Ex-leader of Ecoglasnost, UDF chair July–December 1990.

Table 6.2d PRESIDENTIAL VOTE: 22, 29 October 2006

	1st Round	%	2nd Round[1]	%
Electorate	6,477,126		6,469,224	
Valid Votes	2,779,373	42.9	2,699,875	41.7
Invalid Votes	77,374	1.2	57,560	0.9
Total Votes	2,856,747	44.1	2,757,435	42.6
Georgi Parvanov,[2] Independent	1,780,119	64.0	2,050,488	75.9
Volen Sidorov,[3] Attack	597,175	21.5	649,387	24.1
Nedepcho Beronov,[4] Independent	271,078	9.8	—	—
Georgi Markov, Order, Law, Justice	75,478	2.7	—	—
Petar Beron, Independent	21,812	0.8	—	—
Grigor Velev, Whole Bulgaria	19,857	0.7	—	—
Lyuben Petrov, Independent	13854	0.5	—	—

Source: Central Election Commission, 2006.

[1] Second round held because turnout in the first round did not exceed 50 per cent.

[2] Endorsed by BSP chairman and prime minster (2005–) Sergei Stanishev.

[3] Host of TV talk show 'Attack' and founder of the eponymous party.

[4] Constitutional Court chairman; endorsed by UDF, DSB, and Democratic Party.

Table 6.3a BULGARIA: Votes for the *Narodno Sobranie*

	1990		1991	1994	1997	2001	2005
	List	SMD	List	List	List	List	List
Electorate	6,990,372	6,976,620	6,790,006	6,997,954	6,895,764	6,916,151	6,720,941
Valid Votes	6,124,501	6,090,119	5,540,843	5,202,065	4,255,301	4,568,191	3,648,177
Invalid Votes	208,833	244,296	128,727	62,545	35,963	39,937	99,616
Total Votes	6,333,334	6,334,415	5,669,570	5,264,610	4,291,264	4,608,128	3,747,793
1 Bulgarian Socialist Party	2,887,766	2,775,465	1,836,050	2,262,943	939,308	783,372	1,129,196
2 United Democratic Forces	2,217,798	2,188,547	1,903,567	1,260,374	2,223,714	830,338	280,323
3 Bulgarian Agrarian National Union	491,597	498,017	214,052	—	—	—	—
4 Movement for Rights & Freedoms	368,929	326,420	418,168	283,094	323,429	340,395	467,400
5 BANU–Nikola Petkov	—	—	190,454	—	—	—	—
6 UDF–Centre	—	—	177,295	—	—	—	—
7 UDF–Liberal	—	—	155,902	—	—	—	—
8 Kingdom of Bulgaria	—	—	100,883	73,205	—	—	—
9 Bulgarian Business Bloc	—	—	73,379	245,849	209,796	162	—
10 Bulgarian Communist Party	—	—	39,386	78,606	50,864	—	—
11 People's Union	—	—	—	338,478	—	—	—
12 Dem. Alternative for the Republic	—	—	—	197,057	—	—	—
13 New Choice	—	—	—	77,641	—	—	—
14 Patriotic Union	—	—	—	74,350	—	—	—
15 Euroleft Coalition	—	—	—	—	234,058	44,637	—
16 Union for the King	—	—	—	—	46,765	—	—
17 National Movement Simeon II	—	—	—	—	—	1,952,513	725,314
18 Simeon II Coalition	—	—	—	—	—	157,141	—
19 National Union for Tsar Simeon II	—	—	—	—	—	77,671	—

20 St George's Day–IMRO	—	—	—	—	—	165,927	—
21 Attack Coalition	—	—	—	—	—	—	296,848
22 Democrats for Strong Bulgaria	—	—	—	—	—	—	234,788
23 Bulgarian National Union	—	—	—	—	—	—	189,268
24 New Time	—	—	—	—	—	—	107,758
25 Coalition of the Rose	—	—	—	—	—	—	47,410
26 Euroroma	—	—	—	—	—	—	45,637
Others[1]	158,411	301,670	431,707	310,468	227,367	216,035	124,235

Sources: Central Election Commission, 1991, 2002, 2005, 2006; Koulishev, 1991; Mathematical Collective 'Elections', 2001; Todorov, et al., 1997: 82–83; Todorov, 2002.

[1] In 1990: 36 other parties winning less than 1.0 per cent of the vote. In 1991: 28 other parties and independents with 52,617 votes; in 1994: 49 other parties, independents 12,561 votes; in 1997: 33 other parties, independents 19,335 votes; in 2001: 45 other parties, independents 9,365 votes; in 2005: 11 other parties, independents 12,827 votes.

Table 6.3b BULGARIA: Percentage of Votes for the *Narodno Sobranie*

	1990		1991	1994	1997	2001	2005
	List	SMD	List	List	List	List	List
Valid Votes	87.6	87.3	81.6	74.3	61.7	66.0	54.3
Invalid Votes	3.0	3.5	1.9	0.9	0.5	0.6	1.5
Total Votes	90.6	90.8	83.5	75.2	62.2	66.6	55.8
1 Bulgarian Socialist Party	47.2	45.6	33.1	43.5	22.1	17.1	31.0
2 United Democratic Forces	36.2	35.9	34.4	24.2	52.3	18.2	7.7
3 Bulgarian Agrarian National Union	8.0	8.2	3.9	—	—	—	—
4 Movement for Rights & Freedoms	6.0	5.4	7.5	5.4	7.6	7.5	12.8
5 BANU–Nikola Petkov	—	—	3.4	—	—	—	—
6 UDF–Centre	—	—	3.2	—	—	—	—
7 UDF–Liberal	—	—	2.8	—	—	—	—
8 Kingdom of Bulgaria	—	—	1.8	1.4	—	—	—
9 Bulgarian Business Bloc	—	—	1.3	4.7	4.9	0	—
10 Bulgarian Communist Party	—	—	0.7	1.5	1.2	—	—
11 People's Union	—	—	—	6.5	—	—	—
12 Dem. Alternative for the Republic	—	—	—	3.8	—	—	—
13 New Choice	—	—	—	1.5	—	—	—
14 Patriotic Union	—	—	—	1.4	—	—	—
15 Euroleft Coalition	—	—	—	—	5.5	1.0	—
16 Union for the King	—	—	—	—	1.1	—	—
17 National Movement Simeon II	—	—	—	—	—	42.7	19.9
18 Simeon II Coalition	—	—	—	—	—	3.4	—
19 National Union for Tsar Simeon II	—	—	—	—	—	1.7	—
20 St George's Day–IMRO	—	—	—	—	—	3.6	—

21 Attack Coalition	—	—	—	—	—	—	8.1
22 Democrats for Strong Bulgaria	—	—	—	—	—	—	6.4
23 Bulgarian National Union	—	—	—	—	—	—	5.2
24 New Time	—	—	—	—	—	—	3.0
25 Coalition of the Rose	—	—	—	—	—	—	1.3
26 Euroroma	—	—	—	—	—	—	1.3
Others	2.6	5.0	7.8	6.0	5.3	4.7	3.4

Table 6.3c BULGARIA: Number of Seats in the *Narodno Sobranie*

	1990			1991	1994	1997	2001	2005
	List	SMD	Total	List	List	List	List	List
1 Bulgarian Socialist Party	97	114	211	106	125	58	48	82
2 United Democratic Forces	75	69	144	110	69	137	51	20
3 Bulgarian Agrarian National Union	16	0	16	0	—	—	—	—
4 Movement for Rights & Freedoms	12	11	23	24	15	19	21	34
5 BANU–Nikola Petkov	—	—	—	0	—	—	—	—
6 UDF–Centre	—	—	—	0	—	—	—	—
7 UDF–Liberal	—	—	—	0	—	—	—	—
8 Kingdom of Bulgaria	—	—	—	0	0	—	—	—
9 Bulgarian Business Bloc	—	—	—	0	13	12	0	—
10 Bulgarian Communist Party	—	—	—	0	0	0	—	—
11 People's Union	—	—	—	—	18	—	—	—
12 Dem. Alternative for the Republic	—	—	—	—	0	—	—	—
13 New Choice	—	—	—	—	0	—	—	—
14 Patriotic Union	—	—	—	—	0	—	—	—
15 Euroleft Coalition	—	—	—	—	—	14	0	—
16 Union for the King	—	—	—	—	—	0	—	—
17 National Movement Simeon II	—	—	—	—	—	—	120	53
18 Simeon II Coalition	—	—	—	—	—	—	0	—
19 National Union for Tsar Simeon II	—	—	—	—	—	—	0	—
20 St George's Day–IMRO	—	—	—	—	—	—	0	—
21 Attack Coalition	—	—	—	—	—	—	—	21
22 Democrats for Strong Bulgaria	—	—	—	—	—	—	—	17
23 Bulgarian National Union	—	—	—	—	—	—	—	13
24 New Time	—	—	—	—	—	—	—	0

25 Coalition of the Rose	—	—	—	—	—	—	—	0
26 Euroroma	—	—	—	—	—	—	—	0
Others	0	6[1]	6	0	0	0	0	0
Total	200	200	400	240	240	240	240	240

Sources: Central Electoral Commission, 1991, 2002, 2005, 2006; Koulishev, 1991; Mathematical Collective 'Elections', 2001; Todorov, et al., 1997: 82–83; Todorov, 2002.

[1] Four seats were won by independents associated with the Communist regime and 2 by minor parties.

Table 6.3d BULGARIA: Percentage of Seats in the *Narodno Sobranie*

	1990			1991	1994	1997	2001	2005
	List	SMD	Total	List	List	List	List	List
1 Bulgarian Socialist Party	48.5	57.0	52.7	44.2	52.1	24.2	20	34.2
2 United Democratic Forces	37.5	34.5	36.0	45.8	28.8	57.1	21.3	8.3
3 Bulgarian Agrarian National Union	8.0	0	4.0	0	—	—	—	—
4 Movement for Rights & Freedoms	6.0	5.5	5.7	10.0	6.3	7.9	8.8	14.2
5 BANU–Nikola Petkov	—	—	—	0	—	—	—	—
6 UDF–Centre	—	—	—	0	—	—	—	—
7 UDF–Liberal	—	—	—	0	—	—	—	—
8 Kingdom of Bulgaria	—	—	—	0	0	—	—	—
9 Bulgarian Business Bloc	—	—	—	0	5.4	5.0	0	—
10 Bulgarian Communist Party	—	—	—	0	0	0	—	—
11 People's Union	—	—	—	—	7.5	—	—	—
12 Dem. Alternative for the Republic	—	—	—	—	0	—	—	—
13 New Choice	—	—	—	—	0	—	—	—
14 Patriotic Union	—	—	—	—	0	—	—	—
15 Euroleft Coalition	—	—	—	—	—	5.8	0	—
16 Union for the King	—	—	—	—	—	0	—	—
17 National Movement Simeon II	—	—	—	—	—	—	50.0	22.1
18 Simeon II Coalition	—	—	—	—	—	—	0	—
19 National Union for Tsar Simeon II	—	—	—	—	—	—	0	—
20 St George's Day–IMRO	—	—	—	—	—	—	0	—
21 Attack Coalition	—	—	—	—	—	—	—	8.8
22 Democrats for Strong Bulgaria	—	—	—	—	—	—	—	7.1
23 Bulgarian National Union	—	—	—	—	—	—	—	5.4
24 New Time	—	—	—	—	—	—	—	0

25 Coalition of the Rose	—	—	—	—	—	—	—	0
26 Euroroma	—	—	—	—	—	—	—	0
Others	0	3.0	1.5	0	0	0	0	0

7

CZECHOSLOVAKIA

Czechoslovakia was created as an independent state in 1918, following the collapse of the Habsburg Empire. Previously, Czech lands had been governed as an Austrian domain, and Slovakia as a Hungarian domain. There were differences in their multi-ethnic composition, in their adherence to Catholicism, and in their industrial development, as well as in their experience of political representation (see Krejčí, 1995). The 1920 Czechoslovak constitution established a popularly elected Chamber of Deputies with 300 members and an elected but constitutionally weaker Senate with 150 members. The president was elected by both houses of parliament. Uniquely among Central and East European countries, Czechoslovakia consistently held free and fair elections with universal suffrage during the inter-war period. Between 1920 and 1935 four elections to the National Assembly were held using a proportional representation list system (Berta, et al., 2008).

Party competition reflected a multiplicity of cross-cutting cleavages along class, religion, ethno-linguistic, and urban–rural residence lines. There were also cleavages within each category, for example between Czech and German Social Democrats; between Social Democrats and Communists; and between German and Hungarian as well as Czech and Slovak ethnic groups. Four languages were recognized as official in any area where they were spoken by two-thirds of the population: Czechoslovak, German, Ruthene (that is, Ukrainian), and Hungarian. The result has been described as a hybrid of regional (that is, Czech or Slovak) and Czechoslovak parties (Leff and Mikula, 2002: 304). In the 1925 election, 39 parties contested and 16 won seats; no party gained as much as 14 per cent of the vote. In 1929 16 parties won seats, and in 1935 there were 14 parties (Broklová, 1996: 33–34; Leff, 1988).

The rise of Nazism led to the Munich Agreement of 1938 and the incorporation of German-speaking Sudetenland into the Third Reich. In March 1939 Bohemia and Moravia were formally integrated as a protectorate of the German Reich. Slovakia became a separate republic under Father Tiso and allied with Nazi Germany. It declared war on the Soviet Union in 1941.

In Moscow in March 1945 a National Front was formed to provide civilian government following the liberation of Czechoslovakia by the Soviet army. It was an amalgam of organizations dominated by the Communist Party. An election for a constituent national assembly was called for 25 May 1946. Registration requirements prevented some parties from qualifying for the proportional representation ballot, and an agrarian party was not allowed to form. The Communists won a plurality of votes and seats in Czech lands, but in Slovakia the Democratic Party came first. Communists increasingly undermined other parties. In February 1948 a coup gave the Communists absolute power. A Soviet-style election was called with a single party on the ballot. On a turnout of 93.5 per cent, 89 per cent were reported as voting for the single Communist slate; 11 per cent returned blank ballots (Broklová, 1996: 49). Stalinist purge trials followed under President Klement Gottwald. The Prague Spring movement of 1968 was crushed by Soviet-led armed force. Dissidents who criticized the regime, such as Charter 77, were not allowed to organize as a party.

The Communist regime collapsed abruptly in the Velvet Revolution of autumn 1989 after demonstrations led by Civic Forum in Prague and Public Against Violence in Bratislava. In January 1990, major political representatives agreed to hold a June election for the two houses of the Federal Assembly (*Federální Shromáždění*), the Chamber of the People (*Sněmovna Lidu*), and the Chamber of Nations (*Sněmovna Národů*), and for National Councils (*Národní Rada*) in the Czech lands of Bohemia, Moravia, and part of Silesia, and in Slovakia. The country was renamed the Czech and Slovak Federal Republic. In the 150-seat Chamber of the People seats were awarded to each of the two republics in accordance with its proportion of the electorate, 101 to Czech lands and 49 to Slovakia. All citizens age 18 or older could vote, including residents abroad who returned to vote in person (Gabal, 1996).

An electoral system of proportional representation based on inter-war practice was adopted with only minor alterations. To win seats in either chamber of the federal parliament, a party was required to win at least five per cent of the vote in one of the two republics of the federation. Electors were allowed to show a preference for up to four individuals named on a party list; if at least ten per cent did so, individual preferences would be taken into account. The number of seats assigned in the 12 multi-member constituencies reflected their relative proportion of the electorate. Within each constituency, seats were allotted by the Hagenbach-Bischoff formula. Any unallocated seats were distributed at republic level by the largest-remainder formula (Wightman, 1990: 320). The 1992 electoral law established thresholds for party alliances: seven per cent for alliances of two or three parties and ten per cent for alliances of four or more parties.

The electoral regimes for the Federal Assembly and the two sub-federal legislative bodies, the Czech National Council and the Slovak National Council, were the same, except that the threshold for the Slovak National Council was three per cent in 1990, raised to five per cent in 1992. Changes in the size of the electorate increased the number of seats in Slovakia to 51 and reduced that in Czech lands to 99. There were eight multi-member districts in the Czech Republic returning between 7 and 18 deputies, and four in Slovakia returning between 5 and 18 deputies.

The parties competing in elections differed substantially in the two parts of Czechoslovakia. In 1990 parties contesting seats only in Czech lands won 70 per cent of the vote there, and parties contesting seats only in Slovakia did likewise (Deegan-Krause, 2006). There was a common element insofar as the most successful movements, the Czech Civic Forum and Slovak Public Against Violence, had campaigned together against the Communist regime. Before the 1992 election, both fragmented. Parties confining their campaign to Czech lands won 85 per cent of the vote there, while parties campaigning only in Slovakia won 91 per cent of its vote (Olson, 1993). By the end of the year, the Velvet Revolution was succeeded by the Velvet Divorce, a peaceful division into two independent countries.

DATES OF ELECTIONS

8, 9 June 1990 (Federal, Czech, and Slovak assemblies)
5, 6 June 1992 (Federal, Czech, and Slovak assemblies)

REFERENCES

Bendlová, Jitka, 1997. Foreign Relations Department, Chamber of Deputies. Letter, 28 June.

Berta, Benjamin, et al., 2008. *Volby do zakonodarnych organov na uzemi Slovenska 1920–2006*. Bratislava: Statisticky urad SR.

Brokl, Lubomir, and Zdenka Mansfeldova, 1993. "Czechoslovakia", *European Journal of Political Research* 24, 397–410.

Broklová, Eva, 1996. "Historical Roots for the Restoration of Democracy in Czechoslovakia". In Gabal, 1996, 26–50.

Deegan-Krause, Kevin, 2006. *Elected Affinities: Democracy and Party Competition in Slovakia and the Czech Republic*. Stanford: Stanford University Press.

Gabal, Ivan, ed., 1996. *The 1990 Election to the Czechoslovakian Federal Assembly*. Berlin: Sigma.

Krejčí, Oskar, 1995. *History of Elections in Bohemia and Moravia*. Boulder: East European Monographs. Distributed by Columbia University Press, New York.

Leff, Carol Skalnik, 1988. *National Conflict in Czechoslovakia: The Making and Remaking of a State, 1918–1987*. Princeton: Princeton University Press.

Leff, Carol Skalnik, and Susan B. Mikula, 2002. "Institutionalizing Party Systems in

Multiethnic States: Integration and Ethnic Segmentation in Czechoslovakia, 1918–1992", *Slavic Review* 61, 2, 292–314.
Olson, David, 1993. "Dissolution of the State: Political Parties and the 1992 Election in Czechoslovakia", *Communist and Post-Communist Studies* 26, 3, 301–14.
Wightman, Gordon, 1990. "Czechoslovakia", *Electoral Studies* 9, 4, 319–26.

Table 7.1 CZECHOSLOVAK POLITICAL PARTIES, 1990–1992

CS: On the ballot in both the Czech and Slovak Republics

CS1 *Communist Party of Czechoslovakia* (Komunistická Strana Československa, KSČS). Former ruling party. In 1992 split into Communist Party of Bohemia and Moravia and Party of the Democratic Left. 1990

CS2 *Movement for Self-Governing Democracy–Society for Moravia and Silesia* (Hnutí za Samospravnou Demokracii–Společnost pro Moravu a Slezsko, HSD–SMS). Regional party in eastern Czech Republic. 1990–92

CS3 *Alliance of Peasants and Countryside* (Spojenectví Zemědělcu a Venkova, SZV). Alliance of agrarian groups. 1990

CS4 *Green Party* (Strana Zelených, SZ). Environmentalist party active in Velvet Revolution. Contested 1992 as part of Liberal Social Union. 1990

CS5 *Hungarian Christian Democratic Movement and Coexistence* (Madarské Krestansko-Demokratické Hnutie–Egyuttélés, MKDM–ESWS). Alliance of Hungarians, Poles, Ukrainians, and others, principally in Slovakia. 1990–92

CS6 *Czechoslovak Socialist Party* (Československá Strana Socialistická, ČSS). Part of Communist-era National Front. In 1992 in Liberal Social Union. 1990

CS7 *Association for the Republic–Republican Party of Czechoslovakia* (Sdruzeni pro Republiku–Republikanska Strana Československá, SPR–RSČ). Anti-German, anti-Roma party led by Miroslav Sládek. In 1990 allied with All-People's Democratic Party (Vselidová Demokratická Strana, VDS). 1990–92

CS8 *Free Bloc* (Svobodní Blok, SB). Alliance of several parties. 1990

CS9 *Independent Erotic Initiative* (Nezávislá Erotická Iniciativa, NEI). Promoted availability of pornography. 1992

CS10 *Democrats '92 for a Common State* (Demokraté '92 za Spolecný Stát, D92). Promoted preservation of Czechoslovakia. 1992

CS11 *Party of Labour and Security* (Strana Práce a Istoty, SPI). 1992

C: On the ballot in the Czech Republic only

C1 *Civic Forum* (Občanske Fórum, OF). Formed after 1989 Velvet Revolution. One of its leaders was Václav Havel, former dissident who became president. Fragmented in 1991 into Civic Democratic Party, Civic Movement, Civic Democratic

Alliance, and Club of Active Non-partisans. 1990

C2 *Christian and Democratic Union–Czechoslovak People's Party* (Krestanská a Demokratická Unie–Československá Strana Lidová, KDU–ČSL). Alliance of Christian groups. In 1992 KDU fused with Czechoslovak People's Party, which had been absorbed into Communist National Front in 1948. 1990–92

C3 *Czechoslovak Social Democracy* (Československá Sociální Demokracie, ČSSD). Named after party initially formed in 1878, absorbed into Communist Party in 1948, but re-formed after November 1989 revolution. 1990–92

C4 *Friends of Beer Party* (Strana Přátel Piva, SPP). Anti-establishment party founded as student joke in Pilsen. 1990–92

C5 *Civic Democratic Party* (Občanská Demokratická Strana, ODS). Pro-market party formerly part of Civic Forum. Led by Václav Klaus, head of Czech Republic's government from July 1992, then prime minister of Czech state. 1992

C6 *Communist Party of Bohemia and Moravia* (Komunistická Strana Čech a Moravy, KSČM). Successor to former ruling party. Contested 1992 election as Left Bloc (Levy Blok, LB) with other minor leftist groups. 1992

C7 *Liberal Social Union* (Liberálně Sociální Unie, LSU). Combined Czechoslovak Socialists, Greens, and Agrarians. 1992

C8 *Civic Democratic Alliance* (Občanská Demokratická Aliance, ODA). In 1990 part of Civic Forum. Supported break-up of Czechoslovakia. 1992

C9 *Civic Movement* (Občanske Hnutí, OH). Splinter of Civic Forum led by former dissident and then foreign minister (1989–92) Jirí Dienstbier. 1992

C10 *Movement of Pensioners for Social Guarantees* (Hnutí Důchodců za Životní Jistoty, HDZJ). 1992

C11 *Party of Czechoslovak Entrepreneurs, Small Businesses, and Farmers* (Strana Československych Podnikatelu, Zivnostníku a Rolníku, SČPZR). 1992

C12 *Club of Active Non-partisans* (Klub Angazovanych Nestraniku, KAN). Based on dissident group formed in 1968 during Prague Spring and banned by Communist regime. Part of Civic Forum in 1990. 1992

S: On the ballot in the Slovak Republic only

S1 *Public Against Violence* (Verejnost' Proti Násiliu, VPN). Movement leading protests against Communist regime in 1989. Broke up in 1991. 1990

S2 *Christian Democratic Movement* (Krest'anskodemokratické Hnutie, KDH). Founded in February 1990 by Ján Čarnogurský, Catholic dissident of Communist era, and prime minister of Slovakia (1991–92). 1990–92

S3 *Slovak National Party* (Slovenská Národná Strana, SNS). Nationalist, anti-Hungarian party founded in 1990, claiming descent from party launched 1871.

Defended war-time independent state under Father Tiso. 1990–92

S4 *Democratic Party* (Demokratická Strana, DS). Federalist party revived in 1989 on basis of conservative party founded 1944 and suspended 1948. Slovak equivalent of Czech Civic Democratic Party (ODS). Fought 1992 election in alliance with DS–ODS. 1990–92

S5 *Social Democratic Party in Slovakia* (Sociálnodemokratická Strana na Slovensku, SDSS). Slovak wing of Czechoslovak Social Democracy. Initially led by Alexander Dubček. 1990–92

S6 *Freedom Party* (Strana Slobody, SSL). Former satellite party co-opted by Communist National Front in 1948; broke away in 1989. 1990

S7 *Romanies* (Rómovia). Alliance of Romanies' Democratic Union and Party for Integration of Romanies in Slovakia. 1990

S8 *Movement for Democratic Slovakia* (Hnutie za Demokratické Slovensko, HZDS). National-populist party which split from Public Against Violence in 1991 to press for Slovak autonomy. Led by Vladimír Mečiar, prime minister (1990–91, 1992–94, 1994–98). 1992

S9 *Party of the Democratic Left* (Strana Demokratickej L'avice, SDL). Slovak successor to Communist Party of Czechoslovakia. 1992

S10 *Civic Democratic Union* (Občianska Demokratická Únia, ODU). Anti-Mečiar splinter of Public Against Violence. Opposed break-up of federal state of Czechoslovakia. 1992

S11 *Slovak Christian Democratic Movement* (Slovenské Krestansko-demokratické Hnutí, SKDH). Nationalist break-away from KDH. 1992

S12 *Green Party in Slovakia* (Strana Zelených na Slovensku, SZS). Founded in 1989 as wing of Czechoslovak Green Party, but separated in 1992. 1990–92

S13 *Hungarian Civic Party* (Magyar Polgári Part–Mad'arská Občianska Strana, MPP–MOS). In 1990 election part of Public Against Violence. 1992

Table 7.2a CZECHOSLOVAKIA: Votes for the *Sněmovna Lidu*

	1990			1992		
	Czech	Slovakia	CSFR	Czech	Slovakia	CSFR
Electorate	7,556,084	3,639,512	11,195,596	7,743,048	3,772,651	11,515,699
Valid Votes	7,245,450	3,393,066	10,638,516	6,492,462	3,090,974	9,583,436
Invalid Votes[1]	70,804	75,973	146,777	87,631	79,911	167,542
Total Votes	7,316,254	3,469,039	10,785,293	6,580,093	3,170,885	9,750,978
C1 Civic Forum	3,851,172	—	3,851,172	—	—	—
CS1 Communists–Czechoslovakia	976,996	468,411	1,445,407	—	—	—
S1 Public Against Violence	—	1,104,125	1,104,125	—	—	—
S2 Christian Democratic Movement	—	644,008	644,008	—	277,061	277,061
C2 Chr. & Dem. Union–Czech People	629,359	—	629,359	388,122	—	388,122
CS2 Self-Governing/Moravia & Silesia	572,015	—	572,015	274,489	4,647	279,136
S3 Slovak National Party	—	372,025	372,025	—	290,249	290,249
CS3 Peasants and Countryside	273,175	87,604	360,779	—	—	—
CS4 Green Party	224,432	108,542	332,974	—	—	—
C3 Czechoslovak Social Democracy	278,280	—	278,280	498,030	—	498,030
CS5 Hungarian Chr. Dem.–Coexistence	5,472	291,287	296,759	4,851	227,925	232,776
CS6 Czechoslovak Socialist Party	199,446	2,086	201,532	—	—	—
S4 Democratic Party, DS–ODS	—	149,310	149,310	—	122,226	122,226
CS7 Association–Republican Party	67,781	8,577	76,358	420,848	11,227	432,075
S5 Social Democratic Party of Slovakia	—	64,175	64,175	—	150,095	150,095
CS8 Free Bloc	57,925	6,145	64,070	—	—	—
S6 Freedom Party	—	49,012	49,012	—	—	—
S7 Romanies	—	22,670	22,670	—	—	—

C4 Friends of Beer	8,943	—	8,943	68,985	—	68,985
C5 Civic Democratic Party	—	—	—	2,200,937	—	2,200,937
S8 Movement for a Democratic Slovakia	—	—	—	—	1,036,459	1,036,459
C6 Communists–Bohemia & Moravia	—	—	—	926,228	—	926,228
S9 Party of the Democratic Left	—	—	—	—	446,230	446,230
C7 Liberal Social Union	—	—	—	378,962	—	378,962
C8 Civic Democratic Alliance	—	—	—	323,614	—	323,614
C9 Civic Movement	—	—	—	284,854	—	284,854
C10 Pensioners for Social Guarantees	—	—	—	214,681	—	214,681
C11 Entrepreneurs and Farmers	—	—	—	166,325	—	166,325
C12 Club of Active Non-partisans	—	—	—	129,022	—	129,022
S10 Civic Democratic Union	—	—	—	—	122,359	122,359
S11 Slovak Chr. Dem. Movement	—	—	—	—	106,612	106,612
CS9 Independent Erotic Initiative	—	—	—	76,678	13,139	89,817
S12 Green Party in Slovakia	—	—	—	—	81,047	81,047
S13 Hungarian Civic Party	—	—	—	—	72,877	72,877
CS10 Democrats '92 for a Common State	—	—	—	32,746	35,422	68,168
CS11 Party of Labour and Security	—	—	—	7,118	31,462	38,580
Others[2]	100,454	15,089	115,543	95,972	61,937	157,909

Sources: Brokl and Mansfeldova, 1993: 397–99; Bendlová, 1997; Krejčí, 1995: 340–41, 350ff.

[1] Invalid votes calculated by subtraction.

[2] Includes: 1990: 3 parties on the ballot in both republics winning less than 1.0 per cent of the vote in either Czech lands or Slovakia; in 1992, 2 parties contesting both regions, plus 1 Czech party and 4 Slovak parties.

Table 7.2b CZECHOSLOVAKIA: Percentage of Votes for the *Sněmovna Lidu*

	1990			1992		
	Czech	Slovakia	CSFR	Czech	Slovakia	CSFR
Valid Votes	95.9	93.2	95.0	83.9	81.9	83.2
Invalid Votes	0.9	2.1	1.3	1.1	2.1	1.5
Total Votes	96.8	95.3	96.3	85.0	84	84.7
C1 Civic Forum	53.2	—	36.2	—	—	—
CS1 Communists–Czechoslovakia	13.5	13.8	13.6	—	—	—
S1 Public Against Violence	—	32.5	10.4	—	—	—
S2 Christian Democratic Movement	—	19.0	6.1	—	9.0	2.9
C2 Chr. & Dem. Union–Czech People	8.7	—	5.9	6.0	—	4.0
CS2 Self-Governing/Moravia & Silesia	7.9	—	5.4	4.2	0.2	2.9
S3 Slovak National Party	—	11.0	3.5	—	9.4	3.0
CS3 Peasants and Countryside	3.8	2.6	3.4	—	—	—
CS4 Green Party	3.1	3.2	3.1	—	—	—
C3 Czechoslovak Social Democracy	3.8	—	2.6	7.7	—	5.2
CS5 Hungarian Chr. Dem.–Coexistence	0.1	8.6	2.8	—	7.4	2.4
CS6 Czechoslovak Socialist Party	2.8	0.1	1.9	—	—	—
S4 Democratic Party, DS–ODS	—	4.4	1.4	—	4.0	1.3
CS7 Association–Republican Party	0.9	0.3	0.7	6.5	0.4	4.5
S5 Social Democratic Party of Slovakia	—	1.9	0.6	—	4.9	1.6
CS8 Free Bloc	0.8	0.2	0.6	—	—	—
S6 Freedom Party	—	1.4	0.5	—	—	—
S7 Romanies	—	0.7	0.2	—	—	—
C4 Friends of Beer	0.1	—	0.1	1.1	—	0.7
C5 Civic Democratic Party	—	—	—	33.9	—	23.0

S8 Movement for a Democratic Slovakia	—	—	—	—	33.5	10.8
C6 Communists–Bohemia & Moravia	—	—	—	14.3	—	9.7
S9 Party of the Democratic Left	—	—	—	—	14.4	4.7
C7 Liberal Social Union	—	—	—	5.8	—	4.0
C8 Civic Democratic Alliance	—	—	—	5.0	—	3.4
C9 Civic Movement	—	—	—	4.4	—	3.0
C10 Pensioners for Social Guarantees	—	—	—	3.3	—	2.2
C11 Entrepreneurs and Farmers	—	—	—	2.6	—	1.7
C12 Club of Active Non-partisans	—	—	—	2.0	—	1.3
S10 Civic Democratic Union	—	—	—	—	4.0	1.3
S11 Slovak Chr. Dem. Movement	—	—	—	—	3.4	1.1
CS9 Independent Erotic Initiative	—	—	—	1.2	0.4	0.9
S12 Green Party in Slovakia	—	—	—	—	2.6	0.8
S13 Hungarian Civic Party	—	—	—	—	2.4	0.8
CS10 Democrats '92 for a Common State	—	—	—	0.5	1.1	0.7
CS11 Party of Labour and Security	—	—	—	0.1	1.0	0.4
Others	1.4	0.4	1.1	1.6	2.0	1.7

Table 7.2c CZECHOSLOVAKIA: Number of Seats in the *Sněmovna Lidu*

	1990			1992		
	Czech	Slovakia	CSFR	Czech	Slovakia	CSFR
C1 Civic Forum	68	—	68	—	—	—
CS1 Communists–Czechoslovakia	15	8	23	—	—	—
S1 Public Against Violence	—	19	19	—	—	—
S2 Christian Democratic Movement	—	11	11	—	6	6
C2 Chr. & Dem. Union–Czech People	9	—	9	7	—	7
CS2 Self-Governing/Moravia & Silesia	9	—	9	0	0	0
S3 Slovak National Party	—	6	6	—	6	6
CS3 Peasants and Countryside	0	0	0	—	—	—
CS4 Green Party	0	0	0	—	—	—
C3 Czechoslovak Social Democracy	0	—	0	10	—	10
CS5 Hungarian Chr. Dem.–Coexistence	0	5	5	0	5	5
CS6 Czechoslovak Socialist Party	0	0	0	—	—	—
S4 Democratic Party, DS–ODS	—	0	0	—	0	0
CS7 Association–Republican Party	0	0	0	8	0	8
S5 Social Democratic Party of Slovakia	—	0	0	—	0	0
CS8 Free Bloc	0	0	0	—	—	—
S6 Freedom Party	—	0	0	—	—	—
S7 Romanies	—	0	0	—	—	—
C4 Friends of Beer	0	—	0	0	—	0
C5 Civic Democratic Party	—	—	—	48	—	48
S8 Movement for a Democratic Slovakia	—	—	—	—	24	24
C6 Communists–Bohemia & Moravia	—	—	—	19	—	19
S9 Party of the Democratic Left	—	—	—	—	10	10
C7 Liberal Social Union	—	—	—	7	—	7

C8 Civic Democratic Alliance	—	—	—	0	—	0
C9 Civic Movement	—	—	—	0	—	0
C10 Pensioners for Social Guarantees	—	—	—	0	—	0
C11 Entrepreneurs and Farmers	—	—	—	0	—	0
C12 Club of Active Non-partisans	—	—	—	0	—	0
S10 Civic Democratic Union	—	—	—	—	0	0
S11 Slovak Chr. Dem. Movement	—	—	—	—	0	0
CS9 Independent Erotic Initiative	—	—	—	0	0	0
S12 Green Party in Slovakia	—	—	—	—	0	0
S13 Hungarian Civic Party	—	—	—	—	0	0
CS10 Democrats '92 for a Common State	—	—	—	0	0	0
CS11 Party of Labour and Security	—	—	—	0	0	0
Others	0	0	0	0	0	0
Total	101	49	150	99	51	150

Sources: Brokl and Mansfeldova, 1993: 397–99; Bendlová, 1997; Krejčí, 1995: 340–41, 350ff.

Table 7.2d CZECHOSLOVAKIA: Percentage of Seats in the *Sněmovna Lidu*

	1990			1992		
	Czech	Slovakia	CSFR	Czech	Slovakia	CSFR
C1 Civic Forum	67.3	—	45.3	—	—	—
CS1 Communists–Czechoslovakia	14.9	16.3	15.3	—	—	—
S1 Public Against Violence	—	38.8	12.7	—	—	—
S2 Christian Democratic Movement	—	22.4	7.3	—	11.8	4.0
C2 Chr. & Dem. Union–Czech People	8.9	—	6.0	7.1	—	4.7
CS2 Self-Governing/Moravia & Silesia	8.9	—	6.0	0	0	0
S3 Slovak National Party	—	12.2	4.0	—	11.8	4.0
CS3 Peasants and Countryside	0	0	0	—	—	—
CS4 Green Party	0	0	0	—	—	—
C3 Czechoslovak Social Democracy	0	—	0	10.1	—	6.7
CS5 Hungarian Chr. Dem.–Coexistence	0	10.2	3.3	0	9.8	3.3
CS6 Czechoslovak Socialist Party	0	0	0	—	—	—
S4 Democratic Party, DS–ODS	—	0	0	—	0	0
CS7 Association–Republican Party	0	0	0	8.1	—	5.3
S5 Social Democratic Party of Slovakia	—	0	0	—	0	0
CS8 Free Bloc	0	0	0	—	—	—
S6 Freedom Party	—	0	0	—	—	—
S7 Romanies	—	0	0	—	—	—
C4 Friends of Beer	0	—	0	0	—	0
C5 Civic Democratic Party	—	—	—	48.5	—	32.0
S8 Movement for a Democratic Slovakia	—	—	—	—	47.1	16.0
C6 Communists–Bohemia & Moravia	—	—	—	19.2	—	12.7
S9 Party of the Democratic Left	—	—	—	—	19.6	6.7
C7 Liberal Social Union	—	—	—	7.1	—	4.7

C8 Civic Democratic Alliance	—	—	—	0	—	0
C9 Civic Movement	—	—	—	0	—	0
C10 Pensioners for Social Guarantees	—	—	—	0	—	0
C11 Entrepreneurs and Farmers	—	—	—	0	—	0
C12 Club of Active Non-partisans	—	—	—	0	—	0
S10 Civic Democratic Union	—	—	—	—	0	0
S11 Slovak Chr. Dem. Movement	—	—	—	—	0	0
CS9 Independent Erotic Initiative	—	—	—	0	0	0
S12 Green Party in Slovakia	—	—	—	—	0	0
S13 Hungarian Civic Party	—	—	—	—	0	0
CS10 Democrats '92 for a Common State	—	—	—	0	0	0
CS11 Party of Labour and Security	—	—	—	0	0	0
Others	0	0	0	0	0	0

8

CZECH REPUBLIC

The Czech Republic came into being on 1 January 1993 as a consequence of the break-up of Czechoslovakia. Since that regime was a federal state with separate administrative structures and party systems in each of its two republics, the subordinate body in the Czech half of the federal state, the Czech National Council (*Česká Národní Rada*), became the sole chamber in the parliament of the successor state. In the Czech Republic the members of the National Council of the new state were the candidates elected in the June 1992 vote for the Czechoslovak Federal Assembly. To show continuity, the following tables present votes for the Czech National Council of the Federation in 1990 and 1992, and for the Chamber of Deputies from 1996.

The constitution of the new Czech state provided for a two-chamber parliament but, because of ambivalent attitudes of the leading parties to bicameralism, an election law for the Senate was passed only in 1995. The parliament of the Czech State now comprises the Chamber of Deputies (*Poslanecká Sněmovna*) with 200 deputies elected for a term of four years and a Senate (*Senát*) of 81 members serving six-year terms. One-third of the Senate is elected every two years by majority vote in single-member districts, with a second ballot if necessary. The Chamber of Deputies is the principal chamber of parliament. A majority vote in a joint session of both houses of parliament elects the president for a five-year term.

The electoral law was carried over from the predecessor state. All citizens age 18 or over are eligible to vote. In 1996 seats were distributed by proportional representation with a national threshold of five per cent for a single party, and thresholds of 7, 9, and 11 per cent for alliances of two, three, or four parties. The country was divided into eight districts with from 12 to 42 seats. Citizens voted for a party list and could also cast up to four preferential votes for individual candidates on that list. Allocation of seats occurred in two rounds by the Hagenbach-Bischoff method at the district level and at the national level.

In the year 2000 the Social Democrats and the Civic Democrats, which had concluded a parliamentary pact after the 1998 election, amended the law to make the electoral system less proportional by increasing the number of electoral districts to 35 with four to eight members each. The threshold for electoral alliances to qualify for seats was raised to 10 per cent for alliances of two parties, 15 per cent for three parties, and 20 per cent for four or more parties. At the same time it was proposed to adopt a modified d'Hondt method for allocating seats. The amendments were challenged in the courts by President Václav Havel and the so-called Quad Coalition (Čtyrkoalice) of four opposition parties, the Christian and Democratic Union–Czechoslovak People's Party, Freedom Union, Democratic Union, and Civic Democratic Alliance (ODA). In January 2001 the Constitutional Court declared the above changes unconstitutional except the higher threshold for alliances (Crawford, 2001: 55).

The 2002 election law retains the high threshold but reduces the number of districts to 14. The number of seats allocated to each district is calculated after the election according to its share of national valid votes. At the district level, seats are allocated to parties by the d'Hondt method.

DATES OF ELECTIONS

Czech National Council (*Česká Národní Rada*)	Chamber of Deputies (*Poslanecká Sněmovna*)
8–9 June 1990	31 May–1 June 1996
5–6 June 1992	19–20 June 1998
	14–15 June 2002
	2–3 June 2006

REFERENCES

Crawford, Keith, 2001. "A System of Disproportional Representation", *Representation* 38, 1, 46–58.

Czech Statistical Office, 1996. *Statistical Yearbook of the Czech Republic '96.* Prague: Scientia.

———, 2006. "Volby.cz", http://www.volby.cz.

Deegan-Krause, Kevin, 2006. *Elected Affinities: Democracy and Party Competition in Slovakia and the Czech Republic.* Stanford: Stanford University Press.

Kopecký, Petr, 2004. "The Czech Republic: Entrenching Proportional Representation". In Josep Colomer, ed., *Handbook of Electoral System Choice.* Basingstoke: Palgrave Macmillan, 347–58.

———, 2006. "The Rise of the Power Monopoly: Political Parties in the Czech Republic". In S. Jungerstam-Mulders, ed., *Post-Communist EU Member States: Parties and Party Systems.* Aldershot: Ashgate, 125–45.

Krejčí, Oskar, 1995. *History of Elections in Bohemia and Moravia.* Boulder: East European Monographs and Columbia University Press.

Table 8.1 CZECH POLITICAL PARTIES

(A party number in parentheses cross-refers to its place in Table 7.1.)

CR1 *Civic Forum* (C1 Občanske Fórum, OF). Promoted Velvet Revolution. Václav Havel, president of Czechoslovakia (1990–92) and Czech Republic (1993–2003), a member. In 1991 split into Civic Democratic Party, Civic Movement, Civic Democratic Alliance, and Club of Active Non-partisans. 1990

CR2 *Communist Party of Bohemia and Moravia* (C6 Komunistická Strana Čech a Moravy, KSČM). Successor to former ruling party. Contested 1992 election as Left Bloc (Levy Blok, LB) with minor partners. 1990–

CR3 *Movement for Self-Governing Democracy–Society for Moravia and Silesia* (CS2 Hnutí za Samospravnou Demokracii–Společnost pro Moravu a Slezsko, HSD–SMS). 1990–92

CR4 *Christian and Democratic Union–Czech People's Party* (C2 Krestanská a Demokratická Unie–Československá Strana Lidová, KDU–ČSL). Created by fusion in 1992 of KDU with Czechoslovak People's Party, Catholic party formed in 1918 and absorbed into Communist National Front in 1948. In 2002 part of KDU–ČSL and US–DEU Coalition. 1990–

CR5 *Czech Social Democratic Party* (C3 Česká Strana Sociálně Demokratická, ČSSD, formerly Czechoslovak Social Democracy). Named after party formed in 1878, absorbed into Communist Party in 1948, and re-formed after November 1989. Led by prime ministers Miloš Zeman (1998–2002), Vladimír Špidla (2002–04), Stanislav Gross (2004–05), and Jiří Paroubek (2005–06). 1990–

CR6 *Alliance of Peasants and Countryside* (CS3 Spojenectví Zemědělcu a Venkova, SZV). Alliance of agrarian groups. 1990

CR7 *Green Party* (CS4 Strana Zelenych, SZ). Active in 1989 Velvet Revolution. Contested 1992 election as part of electoral list of Liberal Social Union. Unable to pay deposit to fight 1996 election, but has done so since. 1990–

CR8 *Czechoslovak Socialist Party* (CS6 Československá Strana Socialistická, ČSS). In National Front in Communist era. In 1992 joined LSU. 1990

CR9 *Free Bloc* (CS9 Svobodní Blok, SB). Bloc of minor parties. 1990

CR10 *Association for the Republic–Czech Republican Party* (CS7 Sdruzeni pro Republiku–Republikanska Strana Česká, SPR–RSČ). Anti-German and anti-Roma party led by Miroslav Sládek, unsuccessfully prosecuted for inciting racial hatred. Fought 1990 election as part of alliance with All-People's Democratic Party (Vselidová Demokratická Strana, VDS). SPR–RSČ split and was declared bankrupt in 2001. Some members formed Republicans of Miroslav Sládek (Republikáni Miroslava Sládek, RMS). 1990–2002

CR11 *Friends of Beer Party* (C4 Strana Přátel Piva, SPP). Anti-establishment party founded as a student joke in Pilsen. 1990–92

CR12 *Free Democrats–Liberal Social National Party* (C9 Svobodní Demokrati–Liberalní Sociální Nárondně Strana, SD–LSNS). Free Democrats were splinter of Civic Forum led by former disident Jirí Dienstbier. In 1992 known as Civic Movement (Občanská Hnutí) and in 1993 Free Democrats SD(OH), which in 1995 merged with LSNS, splinter of Liberal Social Union. 1992–96

CR13 *Civic Democratic Party* (C5 Občanská Demokratická Strana, ODS). Pro-market offshoot of Civic Forum. In 1995 absorbed its ally since 1991, Christian Democratic Party (Krest'ansko-Demokratická Strana, KDS). Until 2002 led by Václav Klaus, prime minister (1992–97), and president (2003–). Leader is Mirek Topolánek, prime minister (August 2006–). 1992–

CR14 *Liberal Social Union* (C7 Liberálně Sociální Unie, LSU). Combination of Czechoslovak Socialists, Greens, and Agrarians; split up in 1993. 1992

CR15 *Civic Democratic Alliance* (C8 Občanská Demokratická Aliance, ODA). Founded in 1989. Fought 1990 as part of Civic Forum. Supported break-up of Czechoslovakia. After splits did not contest 1998 election. After further scandals excluded from Quad Coalition of KDU–ČSL and US–DEU. 1992–2002

CR16 *Movement of Pensioners for Social Guarantees* (C10 Hnutí Důchodců za Životní Jistoty, HDZJ). In 2002 named Party for Social Guarantees (Strana za Životní Jistoty). 1992–2002

CR17 *Party of Czechoslovak Entrepreneurs, Small Businesses, and Farmers* (C11 Strana Československych Podnikatelů, Živnostníků a Rolníků, SČPZR). Founded 1992 by Rudolf Baránek. 1992

CR18 *Club of Active Non-partisans* (C12 Klub Angazovanych Nestraniku, KAN). Dissidents during Prague Spring. Part of Civic Forum in 1990. 1992

CR19 *Independent Erotic Initiative* (CS9 Nezávislá Erotická Iniciativa, NEI). Promoted availability of pornography. 1992

CR20 *Movement for Social Justice* (Hnutí za Sociální Spravedlnost, HSS). Ally of Communist Party. 1992

CR21 *Democratic Union* (Demokratická Unie, DEU). Anti-Communist party founded by former dissidents in 1994. Merged with Freedom Union in 2001 to form US–DEU. 1996–98

CR22 *Left Bloc Party* (Strana Levého Blocu, SLB). Minor splinter of KSČM, not to be confused with KSČM-led alliance of the same name in 1992. 1996

CR23 *Freedom Union* (Unie Svobody, US). Splinter from Civic Democratic Party formed in November 1997. Merged with Democratic Union in 2001 to form

US–DEU. Fought 2002 as part of KDU–ČSL/US–DEU alliance. 1998

CR24 *Coalition KDU–ČSL and US–DEU* (Koalice KDU–ČSL, US–DEU). Alliance emerging from parliamentary Quad Coalition (Čtyrkoalice), which included ODA and opposed ČSSD government of Miloš Zeman (1998–2002). ODA expelled in 2002. A merger of Democratic Union and Freedom Union. 2002

CR25 *Association of Independents* (Sdružzení Nezávislých). Pro-European group founded in 2000 by regional politicians. 2002

CR26 *SNK European Democrats* (SNK Evropští Demokraté). Late 2005 merger of Association of Independents with European Democrats, founded in 2002 by former mayor of Prague Jan Kasl. 2006–

Table 8.2a CZECH REPUBLIC: Votes for the *Narodní Rada* 1990–1992 and *Poslanecká Sněmovna* 1996–

	1990	1992	1996	1998	2002	2006
Electorate	7,553,447	7,738,981	7,990,770	8,116,836	8,264,484	8,333,305
Valid Votes	7,211,047	6,473,250	6,059,215	5,969,505	4,768,006	5,348,976
Invalid Votes[1]	92,573	102,776	37,189	25,339	21,139	19,519
Total Votes	7,303,620	6,576,026	6,096,404	5,994,844	4,789,145	5,368,495
CR1 Civic Forum	3,569,201	—	—	—	—	—
CR2 Communist Party	954,690	909,490	626,136	658,550	882,653	685,328
CR3 Self-Governing/Moravia & Silesia	723,609	380,088	—	—	—	—
CR4 KDU-ČSL Christian and Dem.Union	607,134	406,341	489,349	537,013	—[2]	386,706
CR24 KDU–ČSL/US–DEU Coalition	—	—	—	—	680,671	—
CR21 Democratic Union DEU	—	—	169,796	86,431	—	—
CR23 Freedom Union US	—	—	—	513,596	—	—
CR5 Czech Social Democratic Party	296,165	422,736	1,602,250	1,928,660	1,440,279	1,728,827
CR6 Alliance of Peasants & Countryside	296,547	—	—	—	—	—
CR7 Greens	295,844	—[3]	—[4]	67,143	112,929	336,487
CR8 Czechoslovak Socialist Party	192,922	—	—	—	—	—
CR9 Free Bloc	75,242	—	—	—	—	—
CR10 Republican Party	72,048	387,026	485,072	232,965	46,325	—
CR11 Friends of Beer Party	43,632	83,959	—	—	—	—
CR12 Free Democrats	—	297,406	124,165	—	—	—
CR13 Civic Democratic Party	—	1,924,483	1,794,560	1,656,011	1,166,975	1,892,475
CR14 Liberal Social Union	—	421,988	—	—	—	—
CR15 Civic Democratic Alliance	—	383,705	385,369	—	24,278	—
CR16 Pensioners for Social Guarantees	—	244,319	187,455	182,900	41,404	—
CR17 Party Entrepreneurs & Farmers	—	203,654	—	—	—	—

CR18 Club of Active Non-partisans	—	174,006	—	—	—	—
CR19 Independent Erotic Initiative	—	88,823	—	—	—	—
CR20 Movement for Social Justice	—	69,621	—	—	—	—
CR22 Left Bloc Party	—	—	85,122	—	—	—
CR25 Association of Independents	—	—	—	—	132,699	—
CR26 SNK-European Democrats	—	—	—	—	—	111,724
Others[5]	84,013	75,605	109,941	106,236	239,793	207,429

Sources: Czech Statistical Office, 1996, 2006.

[1] Invalid votes calculated by subtraction.

[2] Fought as part of KDU–ČSL/US–DEU Coalition.

[3] Part of Liberal Social Union in 1992.

[4] Unable to pay the required deposit in the 1996 election.

[5] Includes: 1990, 2 parties winning less than 1.0 per cent of the vote; in 1992, 4 parties; in 1996, 6 parties; in 1998, 4 parties; in 2002, 19 parties; in 2006, 20 parties.

Table 8.2b CZECH REPUBLIC: Percentage of Votes for the *Narodní Rada* 1990–1992 and *Poslanecká Sněmovna* 1996–

	1990	1992	1996	1998	2002	2006
Valid Votes	95.5	83.7	75.8	73.5	58.7	64.2
Invalid Votes	1.2	1.3	0.5	0.3	0.3	0.2
Total Votes	96.7	85	76.3	73.8	59.0	64.4
CR1 Civic Forum	49.5	—	—	—	—	—
CR2 Communist Party	13.2	14.0	10.3	11.0	18.5	12.8
CR3 Self-Governing/Moravia & Silesia	10.0	5.9	—	—	—	—
CR4 KDU–ČSL Christian and Dem.Union	8.4	6.3	8.1	9.0	—	7.2
CR24 KDU–ČSL/US–DEU Coalition	—	—	—	—	14.3	—
CR21 Democratic Union DEU	—	—	2.8	1.4	—	—
CR23 Freedom Union US	—	—	—	8.6	—	—
CR5 Czech Social Democratic Party	4.1	6.5	26.4	32.3	30.2	32.3
CR6 Alliance of Peasants & Countryside	4.1	—	—	—	—	—
CR7 Greens	4.1	—	—	1.1	2.4	6.3
CR8 Czechoslovak Socialist Party	2.7	—	—	—	—	—
CR9 Free Bloc	1.0	—	—	—	—	—
CR10 Republican Party	1.0	6.0	8.0	3.9	1.0	—
CR11 Friends of Beer Party	0.6	1.3	—	—	—	—
CR12 Free Democrats	—	4.6	2.1	—	—	—
CR13 Civic Democratic Party	—	29.7	29.6	27.7	24.5	35.4
CR14 Liberal Social Union	—	6.5	—	—	—	—
CR15 Civic Democratic Alliance	—	5.9	6.4	—	0.5	—
CR16 Pensioners for Social Guarantees	—	3.8	3.1	3.1	0.9	—
CR17 Party Entrepreneurs & Farmers	—	3.1	—	—	—	—
CR18 Club of Active Non-partisans	—	2.7	—	—	—	—

CR19 Independent Erotic Initiative	—	1.4	—	—	—	—
CR20 Movement for Social Justice	—	1.1	—	—	—	—
CR22 Left Bloc Party	—	—	1.4	—	—	—
CR25 Association of Independents	—	—	—	—	2.8	—
CR26 SNK–European Democrats	—	—	—	—	—	2.1
Others	1.2	1.2	1.8	1.8	5.0	3.9

Table 8.2c CZECH REPUBLIC: Seats in the *Narodní Rada* 1990–1992 and *Poslanecká Sněmovna* 1996–

	1990	1992	1996	1998	2002	2006
CR1 Civic Forum	127	—	—	—	—	—
CR2 Communist Party	32	35	22	24	41	26
CR3 Self-Governing/Moravia & Silesia	22	14	—	—	—	—
CR4 KDU–ČSL Christian and Dem.Union	19	15	18	20	—[1]	13
CR24 KDU–ČSL/US–DEU Coalition	—	—	—	—	31[1]	—
CR21 Democratic Union DEU	—	—	0	0	—	—
CR23 Freedom Union US	—	—	—	19	—	—
CR5 Czech Social Democratic Party	0	16	61	74	70	74
CR6 Alliance of Peasants & Countryside	0	—	—	—	—	—
CR7 Greens	0	—[2]	—[3]	0	0	6
CR8 Czechoslovak Socialist Party	0	—	—	—	—	—
CR9 Free Bloc	0	—	—	—	—	—
CR10 Republican Party	0	14	18	0	0	—
CR11 Friends of Beer Party	0	0	—	—	—	—
CR12 Free Democrats	—	0	0	—	—	—
CR13 Civic Democratic Party	—	76	68	63	58	81
CR14 Liberal Social Union	—	16	—	—	—	—
CR15 Civic Democratic Alliance	—	14	13	—	0	—
CR16 Pensioners for Social Guarantees	—	0	0	0	0	—
CR17 Party Entrepreneurs & Farmers	—	0	—	—	—	—
CR18 Club of Active Non-partisans	—	0	—	—	—	—
CR19 Independent Erotic Initiative	—	0	—	—	—	—
CR20 Movement for Social Justice	—	0	—	—	—	—
CR22 Left Bloc Party	—	—	0	—	—	—
CR25 Association of Independents	—	—	—	—	0	—

CR26	SNK–European Democrats	—	—	—	—	—	0
	Others	0	0	0	0	0	0
	Total	200	200	200	200	200	200

Source: Czech Statistical Office, 1996, 2006.

[1] Seats distributed as follows: KDU–ČSL, 21; US–DEU, 10.

[2] Part of Liberal Social Union in 1992.

[3] Unable to pay the required deposit in the 1996 election.

Table 8.2d CZECH REPUBLIC: Percentage of Seats in the *Narodní Rada* 1990–1992 and *Poslanecká Sněmovna* 1996–

	1990	1992	1996	1998	2002	2006
CR1 Civic Forum	63.5	—	—	—	—	—
CR2 Communist Party	16.0	17.5	11.0	12.0	20.5	13.0
CR3 Self-Governing/Moravia & Silesia	11.0	7.0	—	—	—	—
CR4 KDU–ČSL Christian and Dem.Union	9.5	7.5	9.0	10.0	—	6.5
CR24 KDU–ČSL/US–DEU Coalition	—	—	—	—	15.5	—
CR21 Democratic Union DEU	—	—	0	0	—	—
CR23 Freedom Union US	—	—	—	9.5	—	—
CR5 Czech Social Democratic Party	0	8.0	30.5	37.0	35.0	37.0
CR6 Alliance of Peasants & Countryside	0	—	—	—	—	—
CR7 Greens	0	—	—	0	0	3.0
CR8 Czechoslovak Socialist Party	0	—	—	—	—	—
CR9 Free Bloc	0	—	—	—	—	—
CR10 Republican Party	0	7.0	9.0	0	0	—
CR11 Friends of Beer Party	0	0	—	—	—	—
CR12 Free Democrats	—	0	0	—	—	—
CR13 Civic Democratic Party	—	38.0	34.0	31.5	29.0	40.5
CR14 Liberal Social Union	—	8.0	—	—	—	—
CR15 Civic Democratic Alliance	—	7.0	6.5	—	0	—
CR16 Pensioners for Social Guarantees	—	0	0	0	0	—
CR17 Party Entrepreneurs & Farmers	—	0	—	—	—	—
CR18 Club of Active Nonpartisans	—	0	—	—	—	—
CR19 Independent Erotic Initiative	—	0	—	—	—	—
CR20 Movement for Social Justice	—	0	—	—	—	—

CR22 Left Bloc Party	—	—	0	—	—	—
CR25 Association of Independents	—	—	—	—	0	—
CR26 SNK–European Democrats	—	—	—	—	—	0
Others	0	0	0	0	0	0

9

SLOVAKIA

Slovakia became independent on 1 January 1993, following the dissolution of Czechoslovakia. Its parliament was established at the 5–6 June 1992 election of the Slovak National Council (*Slovenská Národná Rada*). This subordinate assembly of the old federation became the new parliament of an independent Slovakia (*Národná Rada Slovenskej Republiky*). It is a unicameral parliament.

Members of the 150-seat National Council are elected by proportional representation, and all citizens age 18 or above are eligible to vote. Voters must endorse a party list. In 1990 the threshold to qualify for seats was three per cent. Before the 1992 election it was raised to five per cent for a single party; seven per cent for a two- or three-party alliance; and ten per cent for alliances of four or more parties. Voters may state up to four preferences for individual candidates. These preferences were counted only if the candidate received at least ten per cent of the party vote; before the 2006 election, this threshold was lowered to three per cent of the party vote. Until 1998 there were four multi-member districts with 12 to 50 deputies. Seats were allocated at district level using the Hagenbach-Bischoff method and at national level by the largest-remainder formula.

The governing coalition of Vladimír Mečiar changed the electoral law before the 1998 contest. The powers of the Central Electoral Commission were reduced. The country as a whole was made a single district for allocating PR seats by the Hagenbach-Bischoff method. To qualify for the ballot, a party had to have at least 10,000 members, a requirement that had to be met by each party in an electoral coalition. Likewise, the five per cent threshold to qualify for PR seats was applied to each coalition party. This raised the threshold for a two-party coalition to 10 per cent; for a three-party coalition to 15 per cent; and for a four-party coalition to 20 per cent. Private media were banned from political campaigning, thus favouring the governing party, which controlled television (Malová and Učeň, 1999: 501–03). Despite these measures, an opposition coalition campaigned successfully and Mečiar's party lost power (Bútora, et al., 1999).

In 1999 the Constitutional Court struck down a law prohibiting candidates from belonging to more than one party, thus enabling electoral alliances to be formed by individuals retaining their distinctive party identities. At the 2002 election the threshold for coalitions reverted to seven per cent for two or three parties and ten per cent for four or more parties.

Initially the president was indirectly elected for a five-year term by a majority of three-fifths of the National Council. In 1993 Michal Kováč was chosen as president. In 1997 a referendum was proposed for the direct election of the president, a move backed by opponents of Mečiar. His government deleted the question from the referendum ballot, leading to a boycott of a referendum on other issues. When Kovác's term expired early in 1998, the National Council was unable to produce a three-fifths' majority and the post remained vacant, powers of the president being passed to the government and Prime Minister Mečiar.

In January 1999, the National Council amended the constitution to introduce direct presidential election. If no candidate secures an absolute majority in the first round, a second round between the two leading candidates must be held. Candidates must be 40 years of age, permanent residents of Slovakia, and nominated by 15 deputies or a popular petition signed by 15,000 citizens.

DATES OF ELECTIONS

Slovak National Council
(*Slovenska Národná Rada*)
8, 9 June 1990
5, 6 June 1992

President
5, 29 May 1999
3, 17 April 2004

National Council
(*Národná Rada Slovenskej Republiky*)
30 September, 1 October 1994
25, 26 September 1998
20, 21 September 2002
17 June 2006

REFERENCES

Berta, Benjamin, et al., 2008. *Volby do zakonodarnych organov na uzemi Slovenska 1920–2006*. Bratislava: Statisticky urad SR.

Bútora, Martin, Grigorij Mesežnikov, Zora Bútorová, and Sharon Fisher, eds., 1999. *The 1998 Parliamentary Elections and Democratic Rebirth in Slovakia*. Bratislava: Institute for Public Affairs.

Deegan-Krause, Kevin, 2006. *Elected Affinities: Democracy and Party Competition in Slovakia and the Czech Republic*. Stanford: Stanford University Press.

Malová, Darina, and Peter Učeň, 1999. "Slovakia", *European Journal of Political Research* 36, 3–4, 497–506.

Statistical Office of the Slovak Republic, 2008. "Election Statistics", http://portal.statistics.sk/showdoc.do?docid=3090.

Szomolányi, Sona, and Grigorij Mesežnikov, eds., 1995. *Slovakia Parliamentary Elections 1994*. Bratislava: Slovak Political Science Association/ Friedrich Ebert Foundation.

Table 9.1 SLOVAK POLITICAL PARTIES

(A party number in parentheses cross-refers to its place in Table 7.1.)

SR1 *Public Against Violence* (S1 Verejnost' Proti Násiliu, VPN). Movement of citizens protesting against old regime in 1989. Broke up in 1991. 1990

SR2 *Christian Democratic Movement* (S2 Krest'anskodemokratické Hnutie, KDH). Founded in February 1990 by Ján Čarnogurský, Catholic dissident of Communist era and prime minister of Slovakia (1991–92). Contested 1998 election as part of Slovak Democratic Coalition, but withdrew in late 2000. 1990–

SR3 *Slovak National Party* (S3 Slovenská Národná Strana, SNS). Nationalist, anti-Hungarian party founded in 1990, claiming descent from party launched 1871. Defended wartime independent state under Father Tiso. In 1998 SNS absorbed KSU and Slovak Green Alternative. Led by Ján Slota, 1999 presidential candidate. In 2001 Slota's faction was expelled and formed Real SNS, but splinter merged back in before 2006 elections, with Slota again becoming leader. 1990–

SR4 *Communist Party of Czechoslovakia* (CS1 Komunistická Strana Československa, KSČS). Ruling party, 1948–89. Split into Czech and Slovak parties before 1992 election. 1990

SR5 *Hungarian Christian Democratic Movement–Coexistence* (Mad'arské Krest'anskodemokratické Hnutie–Együttélés/Spolužitie, MKDH–ESWS). Alliance of Hungarians, Poles, Ukrainians, and other minorities. Before 1994 election joined Hungarian Civic Party to form Hungarian Coalition Party. 1990–92

SR6 *Democratic Party* (S4 Demokratická Strana, DS). Federalist party revived in 1989 on basis of a conservative party founded in 1944; it won 1946 election in Slovakia. Fought 1992 election in coalition with Czech Civic Democratic Party (ODS) as DS–ODS. In 1998 DS was part of Slovak Democratic Coalition; in 2002 endorsed voting for SDKU and merged with it in January 2006. 1990–94

SR7 *Green Party* (CS4 Strana Zelených, SZ). Slovak branch of Czechoslovak Green Party, active in 1989 revolution. 1990–92

SR8 *Alliance of Farmers and Countryside* (CS3 Spojenectvo Pol'no-hospodárov a Vidieka, SPV). Slovak branch of an alliance of agrarian groups. 1990

SR9 *Social Democratic Party in Slovakia* (S5 Sociálnodemokratická Strana na

Slovensku, SDSS). Slovak wing of Czechoslovak Social Democracy. Before his death in 1992, led by Alexander Dubček. In 1994 part of Common Choice alliance, and from 1998 to 2002 part of Slovak Democratic Coalition. In 2005 merged into Direction–Social Democracy. 1990–92

SR10 *Freedom Party* (S6 Strana Slobody, SSL). Former satellite party co-opted by Communist National Front in 1948, which broke away in 1989. 1990

SR11 *People's Party–Movement for Democratic Slovakia* (S8 L'udová Strana–Hnutie za Demokratické Slovensko, LS–HZDS). Formerly known as HZDS. Split from Public Against Violence in 1991 to strengthen Slovak influence in the CSFR. Led by Vladimír Mečiar, prime minister of Slovakia (1990–91, 1992–94, 1994–98). In 1994 in alliance with Agrarian Party of Slovakia. In 2003, 'People's Party' (L'udová Strana, LS) was added to its name. 1992–

SR12 *Party of the Democratic Left* (S9 Strana Demokratickej L'avice, SDL). A successor to Communist Party of Slovakia. Adopted present name in 1990. Contested 1994 election in Common Choice alliance; in 1998 and 2000 fought independently; in 2005 merged into Direction–Social Democracy. 1992–2002

SR13 *Civic Democratic Union* (S10 Občianska Demokratická Únia, ODU). Anti-Mečiar splinter of Public Against Violence, opposing separation from Czech Republic. Before 1994 election merged into Democratic Party. 1992

SR14 *Christian Social Union* (Krest'anská Sociálna Unia, KSU). Nationalist splinter of KDH, initially known as Slovak Christian Democratic Movement (Slovenské Krest'anskodemokratické Hnutie, SKDH). 1992–94

SR15 *Hungarian Civic Party* (S13 Magyar Polgári Part–Mad'arská Občianska Strana, MPP–MOS). In 1990 elections part of Public Against Violence. In 1994 joined with MKDH–ESWS to form Hungarian Coalition Party. 1992

SR16 *Green Party in Slovakia* (S12 Strana Zelených na Slovensku, SZS). Slovak break-away of Czechoslovak Green Party. In 1994 election part of Common Choice and in 1998 part of Slovak Democratic Coalition. 1992–2002

SR17 *Hungarian Coalition Party* (Strana Mad'arskej Koalície, SMK). Coalition of Hungarian Christian Democratic Movement–Coexistence and Hungarian Civic Party. Before 1998 election became unitary party to clear PR threshold. 1994–

SR18 *Common Choice* (Spoločná Vol'ba, SV). Alliance formed for 1994 election including Party of the Democratic Left, Social Democratic Party of Slovakia, Green Party in Slovakia, and Farmers' Movement of Slovakia. 1994

SR19 *Democratic Union of Slovakia* (Demokratická Únia Slovenska, DUS). Formed by two splinter groups of Movement for Democratic Slovakia. Contested 1998 as part of Slovak Democratic Coalition; joined SDKU in 2000. 1994

SR20 *Association of Workers of Slovakia* (Združenie Robotníkov Slovenska, ZRS). Splinter of Party of the Democratic Left, led by Ján Lupták, a Communist 'worker-hero'. 1994–98

SR21 *Communist Party of Slovakia* (Komunistická Strana Slovenska, KSS). Hard-line Marxist-Leninist fringe of SDL. 1994–

SR22 *Party Against Corruption, for Order, Work and Money for All Decent Citizens* (Strana Proti Korupcii, za Poriadok, Prácu a Peniaze pre Všestkých Slušných, Občanov SPK). 1994

SR23 *New Slovakia* (Nové Slovensko). Pro-EU party. 1994

SR24 *Movement for a Prosperous Czechia and Slovakia* (Hnutie za Prosperujúce Česko a Slovensko, HZPČS). Supported restoring CSFR state. 1994

SR25 *Roma Civic Initiative* (Rómska Občianska Iniciatíva, ROI). Founded by Gejza Adam in 1990 with the intent of representing diverse Roma groups. 1994

SR26 *Slovak Democratic Coalition* (Slovenská Demokratická Koalícia, SDK). Created as a party in 1998 by KDH, DUS, DS, SZS, and SDSS to avoid high threshold for alliances. KDH and DS withdrew in late 2000. SDK's leader, Prime Minister Mikuláš Dzurinda (1998–2006), also withdrew then to found Slovak Democratic and Christian Union. 1998

SR27 *Party of Civic Understanding* (Strana Občianského Porozumenia, SOP). Founded April 1998 by Rudolf Schuster, who in 1999 became first directly elected president of Slovakia. Many members joined Direction (Smer). 1998

SR28 *Slovak Democratic and Christian Union* (Slovenská Demokratická a Krest'anská Únia, SDKU). Founded on basis of SDK in late 2000 by Mikuláš Dzurinda, prime minister (1998–2006). Merged with DS in early 2006, adding latter's name to new party. 2002

SR29 *Direction* (Smer). Established in 2000 by Robert Fico, a deputy formerly in Party of the Democratic Left, and prime minister (2006–). Carried rubric 'Third Way' (Tretia Cesta) until early 2005, then merged with SDL, SDA, and SDSS to form Direction–Social Democracy (Smer–Sociálna Demokracia). 2002

SR30 *Alliance of the New Citizen* (Aliancia Nového Občiana, ANO, acronym for 'yes'). Led by Pavol Rusko, former chair of a private TV station. 2002–

SR31 *Movement for Democracy* (Hnutie za Demokraciu, HZD). July 2002 splinter of Mečiar's HZDS. In 2004 merged with another HZDS splinter to form People's Union–Movement for Democracy (L'udova Unia–Hnutie za Demokraciu) which together with SNS, smaller nationalist groups, and Smer backed Ivan Gašparovič's successful presidential bid in 2004. 2002–

SR32 *Real Slovak National Party* (Pravá Slovenská Národná Strana, P-SNS). Slovak

National Party splinter led by Ján Slota. Merged with SNS in 2006. 2002

SR33 *Social Democratic Alternative* (Sociálnodemokratická Alternatíva, SDA). Splinter party of SDL formed in 2002. In 2005 merged into Direction–Social Democracy. 2002–

SR34 *Direction–Social Democracy* (Smer–Sociálna Demokracija). Early 2005 merger of Robert Fico's Direction with SDL, SDA, and SDSS, also attracting most members of SOP. 2006–

SR35 *Slovak Democratic and Christian Union–Democratic Party* (Slovenská Demokratická a Kresťanská Únia–Demokratická Strana, SDKU–DS). Merger in January 2006, led by Mikuláš Dzurinda, prime minister (1998–2006). 2006–

SR36 *Free Forum* (Slobodné Fórum). Splinter in 2003 of Slovak Democratic and Christian Union (SDKU). 2006–

Table 9.2 PRESIDENTIAL VOTE: 5, 29 May 1999

	1st Round	%	2nd Round	%
Electorate	4,038,899		4,041,181	
Valid Votes	2,948,402	73.0	3,021,123	74.8
Invalid Votes	33,555	0.8	26,691	0.7
Total Votes	2,981,957	73.8	3,047,814	75.5
Rudolf Schuster, SOP	1,396,950	47.4	1,727,481	57.2
Vladimír Mečiar, HZDS	1,097,956	37.2	1,293,642	42.8
Magdaléna Vášáryová	194,635	6.6	—	—
Ivan Mjartan	105,903	3.6	—	—
Ján Slota, SNS	73,836	2.5	—	—
Boris Zala, SDSS	29,697	1.0	—	—
Juraj Švec	24,077	0.8	—	—
Juraj Lazarčik	15386	0.5	—	—
Michal Kováč[1]	5,425	0.2	—	—
Ján Demikat	4,537	0.2	—	—

Source: Statistical Office of the Slovak Republic, 2008.

[1] Withdrew one week before the first-round vote.

Table 9.3 PRESIDENTIAL VOTE: 3, 17 April 2004

	1st Round	%	2nd Round	%
Electorate	4,204,899		4,202,597	
Valid Votes	1,986,214	47.2	1,801,960	42.9
Invalid Votes	28,405	0.7	25,322	0.6
Total Votes	2,014,619	47.9	1,827,282	43.5
Vladimír Mečiar, LS–HZDS	650,242	32.7	722,368	40.1
Ivan Gašparovič, KNSS[1]	442,564	22.3	1,079,592	59.9
Eduard Kukan, SDKU[2]	438,920	22.1	—	—
Rudolf Schuster	147,549	7.4	—	—
František Mikloško, KDH	129,414	6.5	—	—
Martin Bútora	129,387	6.5	—	—
Ján Králik, SDL	15,873	0.8	—	—
Jozef Kalman, Left Bloc	10,221	0.5	—	—
Július Kubík	7,734	0.4	—	—
Jozef Šesták	6,785	0.3	—	—
Stanislav Bernát	5,719	0.3	—	—
L'ubomír Roman, ANO	1,806	0.1	—	—

Source: Statistical Office of the Slovak Republic, 2008.

[1] Confederation of National Forces of Slovakia. An alliance of HZD, SNS, and smaller nationalist groups. At a late stage in the campaign, Gašparovič was also endorsed by Smer.

[2] Endorsed by ANO candidate L'ubomír Roman shortly before polling day, too late for Roman's name to be withdrawn from the ballot.

Table 9.3a SLOVAKIA: Votes for the *Národná Rada*

	1990	1992	1994	1998	2002	2006
Electorate	3,622,650	3,770,073	3,876,555	4,023,191	4,157,802	4,272,517
Valid Votes	3,377,726	3,082,696	2,875,458	3,359,176	2,875,081	2,303,139
Invalid Votes[1]	77,925	91,740	47,807	26,360	34,917	32,778
Total Votes[2]	3,455,651	3,174,436	2,923,265	3,385,536	2,909,998	2,335,917
SR1 Public Against Violence	991,285	—	—	—	—	—
SR2 Christian Democratic Movement	648,782	273,945	289,987	—[3]	237,202	191,443
SR3 Slovak National Party	470,984	244,527	155,359	304,839	95,633	270,230
SR4 Communist Party of Czechoslovakia	450,855	—	—	—	—	—
SR5 Hungarian Christian Democrats–ESWS	292,636	228,885	—	—	—	—
SR17 Hungarian Coalition Party	—	—	292,936	306,623	321,069	269,111
SR15 Hungarian Civic Party	—	70,689	—	—	—	—
SR6 Democratic Party	148,567	102,058	98,555	—	—	—
SR7 Green Party	117,871	33,372	—	—	—	—
SR8 Alliance of Farmers & Countryside	85,060	—	—	—	—	—
SR10 Freedom Party	60,041	—	—	—	—	—
SR11 Movement for Democratic Slovakia	—	1,148,625	1,005,488	907,103	560,691	202,540
SR12 Party of the Democratic Left	—	453,203	—[4]	492,507	39,163	—
SR18 Common Choice	—	—	299,496	—	—	—
SR9 Social Democratic Party of Slovakia	61,401	123,426	—	—	—	—
SR16 Green Party in Slovakia	—	66,010	—[4]	—[3]	28,365	—
SR13 Civic Democratic Union	—	124,503	—	—	—	—
SR14 Christian Social Union	—	94,162	59,217	—	—	—
SR19 Democratic Union	—	—	246,444	—	—	—
SR20 Association of Workers in Slovakia	—	—	211,321	43,809	—	—

SR21 Communist Party of Slovakia	—	—	78,419	94,015	181,872	89,418
SR22 Party Against Corruption	—	—	37,929	—	—	—
SR23 New Slovakia	—	—	38,369	—	—	—
SR24 Prosperous Czechia & Slovakia	—	—	30,292	—	—	—
SR25 Roma Civic Initiative	—	—	19,542	—	—	—
SR26 Slovak Democratic Coalition	—	—	—	884,497	—	—
SR28 Slovak Dem. & Christian Union SDKU	—	—	—	—	433,953	—
SR35 SDKU–Dem. Party	—	—	—	—	—	422,815
SR27 Party of Civic Understanding	—	—	—	269,343	—	—
SR29 Direction	—	—	—	—	387,100	—
SR34 Direction–Social Democracy	—	—	—	—	—	671,185
SR33 Social Democratic Alternative	—	—	—	—	51,649	—
SR30 Alliance of the New Citizen	—	—	—	—	230,309	32,775
SR31 Movement for Democracy	—	—	—	—	94,324	14,728
SR32 Real Slovak National Party	—	—	—	—	105,084	—
SR36 Free Forum	—	—	—	—	—	79,963
Others[5]	50,244	119,291	12,104	56,440	108,667	58,931

Sources: Statistical Office of the Slovak Republic, 2008.

[1] Invalid votes calculated by subtraction.

[2] Total votes in 1990 and 1992 based on ballots distributed; in other years, turnout based on ballots returned.

[3] Part of Slovak Democratic Coalition in 1998.

[4] Part of Common Choice in 1994.

[5] Includes: 1990: 6 parties winning less than 1.0 per cent of the vote; 1992: 11 parties; 1994: 4 parties; 1998: 9 parties; 2002: 13 parties; 2006: 11 parties.

Table 9.3b SLOVAKIA: Percentage of Votes for the *Národná Rada*

	1990	1992	1994	1998	2002	2006
Valid Votes	93.2	81.8	74.2	83.5	69.2	53.9
Invalid Votes	2.2	2.4	1.2	0.7	0.8	0.8
Total Votes	95.4	84.2	75.4	84.2	70.0	54.7
SR1 Public Against Violence	29.3	—	—	—	—	—
SR2 Christian Democratic Movement	19.2	8.9	10.1	—	8.3	8.3
SR3 Slovak National Party	13.9	7.9	5.4	9.1	3.3	11.7
SR4 Communist Party of Czechoslovakia	13.3	—	—	—	—	—
SR5 Hungarian Christian Democrats–ESWS	8.7	7.4	—	—	—	—
SR17 Hungarian Coalition Party	—	—	10.2	9.1	11.2	11.7
SR15 Hungarian Civic Party	—	2.3	—	—	—	—
SR6 Democratic Party	4.4	3.3	3.4	—	—	—
SR7 Green Party	3.5	1.1	—	—	—	—
SR8 Alliance of Farmers & Countryside	2.5	—	—	—	—	—
SR10 Freedom Party	1.8	—	—	—	—	—
SR11 Movement for Democratic Slovakia	—	37.3	35.0	27.0	19.5	8.8
SR12 Party of the Democratic Left	—	14.7	—	14.7	1.4	—
SR18 Common Choice	—	—	10.4	—	—	—
SR9 Social Democratic Party of Slovakia	1.8	4.0	—	—	—	—
SR16 Green Party in Slovakia	—	2.1	—	—	1.0	—
SR13 Civic Democratic Union	—	4.0	—	—	—	—
SR14 Christian Social Union	—	3.1	2.1	—	—	—
SR19 Democratic Union	—	—	8.6	—	—	—
SR20 Association of Workers in Slovakia	—	—	7.3	1.3	—	—
SR21 Communist Party of Slovakia	—	—	2.7	2.8	6.3	3.9

SR22 Party Against Corruption	—	—	1.3	—	—	—
SR23 New Slovakia	—	—	1.3	—	—	—
SR24 Prosperous Czechia & Slovakia	—	—	1.1	—	—	—
SR25 Roma Civic Initiative	—	—	0.7	—	—	—
SR26 Slovak Democratic Coalition	—	—	—	26.3	—	—
SR28 Slovak Dem. & Christian Union SDKU	—	—	—	—	15.1	—
SR35 SDKU–Dem. Party	—	—	—	—	—	18.4
SR27 Party of Civic Understanding	—	—	—	8.0	—	—
SR29 Direction	—	—	—	—	13.5	—
SR34 Direction–Social Democracy	—	—	—	—	—	29.1
SR33 Social Democratic Alternative	—	—	—	—	1.8	—
SR30 Alliance of the New Citizen	—	—	—	—	8.0	1.4
SR31 Movement for Democracy	—	—	—	—	3.3	0.6
SR32 Real Slovak National Party	—	—	—	—	3.7	—
SR36 Free Forum	—	—	—	—	—	3.5
Others	1.5	3.9	0.4	1.7	3.8	2.6

Table 9.3c SLOVAKIA: Seats in the *Národná Rada*

	1990	1992	1994	1998	2002	2006
SR1 Public Against Violence	48	—	—	—	—	—
SR2 Christian Democratic Movement	31	18	17	—[1]	15	14
SR3 Slovak National Party	22	15	9	14	0	20
SR4 Communist Party of Czechoslovakia	22	—	—	—	—	—
SR5 Hungarian Christian Democrats–ESWS	14	14	—	—	—	—
SR17 Hungarian Coalition Party	—	—	17	15	20	20
SR15 Hungarian Civic Party	—	0	—	—	—	—
SR6 Democratic Party	7	0	0	—	—	—
SR7 Green Party	6	0	—	—	—	—
SR8 Alliance of Farmers & Countryside	0	—	—	—	—	—
SR10 Freedom Party	0	—	—	—	—	—
SR11 Movement for Democratic Slovakia	—	74	61	43	36	15
SR12 Party of the Democratic Left	—	29	—[2]	23	0	—
SR18 Common Choice	—	—	18[2]	—	—	—
SR9 Social Democratic Party of Slovakia	0	0	—	—	—	—
SR16 Green Party in Slovakia	—	0	—[2]	—[1]	0	—
SR13 Civic Democratic Union	—	0	—	—	—	—
SR14 Christian Social Union	—	0	0	—	—	—
SR19 Democratic Union	—	—	15	—	—	—
SR20 Association of Workers in Slovakia	—	—	13	0	—	—
SR21 Communist Party of Slovakia	—	—	0	0	11	0
SR22 Party Against Corruption	—	—	0	—	—	—
SR23 New Slovakia	—	—	0	—	—	—
SR24 Prosperous Czechia & Slovakia	—	—	0	—	—	—
SR25 Roma Civic Initiative	—	—	0	—	—	—

SR26 Slovak Democratic Coalition	—	—	—	42	—	—
SR28 Slovak Dem. & Christian Union SDKU	—	—	—	—	28	—
SR35 SDKU–Dem. Party	—	—	—	—	—	31
SR27 Party of Civic Understanding	—	—	—	13	—	—
SR29 Direction	—	—	—	—	25	—
SR34 Direction–Social Democracy	—	—	—	—	—	50
SR33 Social Democratic Alternative	—	—	—	—	0	—
SR30 Alliance of the New Citizen	—	—	—	—	15	0
SR31 Movement for Democracy	—	—	—	—	0	0
SR32 Real Slovak National Party	—	—	—	—	0	—
SR36 Free Forum	—	—	—	—	—	0
Others	0	0	0	0	0	0
Total	150	150	150	150	150	150

Sources: Statistical Office of the Slovak Republic, 2008.

[1] Part of Slovak Democratic Coalition in 1998.

[2] Seats distributed as follows: Party of the Democratic Left, 13; Social Democratic Party, 2; Green Party in Slovakia, 2; Farmers' Movement of Slovakia: 1.

Table 9.3d SLOVAKIA: Percentage of Seats in the *Národná Rada*

	1990	1992	1994	1998	2002	2006
SR1 Public Against Violence	32.0	—	—	—	—	—
SR2 Christian Democratic Movement	20.7	12	11.3	—	10	9.3
SR3 Slovak National Party	14.7	10.0	6.0	9.3	0	13.3
SR4 Communist Party of Czechoslovakia	14.7	—	—	—	—	—
SR5 Hungarian Christian Democrats–ESWS	9.3	9.3	—	—	—	—
SR17 Hungarian Coalition Party	—	—	11.3	10	13.3	13.3
SR15 Hungarian Civic Party	—	0	—	—	—	—
SR6 Democratic Party	4.7	0	0	—	—	—
SR7 Green Party	4.0	0	—	—	—	—
SR8 Alliance of Farmers & Countryside	0	—	—	—	—	—
SR10 Freedom Party	0	—	—	—	—	—
SR11 Movement for Democratic Slovakia	—	49.3	40.7	28.7	24.0	10.0
SR12 Party of the Democratic Left	—	19.3	—	15.3	0	—
SR18 Common Choice	—	—	12.0	—	—	—
SR9 Social Democratic Party of Slovakia	0	0	—	—	—	—
SR16 Green Party in Slovakia	—	0	—	—	0	—
SR13 Civic Democratic Union	—	0	—	—	—	—
SR14 Christian Social Union	—	0	0	—	—	—
SR19 Democratic Union	—	—	10.0	—	—	—
SR20 Association of Workers in Slovakia	—	—	8.7	0	—	—
SR21 Communist Party of Slovakia	—	—	0	0	7.3	0
SR22 Party Against Corruption	—	—	0	—	—	—
SR23 New Slovakia	—	—	0	—	—	—
SR24 Prosperous Czechia & Slovakia	—	—	0	—	—	—
SR25 Roma Civic Initiative	—	—	0	—	—	—

SR26 Slovak Democratic Coalition	—	—	—	28.0	—	—
SR28 Slovak Dem. & Christian Union SDKU	—	—	—	—	18.7	—
SR35 SDKU–Dem. Party	—	—	—	—	—	20.7
SR27 Party of Civic Understanding	—	—	—	8.7	—	—
SR29 Direction	—	—	—	—	16.7	—
SR34 Direction–Social Democracy	—	—	—	—	—	33.3
SR33 Social Democratic Alternative	—	—	—	—	0	—
SR30 Alliance of the New Citizen	—	—	—	—	10.0	0
SR31 Movement for Democracy	—	—	—	—	0	0
SR32 Real Slovak National Party	—	—	—	—	0	—
SR36 Free Forum	—	—	—	—	—	0
Others	0	0	0	0	0	0

10

ESTONIA

Estonia was a part of the Russian Empire until 24 February 1918, when nationalists proclaimed independence and a provisional government was formed. Power was then seized by German military forces and held until the First World War ended. The Red Army attacked Estonia in late November 1918 but were driven out early the following year. The independence of Estonia was recognized and peace secured by the Tartu Treaty with the Soviet Union on 2 February 1920. In ethnic terms, 88 per cent of the population was Estonian.

The Constitution of 1920 created a single-chamber parliament (*Riigikogu*) of 100 members elected by proportional representation. All citizens age 20 or over had the right to vote. The prime minister was head of state as well as head of government. Between 1919 and 1933 Estonia held five free elections. Parties on the democratic left won between 20 and 29 seats; the centre, 23 to 36 seats; right-wing agrarian parties 21 to 42 seats; ethnic minority parties – Russian, German, and Swedish – together won five to eight seats. The Communist Party, which staged an unsuccessful armed coup in 1924, won five to ten seats (Parming, 1975: 11). In the early 1930s agitation by the League of Veterans of the War of Independence led to a new constitution granting broad executive power. Konstantin Päts, the acting head of government, took emergency powers and in 1934 became a dictator.

Under the terms of the Nazi–Soviet Pact, Estonia was occupied by the Soviet Union on 17 June 1940. Soviet forces established a transitional people's government led by Communists at a time when the Estonian Communist Party had barely 100 members. In the election of a people's assembly on 14–15 July 1940, only Communist-sponsored candidates were on the ballot, secret voting was discouraged, and fraud was widespread. Turnout was reported as 81.6 per cent and the vote for the Working People's League was 92.2 per cent (Misiunas and Taagepera, 1993: 20ff.). Estonia was incorporated into the Soviet Union in August 1940.

When Nazi Germany declared war on the Soviet Union, Estonia was occupied by Germany. In 1944 it was re-occupied by Soviet forces. Single-candidate elections were held in Estonia for the Supreme Soviet of the USSR in February 1946. Deportations, the flight of Estonians, and an influx of Russians reduced Estonians from 95 per cent to 62 per cent of the population.

Following the 1985 introduction of glasnost by Mikhail Gorbachev, Estonians began to voice demands for national independence, starting with a large public demonstration in Tallinn on 23 August 1987. As part of perestroika, semi-competitive elections began to be held. In the election of the USSR Congress of People's Deputies in March 1989, three-quarters of the Estonian seats were won by candidates from the Popular Front of Estonia, including some low-ranking officials in the Estonian Communist Party (Misiunas and Taagepera, 1993: 311–35).

A single transferable vote election was held for the Supreme Soviet of the Estonian Soviet Socialist Republic on 18 March 1990. The 105 seats were distributed among 28 districts electing one to five members, plus a four-seat district in which only Soviet military personnel voted. At a time when candidates' allegiances were rapidly shifting from Moscow to Estonia, the STV ballot avoided any need to identify candidates by party labels. Within the pro-independence movement, there were disputes about whether to take part in the election, with a boycott advocated by those opposed to any recognition of Soviet sovereignty. All residents, including Russian immigrants, were eligible to vote. On a turnout of 78.2 per cent, the pro-independence Popular Front of Estonia claimed at least 41 seats; the Communist Free Estonia group and its allies at least 25 seats; the anti-independence Joint Council of Work Collectives, 26 seats; and the allegiances of 13 deputies were unclear (Taagepera, 1990: 308). Twelve days after the election, by a vote of 78 to 8 the new Estonian Supreme Soviet declared the country was in transition to independence.

When Mikhail Gorbachev called a referendum on the future of the Soviet Union, the Estonian Supreme Soviet turned it into a vote on independence, in which all permanent residents of the republic were eligible to vote. In the 3 March 1991 referendum turnout was 83.0 per cent, and 77.7 per cent voted for independence, including almost all ethnic Estonians and more than a quarter of non-Estonians (Raun, 1997: 348). Full independence was declared on 20 August 1991 and was accepted by Moscow on 6 September.

The declaration of independence called for an Assembly of 60 members, half from the Supreme Soviet and half from the *Eesti Kongress,* a pro-independence movement of ethnic Estonians. While the Assembly was at work, the Estonian Supreme Soviet adopted a law that restricted citizenship to individuals who were citizens in June 1940 – that is, prior to Soviet occupation – or their descendants. In 1989 Russians and other Soviet nationalities who had entered Estonia after 1940 were 36 per cent of the population. In a referendum on 28 June 1992, the constitution was approved by 91.3 per cent of the voters on a 66.8 per cent turnout of citizens.

The constitution established a single-chamber National Assembly, the *Riigikogu,* with 101 deputies elected for a four-year term. The *Riigikogu* is elected by proportional representation in which each elector votes for a single candidate on a party list and the vote is counted for both the individual and the party (Ishiyama, 1996). In the first stage of allocating seats in a district, individual candidates winning a Hare quota are awarded seats. In the second stage, unallocated seats are awarded to parties that win full Hare quotas, and a party's seats go to candidates in the order of their personal votes. Third, unallocated seats are distributed at the national level by a modified d'Hondt formula with divisors of 1, 1.87, 2.69, 3.48, *et sequentiae.* These seats go to parties receiving at least five per cent of the nationwide vote, and to candidates in the order of their ranking on their party's national list. In 1992 there were 12 multi-member districts, in 1995 and 1999 11 districts, and since 2003 12 districts. In 2007 there were from 6 to 13 deputies returned per district. Shortly before the 1999 election, a new law required that each party have at least 1,000 members and that parties in electoral alliances form a single party in the *Riigikogu* rather than separate parties. The number of parties on the ballot fell from 16 to 12.

All citizens over the age of 18 are eligible to vote, except for prisoners and the mentally incapacitated. To qualify for citizenship, one must pass an Estonian-language test. Non-citizens are eligible to vote in local elections. In 1998 a law was enacted allowing children of non-citizens born in Estonia after 26 February 1992 to become citizens without a language test. Persons who are not ethnic Estonians now constitute about one-sixth of the electorate (Statistics Estonia, 2007). In 1995 and 1999 Russian parties won six seats but then split (Mikkel, 2006: 27f.) and in the 2007 election won only 1.0 per cent of the vote.

The 2007 election was the first national election in which electors could vote over the internet, using state ID cards fitted with a computer chip. Internet voting account for 30,275 votes, 5.5 per cent of the total cast (Trechsel, 2007).

The constitution stipulated that the first president was to be elected for a four-year term by a popular vote and, if no candidate won an absolute majority, the *Riigikogu* would choose between the top two candidates. In a four-candidate presidential ballot on 20 September 1992, no one received half the vote. The Assembly chose the second-place presidential candidate, Lennart Meri, a writer active in the independence movement, in preference to Arnold Rüütel, chair of the Estonian Supreme Soviet (1983–90) and of the transitional assembly (1990–92). The constitution provided that subsequent presidential elections should be by parliament for a fixed five-year term. A two-thirds' majority is required. If this is not achieved in the first round, new candidates can be nominated. If a two-thirds' majority is not achieved in the second round, a third is held between the two leading candidates. If a two-thirds' majority is still not achieved, as happened both in 1996 and in 2001, an electoral college composed of MPs and a larger number of local government councillors elects the president by a majority vote, with a second-round run-off election if necessary.

DATES OF ELECTIONS

President	*Riigikogu* (National Assembly)
20 September 1992	20 September 1992
	5 March 1995
	7 March 1999
	2 March 2003
	4 March 2007

REFERENCES

Estonian National Electoral Committee, 1992. *Vabariigi presidendi ja Riigikogu valimised 1992: dokumente ja materjale*. Tallinn: Estonian National Electoral Committee.

———, 2007. "Vabariigi Valimiskomisjon", http://www.vvk.ee.

Ishiyama, J., 1996. "Electoral Systems Experimentation in the New Eastern Europe: The Single Transferable Vote and the Additional Member System in Estonia and Hungary", *East European Quarterly* 29, 4, 487–507.

Mikkel, Evald, 2006. "Patterns of Party Formation in Estonia". In Susanne Jungerstamm-Mulders, ed., *Post-Communist EU Member States: Parties and Party Systems*. Aldershot: Ashgate, 23–50.

Misiunas, Romuald, and Rein Taagepera, 1993. *The Baltic States: Years of Dependence, 1940–1990*. London: C. Hurst, 2nd edition.

Parming, T., 1975. *The Collapse of Liberal Democracy and the Rise of Authoritarianism in Estonia*. London: Sage Professional Papers in Comparative Political Sociology No. 6.

Raun, Toivo U., 1997. "Democratization and Political Development in Estonia, 1987–96". In K. Dawisha and Bruce Parrott, eds., *The Consolidation of Democracy in East-Central Europe*. Cambridge: Cambridge University Press, 334–74.

Statistics Estonia, 2007. "Table PC225", http://www.stat.ee/statistics.

Taagepera, Rein, 1990. "The Baltic States", *Electoral Studies* 9, 4, 303–11.

Trechsel, Alexander H., 2007. *Internet Voting in the March, 2007 Parliamentary Elections in Estonia*. Florence: European University Institute.

Table 10.1 ESTONIAN POLITICAL PARTIES

1 *Estonian National Independence Party* (Eesti Rahvusliku Sõltumatuse Partei, ERSP). Anti-Communist party founded 20 August 1988 to campaign for Estonian independence. In 1995 merged into Pro Patria Union. 1992

2 *Pro Patria National Coalition* (Rahvuslik Koonderakond Isamaaliit, RKEI). Formed in early 1992 by anti-Communist groups. Leaders included Lennart Meri, president (1992–2001), and Mart Laar, prime minister (1999–2002). After 1995 election merged with ERSP to form Pro Patria Union (Isamaaliit). 1992–95

3 *Estonian Coalition Party* (Eesti Koonderakond, EK). Formed in December 1991 under prime minister Tiit Vähi (1991–92, 1995–97). In 1992 main partner in coalition *Secure Home* (Kindel Kodu) and supported presidential bid of Arnold Rüütel. In 1995 led the electoral alliance Coalition Party and Rural Union (Koonderakond ja Maarahva Ühendus, KMÜ). 1992–99

4 *Estonian Centre Party* (Eesti Keskerakond, EKe). Organized in 1991 by Prime Minister Edgar Savisaar (1990–92) as offshoot of Estonian Popular Front (pro-independence movement); for two years kept the name Front. 1992–

5 *Social Democratic Party* (Sotsiaaldemokraatlik Erakond, SDE). Organized in 1990 as coalition of Estonian Social Democratic Party, revival of party founded in 1905, and Estonian Rural Centre Party, which supported restitution of land based on pre-war property rights. Contested 1992–2003 elections as Moderates (Mõõdukad). In 1999 allied with Estonian People's Party (Eesti Rahverakond) and joined it after election. 1992–

6 *Estonian Royalist Party* (Eesti Rojalistlik Partei, ERP). Founded in 1989 to promote a monarchy. Initially favoured an English royal and then a Swedish prince. In 1995 joined in Fourth Force with Estonian Greens. 1992

7 *Better Estonia and Estonian Citizen* (Parem Eesti ja Eesti Kodanik, PE–EK). Nationalist bloc, in 1992 called Estonian Citizen. 1992–95

8 *Estonian Pensioners' and Families League* (Eesti Pensionäride ja Perede Liit, EPPL). Formerly known as Estonian Democratic Justice Union and Pensioners' League. Part of KMÜ in 1995. Fielded candidates on Coalition Party list in 1999 and in 2000 joined People's Union. 1992

9 *Farmers' Assembly* (Põllumeeste Kogu, PK). Agrarian party founded 1992. In 1995 contested as part of Coalition Party and Rural Union. 1992–99

10 *Estonian Greens* (Eesti Rohelised, ER). Coalition of environmental organizations. Contested 1995 election as part of electoral list of Fourth Force. Insufficient members to register as a political party in the 1999 and 2003 elections. Registered in 2006. 1992–

11 *Estonian Entrepreneurs' Party* (Eesti Ettevõtjate Erakond, EEE). Pro-business party led by Tiit Made. Absorbed by Centre Party in 1995. 1992

12 *Left Alternative* (Vasakvõimalus). Successor to Communist Party. 1992

13 *Coalition Party and Rural Union* (Koonderakond ja Maarahva Ühendus, KMÜ). Alliance of Coalition Party with Rural Union, Estonian Country People's Party, Pensioners and Families' League, and Farmers' Assembly. 1995

14 *Estonian Reform Party* (Eesti Reformierakond, ER). Founded in 1994 by Siim Kallas, former president of Bank of Estonia and prime minister (2002–03), with elements previously part of Pro Patria (Isamaaliit). Led by Prime Minister Andrus Ansip (2005–). 1995–

15 *Our Home Is Estonia* (Meie Kodu on Eestimaa, MKE). Formed by Estonian United People's Party, Russian Party in Estonia, and Russian People's Party of Estonia. 1995

16 *Right-Wingers' Party* (Vabariiklaste ja Konservatiivide Rahvaerakond/ Parempoolsed VKR/P). Also known as Republican and Conservative People's Party. Formed in 1994 by groups formerly part of Pro Patria. In 1998 merged with Estonian Farmers' Party to form Estonian People's Party. 1995

17 *Future Estonia Party* (Tuleviku Eesti Erakond, TEE). Nationalist party led by Jaanus Raidal. 1995

18 *Justice* (Õiglus). Coalition of parties descended from former ruling Communist Party of Estonia. 1995

19 *Estonian Farmers' Party* (Eesti Talurahva Erakond, ETRE). Founded in 1994. In 1998 merged with VKR/P to form Estonian People's Party. 1995

20 *Fourth Force* (Neljas Jõud, NJ). Alliance of Estonian Royalist Party and Estonian Greens. 1995

21 *Estonian Blue Party* (Eesti Sinine Erakond, ESE). Founded in 1994 under leadership of Neeme Kuningas. 1995–99

22 *Pro Patria Union* (Isamaaliit). December 1995 union of Pro Patria National Coalition and Estonian National Independence Party. In 2006 merged with Res Publica to form Pro Patria and Res Publica Union. 1999–2003

23 *Estonian Country People's Party* (Eesti Maarahva Erakond, EME). Founded in 1994 by Arnold Rüütel, chair of Estonian Supreme Soviet (1983–90). Contested 1995 with the Coalition Party and Rural Union. After 1999 election in People's Union. 1999

24 *Constitutional Party* (Konstitutsioonierakond). Seeks citizenship for Russian ethnics. Founded as *Estonian United People's Party* (Eestimaa Ühendatud Rahvapartei, EÜRP). In 2003 added 'Russian' (Vene) to name. Name changed to

Constitutional Party in 2006. 1999–

25 *Party of Estonian Christian Democrats* (Erakond Eesti Kristlikud Demokraadid). Eurosceptic party led by Aldo Vinkel. Contested 1999–2003 elections as Estonian Christian People's Party (Eesti Kristlik Rahvapartei, EKRP). 1999–

26 *Russian Party in Estonia* (Vene Erakond Eestis, VEE). Founded in 1994. Contested 1995 as part of Our Home Is Estonia bloc. 1999–2003

27 *Union for the Republic: Res Publica* (Ühendus Vabariigi Eest–Res Publica, ResP). Founded by anti-Soviet activists. Led by Rein Taagepera, presidential candidate in 1992, then by Juhan Parts, prime minister (2003–05). In 2006 merged with Pro Patria Union. 2003

28 *People's Union of Estonia* (Eestimaa Rahvaliit, ERL). Founded in 1999 by Estonian Country People's Party and joined in 2000 by Estonian Pensioners' and Families' League (EPPL). Led by Arnold Rüütel. 2003–

29 *Union of Pro Patria and Res Publica* (Isamaa ja Res Publica Liit, IresPL). Two eponymous parties merged in 2006. 2007–

Table 10.2 PRESIDENTIAL VOTE: 20 September 1992

Electorate	689,608	%
Valid Votes	463,528	67.2
Invalid Votes	5,077	0.7
Total Votes	468,605	67.9
Arnold Rüütel, Secure Home	195,743	42.2
Lennart Meri, Pro Patria[1]	138,317	29.8
Rein Taagepera, Popular Front	109,631	23.7
Lagle Parek, Estonian National Independence Party	19,837	4.3

Source: Estonian National Electoral Committee, 2007.

[1] Winner by *Riigikogu*'s choice between top two candidates.

Table 10.3a ESTONIA: Votes for the *Riigikogu*

	1992	1995	1999	2003	2007
Electorate	689,319	790,392	857,270	859,714	897,243
Valid Votes	458,247	540,699	484,239	494,888	550,213
Invalid Votes[1]	9,381	5,126	8,117	5,798	5,250
Total Votes	467,628	545,825	492,356	500,686	555,463
1 Estonian National Independence Party	40,260	—	—	—	—
2 Pro Patria National Coalition	100,828	42,493	—	—	—
22 Pro Patria Union	—	—	77,917	36,169	—
3 Estonian Coalition Party	62,329	—[2]	36,692	—	—
13 Estonian Coalition Party and Rural Union	—	174,248	—	—	—
8 Estonian Pensioners' League	17,011	—[2]	—	—	—
9 Farmers' Assembly	13,356	—[2]	2,421	—	—
23 Estonian Country People's Party	—	—[2]	35,204	—	—
4 Estonian Centre Party	56,124	76,634	113,378	125,709	143,518
5 Social Democratic Party	44,577	32,381	73,630	34,837	58,363
6 Estonian Royalist Party	32,638	—	—	—	—
20 Fourth Force	—	4,377	—	—	—
10 Estonian Greens	12,009	—	—	—	39,279
7 Better Estonia/Estonian Citizen	31,553	19,529	—	—	—
11 Estonian Entrepreneurs' Party	10,946	—	—	—	—
12 Left Alternative	7,374	—	—	—	—
14 Estonian Reform Party	—	87,531	77,088	87,551	153,044
15 Our Home Is Estonia	—	31,763	—	—	—
24 Constitutional Party	—	—	29,682	11,113	5,464
26 Russian Party in Estonia	—	—	9,825	990	—

16 Right-Wingers' Party	—	27,053	—	—	—
17 Future Estonia Party	—	13,907	—	—	—
18 Justice	—	12,248	—	—	—
19 Estonian Farmers' Party	—	8,146	—	—	—
21 Estonian Blue Party	—	1,913	7,745	—	—
25 Estonian Christian Democrats	—	—	11,745	5,275	9,456
28 People's Union	—	—	—	64,463	39,215
27 Res Publica	—	—	—	121,856	—
29 Pro Patria and Res Publica Union	—	—	—	—	98,347
Others[3]	29,242	8,476	8,912	6,925	3,527

Sources: Estonian National Electoral Committee, 1992, 2007.

[1] Invalid votes calculated by subtraction.

[2] Part of Estonian Coalition Party and Rural Union in 1995.

[3] Includes: 1992: 5 parties winning less than 1.0 per cent of the vote and 19,753 votes for independents; 1995: 3 parties and 1,444 votes for independents; 1999: 1 party and 7,058 votes for independents; 2003: 2 parties and 2,161 votes for independents; 2007: 3 parties and 563 votes for independents.

Table 10.3b ESTONIA: Percentage of Votes for the *Riigikogu*

	1992	1995	1999	2003	2007
Valid Votes	66.5	68.4	56.5	57.6	61.3
Invalid Votes	1.4	0.6	0.9	0.7	0.6
Total Votes	67.9	69.0	57.4	58.3	61.9
1 Estonian National Independence Party	8.8	—	—	—	—
2 Pro Patria National Coalition	22.0	7.9	—	—	—
22 Pro Patria Union	—	—	16.1	7.3	—
3 Estonian Coalition Party	13.6	—	7.6	—	—
13 Estonian Coalition Party and Rural Union	—	32.2	—	—	—
8 Estonian Pensioners' League	3.7	—	—	—	—
9 Farmers' Assembly	2.9	—	0.5	—	—
23 Estonian Country People's Party	—	—	7.3	—	—
4 Estonian Centre Party	12.2	14.2	23.4	25.4	26.1
5 Social Democratic Party	9.7	6.0	15.2	7.0	10.6
6 Estonian Royalist Party	7.1	—	—	—	—
20 Fourth Force	—	0.8	—	—	—
10 Estonian Greens	2.6	—	—	—	7.1
7 Better Estonia/Estonian Citizen	6.9	3.6	—	—	—
11 Estonian Entrepreneurs' Party	2.4	—	—	—	—
12 Left Alternative	1.6	—	—	—	—
14 Estonian Reform Party	—	16.2	15.9	17.7	27.8
15 Our Home Is Estonia	—	5.9	—	—	—
24 Constitutional Party	—	—	6.1	2.2	1.0
26 Russian Party in Estonia	—	—	2.0	0.2	—
16 Right-Wingers' Party	—	5.0	—	—	—

17 Future Estonia Party	—	2.6	—	—	—
18 Justice	—	2.3	—	—	—
19 Estonian Farmers' Party	—	1.5	—	—	—
21 Estonian Blue Party	—	0.4	1.6	—	—
25 Estonian Christian Democrats	—	—	2.4	1.1	1.7
28 People's Union	—	—	—	13.0	7.1
27 Res Publica	—	—	—	24.6	—
29 Pro Patria and Res Publica Union	—	—	—	—	17.9
Others	6.4	1.6	1.8	1.4	0.6

Table 10.3c ESTONIA: Number of Seats in the *Riigikogu*

	1992	1995	1999	2003	2007
1 Estonian National Independence Party	10	—	—	—	—
2 Pro Patria National Coalition	29	8	—	—	—
22 Pro Patria Union	—	—	18	7	—
3 Estonian Coalition Party	17	—[1]	7	—	—
13 Estonian Coalition Party and Rural Union	—	41[1]	—	—	—
8 Estonian Pensioners' League	0	—[1]	—	—	—
9 Farmers' Assembly	0	—[1]	0	—	—
23 Estonian Country People's Party	—	—[1]	7	—	—
4 Estonian Centre Party	15	16	28	28	29
5 Social Democratic Party	12	6	17	6	10
6 Estonian Royalist Party	8	—	—	—	—
20 Fourth Force	—	0	—	—	—
10 Estonian Greens	1	—	—	—	6
7 Better Estonia/Estonian Citizen	8	0	—	—	—
11 Estonian Entrepreneurs' Party	1	—	—	—	—
12 Left Alternative	0	—	—	—	—
14 Estonian Reform Party	—	19	18	19	31
15 Our Home Is Estonia	—	6	—	—	—
24 Constitutional Party	—	—	6	0	0
26 Russian Party in Estonia	—	—	0	0	—
16 Right-Wingers' Party	—	5	—	—	—
17 Future Estonia Party	—	0	—	—	—
18 Justice	—	0	—	—	—
19 Estonian Farmers' Party	—	0	—	—	—
21 Estonian Blue Party	—	0	0	—	—

25 Estonian Christian Democrats	—	—	0	0	0
28 People's Union	—	—	—	13	6
27 Res Publica	—	—	—	28	—
29 Pro Patria and Res Publica Union	—	—	—	—	19
Others	0	0	0	0	0
Total	101	101	101	101	101

Sources: Estonian National Electoral Committee, 1992, 2007.

[1] Seats shared as follows: Estonian Coalition Party, 18; Rural Union, 8; Estonian Country People's Party, 7; Estonian Pensioners' League, 6; Farmers' Assembly, 2.

Table 10.3d ESTONIA: Percentage of Seats in the *Riigikogu*

	1992	1995	1999	2003	2007
1 Estonian National Independence Party	9.9	—	—	—	—
2 Pro Patria National Coalition	28.7	7.9	—	—	—
22 Pro Patria Union	—	—	17.8	6.9	—
3 Estonian Coalition Party	16.8	—	6.9	—	—
13 Estonian Coalition Party and Rural Union	—	40.6	—	—	—
8 Estonian Pensioners' League	0	—	—	—	—
9 Farmers' Assembly	0	—	0	—	—
23 Estonian Country People's Party	—	—	6.9	—	—
4 Estonian Centre Party	14.9	15.8	27.7	27.7	28.7
5 Social Democratic Party	11.9	5.9	16.8	5.9	9.9
6 Estonian Royalist Party	7.9	—	—	—	—
20 Fourth Force	—	0	—	—	—
10 Estonian Greens	1.0	—	—	—	5.9
7 Better Estonia/Estonian Citizen	7.9	0	—	—	—
11 Estonian Entrepreneurs' Party	1.0	—	—	—	—
12 Left Alternative	0	—	—	—	—
14 Estonian Reform Party	—	18.8	17.8	18.8	30.7
15 Our Home Is Estonia	—	5.9	—	—	—
24 Constitutional Party	—	—	5.9	0	0
26 Russian Party in Estonia	—	—	0	0	—
16 Right-Wingers' Party	—	5.0	—	—	—
17 Future Estonia Party	—	0	—	—	—
18 Justice	—	0	—	—	—
19 Estonian Farmers' Party	—	0	—	—	—
21 Estonian Blue Party	—	0	0	—	—

25 Estonian Christian Democrats	—	—	0	0	0
28 People's Union	—	—	—	12.9	5.9
27 Res Publica	—	—	—	27.7	—
29 Pro Patria and Res Publica Union	—	—	—	—	18.8
Others	0	0	0	0	0

11

HUNGARY

The *Ausgleich* of 1867 created a Hungarian government with its own parliament as one part of the Habsburg monarchy's Austro-Hungarian Empire. The population was divided almost equally between Hungarians and a multiplicity of non-Hungarian nationalities. Elections in single-member districts for the national assembly in Budapest were held under conditions designed to ensure a majority for the Hungarian elite. The franchise was restricted to men of property or education; thus, only six per cent of the population had the right to vote. Voting was open, not secret; large landowners could influence the vote of those dependent on them. Districts were very unequal in size. In an electorate of 1,025,000 persons, in 1901 a total of 125 of the 413 deputies won their seats with fewer than 100 votes. Hungarian officials administering the election discriminated against non-Hungarian electors (Seymour and Frary, 1918: vol. II, 69ff.).

The First World War led to the collapse of the Habsburg Empire and to the independence of Hungary. After the end of a short-lived Communist republic in 1919, Admiral Miklos Horthy became regent, even though there was no royal family. The 1920 Treaty of Trianon recognized Hungary's independence with much reduced borders that excluded the great majority of the non-Hungarian population formerly governed from Budapest. It also ceded areas with Hungarian-speaking populations to Romania, Slovakia, and Yugoslavia. In 1920 an election was held with a franchise allowing all males to vote in a secret ballot; the result was negated by political upheavals. Before the 1922 election the secret ballot was abolished in rural districts. Subsequent elections were neither free nor fair (Bachmann, 1969).

During the Second World War Hungary sided with Germany and was occupied by the Soviet army in autumn 1944. A proportional representation election was held on 4 November 1945 with a secret ballot. All adult men and women were eligible to vote with the exception of ethnic Germans and leaders of fascist parties. The Independent Smallholders' Party won an absolute majority of votes and seats; the Social Democratic Party came second; and the Communist Party third (Table 11.1). A five-party coalition, including Communists, formed an Independence Popular Front government. The Interior Ministry and police were under Communist control. In early 1947 the Communists forced Prime Minister Ferenc Nagy to resign.

Table 11.1 HUNGARIAN ELECTION: 4 November 1945

		%		
Electorate	5,167,180			
Valid Votes	4,730,409	91.5		
Invalid Votes	44,244	0.9		
Total Votes	4774653	92.4		
	Votes	%	Seats	%
Independent Smallholders	2,697,503	57.0	245	59.0
Social Democratic Party	823,314	17.4	76	18.4
Communist Party	802,122	17.0	69	16.6
National Peasants' Party	325,284	6.9	23	5.5
Civic Democrats	76,424	1.6	2	0.5
Radical Party	5,762	0.1	0	0
Total Seats			415	

Source: Földes and Hubai, 1994: 231–32.

Before the election of 31 August 1947 an additional 460,000 people were excluded from the franchise on political grounds. On a reported turnout of 94 per cent, the governing Front secured 61 per cent of the reported vote and 271 of the 411 seats in parliament. The Communists won 22.3 per cent of the vote. In early 1948 the Social Democrats were forced to merge with the Communists to form the Hungarian Workers' Party. In the May 1949 election the Communist-led Front was the only party to nominate candidates. The Hungarian People's Republic was proclaimed and competitive party elections ended (Dessewffy and Hammer, 1995: 11ff.).

Hungary was a party-state but not monolithic. In 1983 an election law was adopted that permitted multi-candidate elections at local and National Assembly levels (Barany, 1990). In September 1987 the Hungarian Democratic Forum was organized and the Alliance of Young Democrats was formed in March 1988. Round-table negotiations about a new electoral law, involving non-Communist as well as Communist groups, began in June 1989 (Schiemann, 2001; Enyedi, 2007). There was disagreement about whether the president should be elected. Communists favoured direct election in the belief that they had a popular candidate who would win, Imre Pozsgay. The opposition forced a referendum vote about postponing a presidential election until after the parliamentary election. In the 26 November 1989 referendum 50.07 per cent voted for delay; turnout was 58.1 per cent. In the post-election referendum on 29 July 1990, 86.4 per cent of valid votes favoured the direct election of a president but, since the turnout was only 13.9 per cent, it fell far short of the 50 per cent required to make the result legally binding. The president of Hungary is elected for a maximum of two five-year terms by a two-thirds' majority of parliament in a first- or second-round ballot. If this is not achieved, a run-off is held between the top two second-round candidates.

The election law adopted in autumn 1989 gave universal suffrage to citizens age 18 and above, subject to very minor restrictions. The election of the single-chamber parliament of 386 deputies, the *Országgyûlés,* is by a mixed system. Each elector has two votes, one for a candidate in a single-member district and one for a closed party list in a multi-member proportional representation district.

A total of 176 deputies are elected in single-member districts. To win in the first round, a candidate must have an absolute majority of the votes and turnout must be at least 50 per cent. More than half a dozen candidates normally contest a district. If none wins an absolute majority, the three leading candidates, plus any other candidates winning 15 per cent of the vote, are eligible to contest the second round. If turnout in the first round is less than 50 percent, all candidates may stand in the second round. A plurality is enough for victory in the second round and the minimum turnout requirement is 25 per cent.

Deputies are elected by different proportional representation rules in regional and national multi-member constituencies. A total of 152 deputies are elected from party lists in 20 regional constituencies varying in size from 4 to 28 seats. A turnout of 50 per cent in a region is required for a valid first-round result, and 25 per cent if a second round is required. Initially, the threshold to qualify for regional list seats was four per cent of the nationwide vote. In December 1993 it was raised to 5 per cent, 10 per cent for alliances of two parties, and 15 per cent for groups of three or more. Seats are allocated to regional lists passing the threshold with a Hagenbach-Bischoff quota. When the remainder reaches two-thirds of the quotient required to win a seat, any unallocated seats are added to the national pool of 58 seats. National seats are distributed by the d'Hondt method among parties nominating lists in at least seven regions on the basis of votes wasted in single-member districts and in multi-member districts. The tables below report results for the first-round ballot in single-member districts and in the regional ballot for proportional representation seats.

DATES OF ELECTIONS FOR THE ORSZÁGGYÛLÉS

25 March, 8 April 1990
8, 29 May 1994
10, 24 May 1998
7, 21 April 2002
9, 23 April 2006

REFERENCES

Bachmann, G., 1969. "Ungarn". In D. Sternberger and B. Vogel, eds., *Die Wahl der Parlamente und anderer Staatsorgane: ein Handbuch*, I:ii, *Europa*. Berlin: Walter de Gruyter, 1365–1405.

Barany, Z., 1990. "Elections in Hungary". In R. Furtak, ed., *Elections in Socialist States*. London: Harvester/Wheatsheaf, 71–97.

Dessewffy, Tibor, and Ferenc Hammer, 1995. "The Transition in Hungary". In Gabor Tóka, ed., *The 1990 Election to the Hungarian National Assembly*. Berlin: Sigma, 11–31.

Enyedi, Zsolt, 2007. "The Survival of the Fittest: Party System Concentration in Hungary". In Susanne Jungerstamm-Mulders, ed., *Post-Communist EU Member States: Parties and Party Systems*. Aldershot: Ashgate, 177–202.

Földes, G., and L. Hubai, eds., 1994. *Parlamenti Kepviselöválasztások 1920–1990: Tanulmányok*. Budapest: Politikatörténeti Alapítvány.

Ilonszki, Gabriella, and Sandor Kurtán, 1995. "Hungary", *European Journal of Political Research* 28, 3–4, 359–68.

Ministry of the Interior, Central Data Processing, Election and Registration Office, 2002. http://www.election.hu/index_en.htm.

———, 2006. "Election History Archive", http:// www.valasztas.hu.

Schiemann, John W., 2001. "Hedging Against Uncertainty: Regime Change and the Origins of Hungary's Mixed-Member System". In Matthew Soberg Shugart and Martin P. Wattenberg, eds., *Mixed Member Electoral Systems: The Best of Both Worlds?* Oxford: Oxford University Press, 231–54.

Seymour, Charles, and Donald Paige Frary, 1918. *How the World Votes*. Springfield, MA.: C. A. Nichols, 2 vols.

Tóka, Gabor, ed., 1995. *The 1990 Election to the Hungarian National Assembly*. Berlin: Sigma.

Table 11.2 HUNGARIAN POLITICAL PARTIES

1 *Hungarian Democratic Forum* (Magyar Demokrata Fórum, MDF). Group formed in 1987 to promote free elections. Formerly led by József Antall, prime minister (1990–93). In 2002 ran a joint list with Fidesz. In 2006 the two parties ran separate sets of candidates with few exceptions. 1990–

2 *Alliance of Free Democrats* (Szabad Demokraták Szövetsége, SZDSZ). Party of Árpád Göncz, president (1990–2000). After first round of 2006 election, withdrew 55 SMD candidates in favour of MSZP and fielded joint candidates with that party in ten districts. 1990–

3 *Independent Party of Smallholders, Agrarian Workers, and Citizens* (Független Kisgazda, Földmunkás és Polgári Párt, FKGP). Founded November 1988 in tradition of a party created in 1930. Favoured restitution of land to pre-collectivization owners. Collapsed in 2001 after corruption scandals. 1990–2002

4 *Hungarian Socialist Party* (Magyar Szocialista Párt, MSZP). Reformist successor of governing party under old regime, Hungarian Socialist Workers' Party. Party of Prime Ministers Gyüla Horn (1994–98), Peter Medgyessy (2002–04), and Ferenc Gyurcsány (2004–). In 2006 election ran joint candidates with SZDSZ in ten single-member districts. 1990–

5 *Fidesz–Hungarian Civic Alliance* (Fidesz–Magyar Polgári Szövetség, Fidesz–MPS). Formed 1988 as Alliance of Young Democrats (Fiatal Demokraták Szövetsége, FIDESZ). Until 1993 membership restricted to those under 35. In 1995 added Hungarian Civic Party (MPP, later MPS) to its name. Led by Viktor Orbán, prime minister (1998–2002). In 2002 part of an alliance with MDF and in 2006 with KDNP. 1990–

6 *Christian Democratic People's Party* (Kereszténydemokrata Néppárt, KDNP). Claims descent from Democratic People's Party, leading opposition party in 1947 election. After losing all its seats in 1998, the party split. In 2002 part of Centre Party. In 2006 formed alliance with Fidesz. 1990–

7 *Hungarian Communist Workers' Party* (Magyar Kommunista Munkáspárt, MP). Orthodox Communist Party. Formerly known as Workers' Party. Adopted present name in 2005 after splits. 1990–

8 *Social Democratic Party of Hungary* (Magyarországi Szociáldemokrata Párt, MSZDP). Revival of party founded in 1890 and forcibly merged with Hungarian Socialist Workers' Party in 1948. 1990–2002

9 *Agrarian Alliance* (Agrárszövetség, ASZ). Opposed to land privatization. In 1998 absorbed into Hungarian Socialist Party. 1990–94

10 *Party of Entrepreneurs* (Vállalkozók Pártja). Also known as Liberal Citizens' Alliance (Liberális Polgári Szövetség, LPS). Fought 2002 election as part of Centre Party. 1990–98

11 *Patriotic Election Coalition* (Hazafias Választási Koalíció, HVK). Alliance of 16 organizations headed by Central Council of Trade Unions. 1990

12 *Hungarian People's Party* (Magyar Néppárt, MNP). Revival of National Peasant Party founded in 1939. 1990

13 *Green Party of Hungary* (Magyarországi Zöld Párt, MZP). An anti-establishment party . After 1990 election a split led to formation of Green Democrats (Zöld Demokraták). 1990–94

14 *Party of the Republic* (Köztársaság Párt, KP). Founded in 1992 by János Palotás, chair of National Federation of Entrepreneurs. 1994

15 *Hungarian Justice and Life* (Magyar Igazság és Élet Párt, MIÉP). Anti-Semitic party founded by Istvan Csurka, expelled from MDF in 1993. Seeks revision of state borders. In 2006 contested jointly with Movement for a Better Hungary (Jobbik Magyarországért Mozgalom). 1994–

16 *National Democratic Alliance* (Nemzeti Demokrata Szövetség, NDSZ). Group launched in 1991 by Imre Pozsgay, a Communist leader. 1994

17 *Hungarian Democratic People's Party* (Magyar Demokrata Néppárt, MDNP). Splinter of MDF formed 1996. In 2002 part of Centre Party. 1998

18 *Fidesz–Hungarian Democratic Forum–MDF* (Fiatal Demokraták Szövetsége–Magyar Demokrata Fórum, Fidesz–MDF). Joint list for one election. 2002

19 *Centre Party* (Centrumpárt). Founded as Centre of Solidarity for Hungary (Összefogás Magyarországért Centrum, OMC) by 25 groups including KDNP, Party of Entrepreneurs, Green Democrats, and MDNP. Before 2006 election KDNP allied with Fidesz and MDNP merged into MDF. 2002–

20 *Fidesz–Hungarian Civic Party–KDNP* (Fiatal Demokraták Szövetsége–Magyar Polgári Szövetség–Kereszténydemokrata Néppárt, Fidesz–MPS–KDNP). Joint list formed for 2006 election. 2006

Table 11.3a HUNGARY: Votes for the *Országgyûlés*

	1990		1994		1998		2002		2006	
	List	SMD	List	SMD	List	SMD	List	SMD	List	SMD
Electorate[1]	7,822,764	7,798,018	7,959,228	7,873,937	8,062,708		8,061,101		8,046,129	
Valid Votes	4,911,241	4,958,580	5,400,196	5,400,926	4,483,974[2]	4,467,940	5,616,750	5,624,595	5,408,050	5,403,675
Invalid Votes[3]	172,138	109,730	80,191	84,692	52,280	64,103	68,905	55,875	49,503	51,402
Total Votes	5,083,379	5,068,310	5,480,387	5,485,618	4,536,254	4,532,043	5,685,655	5,680,470	5,457,553	5,455,077
2 Free Democrats	1,050,799	1,077,386	1,065,889	1,005,658	353,186	456,008	313,084	380,982	351,612	394,895[4]
4 Hung. Socialists	535,064	508,753	1,781,504	1,688,835	1,445,909	1,332,178	2,361,997	2,277,737	2,336,705	2,275,782[4]
1 MDF	1,214,359	1,186,668	633,770	649,872	139,934	343,089	—[5]	—[5]	272,831	238,566
5 Fidesz	439,649	235,558	379,344	416,116	1,263,522	956,008	—	—	—	—
18 Fidesz–MDF	—	—	—	—	—	—	2,306,763	2,217,755	—	—
20 Fidesz–KDNP	—	—	—	—	—	—	—	—	2,272,979	2,269,241
6 KDNP	317,278	287,578	379,523	397,873	116,065	129,787	—	—	—	—
3 Smallholders	576,315	529,270	476,272	425,346	617,740	594,023	42,338	67,401	—	—
7 Workers' Party	180,964	131,422	172,109	177,416	183,064	165,455	121,503	108,732	21,955	16,379
8 Social Democrats	174,434	104,010	51,110	32,912	5,689	11,845	912	590	—	—
9 Agrarians	154,004	161,052	113,386	132,173	—	—	—	—	—	—
10 Entrepreneurs	92,689	82,477	33,367	42,951	3,962	8,874	—	—	—	—
11 Patriot Coalition	91,922	161,841	—	—	—	—	—	—	—	—
12 H. People's Party	37,047	38,647	—	—	—	—	—	—	—	—
13 Green Party	17,951	19,434	8,809	4,766	—	—	—	—	—	—
14 Republic Party	—	—	137,561	104,253	—	—	—	—	—	—
15 H. Justice & Life	—	—	85,737	67,162	248,825	249,127	245,326	257,430	119,007	92,798
16 National Dem.	—	—	28,075	32,258	—	—	—	—	—	—
17 H. Dem. People	—	—	—	—	62,568	87,971	—	—	—	—

19 Centre Party	—	—	—	—	—	—	219,029	182,253	17,431	14,126
Others	28,766[6]	434,484[7]	53,740[8]	223,335[9]	43,510[10]	133,575[11]	5,798[12]	131,715[13]	15,530[14]	101,888[15]

Sources: Ilonzski and Kurtan, 1995: 359–60; Tóka, 1995: 55–66; Ministry of the Interior, 2002, 2006.

[1] From 1998 onwards, election law provides for a common electoral roll for both single-member and list votes.

[2] Includes first-round vote in two list districts where the initial ballot was invalid because turnout was below 50 per cent.

[3] Invalid votes are calculated by subtraction.

[4] Includes 10 joint Socialist–Free Democrat candidates, winning a total of 154,619 votes, of which 100,470 went to the Socialists and 54,149 to the Free Democrats.

[5] Contested in 2002 as part of Fidesz–MDF joint list.

[6] Six other parties with less than 1.0 per cent of the vote.

[7] Includes: independents winning 342,544 votes; joint candidates of Free Democrats and FIDESZ with 29,113 votes and a joint candidate of Free Democrats, FIDESZ, and KDNP with 6,473 votes.

[8] Five other parties with less than 1.0 per cent.

[9] Includes independents with 122,190 votes and a joint candidate of Entrepreneurs, FIDESZ, Free Democrats, and the Agrarians with 6,440 votes.

[10] Four other parties with less than 1.0 per cent of the vote.

[11] Includes: independents with 75,695 votes.

[12] Five other parties winning less than 1.0 per cent of the vote.

[13] Includes: independents with 43,219 votes, two joint candidates of Socialists and Free Democrats with 27,892 votes, and four joint Socialist–Social Democrat candidates with 41,461 votes.

[14] Fifteen other parties winning less than 1.0 per cent of the vote.

[15] Includes: independents with 18,054 votes; two joint Fidesz–KDNP–MDF candidates with 34,109 votes.

Table 11.3b HUNGARY: Percentage of Votes for the *Országgyûlés*

	1990		1994		1998		2002		2006	
	List	SMD	List	SMD	List	SMD	List	SMD	List	SMD
Valid Votes	62.8	63.6	67.8	68.6	55.6	55.4	69.7	69.8	67.2	67.2
Invalid Votes	2.2	1.4	1.0	1.1	0.6	0.8	0.9	0.7	0.6	0.6
Total Votes	65.0	65.0	68.8	69.7	56.2	56.2	70.6	70.5	67.8	67.8
2 Free Democrats	21.4	21.7	19.7	18.6	7.9	10.2	5.6	6.8	6.5	7.3
4 Hungarian Socialists	10.9	10.3	33.0	31.3	32.2	29.8	42.1	40.5	43.2	42.2
1 Hungarian Democratic Forum	24.7	23.9	11.7	12.0	3.1	7.7	—	—	5.0	4.4
5 Fidesz	9.0	4.8	7.0	7.7	28.2	21.4	—	—	—	—
18 Fidesz–MDF	—	—	—	—	—	—	41.1	39.4	—	—
20 Fidesz–KDNP	—	—	—	—	—	—	—	—	42.0	42.0
6 KDNP	6.5	5.8	7.0	7.4	2.6	2.9	—	—	—	—
3 Independent Smallholders	11.7	10.7	8.8	7.9	13.8	13.3	0.8	1.2	—	—
7 Workers' Party	3.7	2.7	3.2	3.3	4.1	3.7	2.2	1.9	0.4	0.3
8 Social Democrats	3.6	2.1	0.9	0.6	0.1	0.3	0	0	—	—
9 Agrarian Alliance	3.1	3.2	2.1	2.4	—	—	—	—	—	—
10 Entrepreneurs	1.9	1.7	0.6	0.8	0.1	0.2	—	—	—	—
11 Patriotic Coalition	1.9	3.3	—	—	—	—	—	—	—	—
12 Hungarian People's Party	0.8	0.8	—	—	—	—	—	—	—	—
13 Green Party	0.4	0.4	0.2	0.1	—	—	—	—	—	—
14 Party of the Republic	—	—	2.5	1.9	—	—	—	—	—	—
15 Hung. Justice & Life Party	—	—	1.6	1.2	5.5	5.6	4.4	4.6	2.2	1.7
16 National Democratic Alliance	—	—	0.5	0.6	—	—	—	—	—	—
17 Hung. Democratic People's Party	—	—	—	—	1.4	2	—	—	—	—
19 Centre Party	—	—	—	—	—	—	3.9	3.2	0.3	0.3
Others	0.6	8.8	1	4.1	0.9	3	0.1	2.3	0.2	1.8

Table 11.3c HUNGARY: Number of Seats[1] in the *Országgyûlés*

	1990				1994				1998				2002				2006			
	Reg	Nat	SMD	All	Reg	Nat	SMD	All	Reg	Nat	SMD	All	Reg	Nat	SMD	All	Reg	Nat	SMD	All
2 Free Democrats	34	23	35	92	28	25	16	69	5	17	2	24	4	13	2	19	4	11	5[2]	20[2]
4 Socialists	14	18	1	33	53	7	149	209	50	30	54	134	69	31	78	178	71	17	102[2]	190[2]
1 MDF	40	10	114	164	18	15	5	38	0	0	17	17	—[3]	—[3]	—[3]	—[3]	2	9	0	11
5 Fidesz	8	12	1	21	7	13	0	20	48	10	90	148	—	—	—	—	—	—	—	—
18 Fidesz–MDF	—	—	—	—	—	—	—	—	—	—	—	—	67	26	95	188[4]	—	—	—	—
20 Fidesz–KDNP	—	—	—	—	—	—	—	—	—	—	—	—	—	—	—	—	69	27	68	164[5]
6 KDNP	8	10	3	21	5	14	3	22	0	0	0	0	—	—	—	—	—	—	—	—
3 Smallholders	16	17	11	44	14	11	1	26	22	14	12	48	0	0	0	0	—	—	—	—
7 Workers' Party	0	0	0	0	0	0	0	0	0	0	0	0	0	0	0	0	0	0	0	0
8 Soc. Democrats	0	0	0	0	0	0	0	0	0	0	0	0	0	0	0	0	—	—	—	—
9 Agrarians	0	0	2[6]	2[6]	0	0	1	1	—	—	—	—	—	—	—	—	—	—	—	—
10 Entrepreneurs	0	0	0	0	0	0	1	1	0	0	0	0	—	—	—	—	—	—	—	—
11 Patriot Coalition	0	0	0	0	—	—	—	—	—	—	—	—	—	—	—	—	—	—	—	—
12 People's Party	0	0	0	0	—	—	—	—	—	—	—	—	—	—	—	—	—	—	—	—
13 Green Party	0	0	0	0	0	0	0	0	—	—	—	—	—	—	—	—	—	—	—	—
14 P. of Republic	—	—	—	—	0	0	0	0	—	—	—	—	—	—	—	—	—	—	—	—
15 Justice & Life	—	—	—	—	0	0	0	0	3	11	0	14	0	0	0	0	0	0	0	0
16 National Dem.	—	—	—	—	0	0	0	0	—	—	—	—	—	—	—	—	—	—	—	—
17 Dem. People	—	—	—	—	—	—	—	—	0	0	0	0	—	—	—	—	—	—	—	—
19 Centre Party	—	—	—	—	—	—	—	—	—	—	—	—	0	0	0	0	0	0	0	0
Others	0	0	9[7]	9[7]	0	0	0	0	0	0	1[8]	1[8]	0	0	1[9]	1[9]	0	0	1	1
Total	120	90	176	386	125	85	176	386	128	82	176	386	140	70	176	386	146	64	176	386

Sources: Ilonzski and Kurtan, 1995: 359–60; Tóka, 1995: 55–66; Ministry of the Interior, 2002, 2006.

[1] Regional seats are allocated according to votes in the list ballot and national seats in proportion to the total votes a party has 'wasted'

when not awarded seats in the list and single-member districts.

[2] Six joint Socialist–Free Democrat candidates won seats in single-member districts in 2006. At the opening of parliament, 4 joined the Socialists and 2 joined the Free Democrats. They are counted here in the totals for their respective parties.

[3] MDF contested in 2002 as part of the Fidesz–MDF joint list.

[4] Of the joint list's total seats, Fidesz won 164 and MDF 24.

[5] Of the joint list's total seats, Fidesz won 141 and KDNP 23.

[6] At the opening of parliament, 1 deputy joined the Free Democrats and 1 the independents' group.

[7] Includes: 6 independent candidates, of whom 1 joined MDF in parliament; 1 joint candidate of the Free Democrats, FIDESZ, and KDNP who joined the independents group in parliament; 2 joint candidates of Free Democrats and FIDESZ, 1 of whom joined FIDESZ and the other the Free Democrats.

[8] Independent candidate.

[9] Joint Socialist–Free Democrats candidate. In parliament joined Free Democrats.

Table 11.3d HUNGARY: Percentage of Seats in the *Országgyûlés*

	1990				1994				1998				2002				2006			
	Reg	Nat	SMD	All	Reg	Nat	SMD	All	Reg	Nat	SMD	All	Reg	Nat	SMD	All	Reg	Nat	SMD	All
2 Free Democrats	28.3	25.6	20.5	24.1	22.4	29.4	9.1	17.9	3.9	20.7	1.1	6.2	2.9	18.6	1.1	4.9	2.7	17.2	2.8	5.2
4 Hun. Socialists	11.7	20.0	0.6	8.5	42.4	8.2	84.7	54.1	39.1	36.6	30.7	34.7	49.3	44.3	44.3	46.1	48.6	26.6	58.0	49.2
1 MDF	33.3	11.1	64.8	42.5	14.4	17.6	2.8	9.8	0	0	9.7	4.4	—	—	—	—	1.4	14.1	0	2.8
5 Fidesz	6.7	13.3	1.1	5.7	5.6	15.3	0	5.2	37.5	12.2	51.1	38.3	—	—	—	—	—	—	—	—
18 Fidesz–MDF	—	—	—	—	—	—	—	—	—	—	—	—	47.9	37.1	54.0	48.7	—	—	—	—
20 Fidesz–KDNP	—	—	—	—	—	—	—	—	—	—	—	—	—	—	—	—	47.3	42.2	38.6	42.5
6 KDNP	6.7	11.1	1.7	5.4	4.0	16.5	1.7	5.7	0	0	0	0	—	—	—	—	—	—	—	—
3 Smallholders	13.3	18.9	6.3	11.4	11.2	12.9	0.6	6.7	17.2	17.1	6.8	12.4	0	0	0	0	—	—	—	—
7 Workers' Party	0	0	0	0	0	0	0	0	0	0	0	0	0	0	0	0	0	0	0	0
8 Soc. Democrats	0	0	0	0	0	0	0	0	0	0	0	0	0	0	0	0	—	—	—	—
9 Agrarians	0	0	1.1	0.5	0	0	0.6	0.3	—	—	—	—	—	—	—	—	—	—	—	—
10 Entrepreneurs	0	0	0	0	0	0	0.6	0.3	0	0	0	0	—	—	—	—	—	—	—	—
11 Patriot Coalition	0	0	0	0	—	—	—	—	—	—	—	—	—	—	—	—	—	—	—	—
12 People's Party	0	0	0	0	—	—	—	—	—	—	—	—	—	—	—	—	—	—	—	—
13 Green Party	0	0	0	0	0	0	0	0	—	—	—	—	—	—	—	—	—	—	—	—
14 P. of Republic	—	—	—	—	0	0	0	0	—	—	—	—	—	—	—	—	—	—	—	—
15 Justice & Life	—	—	—	—	0	0	0	0	2.3	13.4	0	3.6	0	0	0	0	0	0	0	0
16 National Dem.	—	—	—	—	0	0	0	0	—	—	—	—	—	—	—	—	—	—	—	—
17 H. Dem. People	—	—	—	—	—	—	—	—	0	0	0	0	—	—	—	—	—	—	—	—
19 Centre Party	—	—	—	—	—	—	—	—	—	—	—	—	0	0	0	0	0	0	0	0
Others	0	0	4.0	1.8	0	0	0	0	0	0	0.6	0.3	0	0	0.6	0.3	0	0	0.6	0.3

12

LATVIA

In early medieval times the territory of Latvia was part of Livonia, ruled by a Germanic order of knights, and Riga was a Hanseatic city-state. Subsequently the land was under Swedish rule and in the early eighteenth century it became part of the empire of the Russian tsar. In 1920, following the First World War and fighting between Bolshevik and anti-Bolshevik forces, Latvia was recognized as an independent state. Minorities, principally Russian, Jewish, and German, comprised more than one-fifth of the population. The adoption of a constitution in 1922 was followed by four proportional representation elections in 1922, 1925, 1928, and 1931, in which all citizens age 21 or above could vote. In the 100-seat *Saeima* (parliament), a total of 39 parties won seats at least once. The socialists and the agrarian parties each won up to one-third of seats, minorities won one-sixth, and the remainder were divided between different centre parties and parties of the right (RIIA, 1938: 52). In each election at least 22 parties won seats. After parliament refused to pass a bill strengthening executive powers, in May 1934 Prime Minister Kärlis Ulmanis staged a coup; parliament was dissolved and parties were banned.

Following the Nazi–Soviet Pact of August 1939, Soviet troops entered Latvia, and a Soviet-style election in July 1940 was followed in August by Latvia's being annexed as part of the Soviet Union (Rauch, 1974). After being driven out by the German army in 1941, Soviet troops re-entered Latvia in 1944 and the country was governed as a republic of the Soviet Union, with a regional Communist Party and controlled single-party elections. Riga became the headquarters of the Baltic Military District of the Soviet Union.

The ethnic composition of the country was radically changed by the killing of Jews, massive deportations of Latvians, the flight of ethnic Germans and Latvians, and, after the Second World War, an influx of migrants from the USSR. The 1989 census reported that 52 per cent of the population was Latvian. While a majority of Latvians had become fluent in Russian, only one-fifth of those whose first language was Russian claimed fluency in Latvian (Misiunas and Taagepera, 1993).

In the wake of Mikhail Gorbachev's call for reforms in the Soviet Union, in 1988 Latvians began public demonstrations demanding independence, led by the Latvian National Independence Movement and the Latvian Popular Front, which attracted some Communist leaders. Competitive elections for 201 single-member seats in the Latvian Supreme Soviet took place on 18 March 1990. With all legal residents eligible to vote, the turnout was 81.3 per cent. To win a seat in the first round, a candidate had to receive 50 per cent of the valid votes cast and at least half the electors had to participate. In this way 170 seats were filled; to meet the turnout requirement, run-off elections were required for the remaining seats. The election was competitive but not along strict party lines, as many candidates listed more than one affiliation and single-member districts encouraged this. Pro-independence candidates won 131 seats; of these 111 were affiliated with the Latvian Popular Front and 55 had a secondary or primary Communist Party affiliation. Fifty-five elected members favoured remaining in the USSR and all but one belonged to the Communist Party of the Soviet Union. The remaining 15 seats went to uncommitted candidates (Taagepera, 1990: 309).

The newly elected Latvian assembly reclaimed independence in a declaration on 4 May 1990 and reinstated its 1922 constitution. In January 1991, clashes occurred in Riga between pro-independence forces and those loyal to Moscow, including the leadership of the Latvian Communist Party and Interfront, an anti-independence organization created in 1989. In anticipation of a USSR referendum, an advisory referendum was held in Latvia on 3 March 1991, asking whether voters approved a 'democratic and independent Republic of Latvia'. With a turnout of 87.6 per cent, 73.7 per cent voted in favour, 24.7 per cent against, and 1.6 per cent were invalid. This indicates that a substantial proportion of Russian residents favoured independence. At the same time as the hardline coup against Gorbachev collapsed in Moscow, on 21 August 1991, Latvia's Supreme Soviet declared full sovereignty. It was accepted by the Soviet Union on 6 September (Karklins, 1994; Plakans, 1997).

The constitution's electoral law authorized the parliament, the 100-member *Saeima,* to be elected by proportional representation for a term of three years; this was changed to four years in December 1997. There are five multi-member districts with 14 to 28 seats. Seats are allocated to the parties at district level according to the Sainte-Laguë formula, initially with a threshold of four per cent of the national vote, raised to five per cent before the 1995 election. Electors vote for a party list, and may express positive or negative preferences for individual candidates. Each list's candidates are awarded seats according to the number of their individual preferences minus their negative votes. The president is elected for a four-year term by an absolute majority of the *Saeima.*

Citizenship is a requirement of voting. It is conferred as of right on pre-1940 Latvian citizens and their descendants, a group that includes a small proportion of non-ethnic Latvian residents. All citizens age 18 and above are entitled to vote, subject to disqualifications for incapacity and imprisonment. A 1994 law provided for the potential naturalization of immigrants of at least ten years' residence or non-ethnic Latvians born in the country, subject to a test in the Latvian language and history and an oath of allegiance. In a referendum held in conjunction with the 1998 parliamentary election, 53 per cent endorsed liberalizing laws on citizenship, so that non-citizens' children born after 21 August 1991 could automatically receive citizenship if their parents requested it. As of 2007, 41 per cent of the population of the country were not ethnic Latvians; they divided into 42 per cent who were citizens and 58 per cent who were not. Of the country's total citizens, 73 per cent are Latvian and 27 per cent non-Latvian (Central Statistical Bureau, 2007).

In September 1991, the Latvian Supreme Soviet passed a decree banning the Latvian Communist Party, Interfront, and other organizations opposed to Latvian independence. As a result of these and related measures, those active in such groups after 13 January 1991 have been banned from participation in elections to the *Saeima* and municipal elections, and those without citizenship have faced restrictions on naturalization. In 1998, Tatyana Zhdanok (in Latvian, Ždanoka), a former Interfront leader, was barred from running for the *Saeima*, and the following year deprived of her seat in Riga city council. She sued Latvia in the European Court of Human Rights (ECHR). In June 2004, she was elected a member of the European Parliament and won her court case a few days later. Latvia appealed to the Grand Chamber of the ECHR on the grounds that Latvia's occupation and experience of totalitarian rule had not been properly taken into consideration. The Grand Chamber ruled in Latvia's favour in 2006 (Hoogers, 2007).

DATES OF ELECTIONS TO THE SAEIMA

5, 6 June 1993
30 September, 1 October 1995
3 October 1998
5 October 2002
7 October 2006

REFERENCES

Central Electoral Commission, 2007. "7. Saeimas vēlēšanas", "8. Saeimas vēlēšanas", and "9. Saeimas vēlēšanas", http://www.cvk.lv.

Central Statistical Bureau, 2007. 04 Population, http://data.csb.gov.lv/DATABASEEN/Iedzsoc/Annual%20statistical%20data/04.%20Population/04.%20Population.asp.

Davies, Philip John, and A. V. Ozolins, 2004. "The Parliamentary Election in Latvia, October 2002", *Electoral Studies* 23, 4, 821–45.

Hoogers, H. G., 2007. "European Court of Human Rights: The Boundaries of the Right to be Elected under Article 3 of the First Protocol to the European Convention on Human Rights. Judgment of 16 March 2006, Ždanoka v. Latvia, Application No. 58278/00", *European Constitutional Law Review* 3, 2, 307–23.

Karklins, Rasma, 1994. *Ethnopolitics and Transition to Democracy: The Collapse of the USSR and Latvia.* Washington, DC: Woodrow Wilson Center Press.

Misiunas, Romuald, and Rein Taagepera, 1993. *The Baltic States: Years of Dependence, 1940–1990.* London: C. Hurst, 2nd edition.

Plakans, Andrejs, 1997. "Democratization and Political Participation in Postcommunist Societies: The Case of Latvia". In K. Dawisha and B. Parrott, eds., *The Consolidation of Democracy in East-Central Europe.* Cambridge: Cambridge University Press, 245–89.

Pujāte, Inta, Librarian of the Chancellery of the Latvian Parliament, 1997. Letter, 18 March.

Rauch, G. von, 1974. *The Baltic States: The Years of Independence.* London: Hurst.

RIIA (Royal Institute of International Affairs), 1938. *The Baltic States.* London: Oxford University Press.

Taagepera, Rein, 1990. "The Baltic States", *Electoral Studies* 9, 4, 303–11.

Table 12.1 LATVIAN POLITICAL PARTIES

1 *Latvia's Way Alliance* (Savienība Latvijas Ceļš, LC). Established by Latvian Popular Front activists and Anatolijs Gorbunovs, head of state (1990–93). Party of Prime Minister Andris Berzins (2000–02). In 2006 part of a joint list with Latvia's First Party. Member of Liberal International. 1993–2002

2 *Latvian National Conservative Party* (Latvijas Nacionāli Konservatīvā Partija, LNNK). Founded in 1988 as Latvian National Independence Movement (Latvijas Nacionālas Neatkarības Kustība, LNNK). Changed name in June 1994. Contested 1995 election with Latvian Green Party. In 1997 merged with For Fatherland and Freedom. 1993–95

3 *National Harmony Party* (Tautas Saskaņas Partija, TSP). Supports rights of Russians. In 1993 fought as *Harmony for Latvia–Rebirth of the Economy* (Saskana Latvijai– Ekonomiska Ardzimsana, SL–EA). Changed name after splits in 1994. In 1998 Equality and Latvian Socialist Party fought under TSP label. In 2002, TSP contested as part of PCTVL and in 2006 as part of Harmony Centre. 1993–98

4 *Equality/Latvian Socialist Party* (Līdztiesība/Latvijas Sociālistiskā Partija, LSP).

Equality was founded in 1993 to promote interests of ethnic Russians. One of its leaders, Alfrēds Rubiks, was elected in 1993 but not seated and received an 8-year prison sentence for supporting the 1991 Moscow coup. In 1995 Equality's candidates fought under the LSP label with Rubiks headings its list. The group fought on the TSP list in 1998 and the PCTVL list in 2002 and 2006. LSP joined Harmony Centre before the 2006 election. 1993–95

5 *Latvian Farmers' Union* (Latvijas Zemnieku Savenība, LZS). Based on pre-war party of Kārlis Ulmanis, founded 1917. In 1995 part of United List. 1993–98

6 *For Fatherland and Freedom* (Apvienība Tēzvemei un Brīvībai, TB). Nationalist-populists. Merged with Latvian National Conservative Party in 1997 to form TB–LNNK. 1993–95

7 *Latvian Christian Democratic Union* (Latvijas Kristīgo Demokrātu Savienība, LKDS). Catholic party. Contested in 1995 as part of United List, and in 1998 as part of alliance with Labour Party and Greens. 1993

8 *Democratic Party–Saimnieks* (Demokrātiskā Partija Saimnieks, DPS). Revival of pre-war Democratic Centre Party (Demokrātiskā Centra Partija, DCP). In 1994 merged with Saimnieks (meaning 'in charge') adopting DPS name. 1993–98

9 *Latvian Popular Front* (Latvijas Tautas Fronte, LTF). Remnant of nationalist movement founded in 1988. 1993–95

10 *Latvian Green Party* (Latvijas Zaļā Partija, LZP). Founded 1990. Fought 1995 election with LNNK, and in 1998 part of DP–KDS–LZPA alliance. 1993

11 *Russian Citizens of Latvia* (Latvijas Krievu Pilşonu Partija, LKPP). In 1993 known as Russian National Democratic List (Krievu Nacionālais Deokrātiskais Saraksts, KNDS). 1993–95

12 *Popular Movement for Latvia–Siegerist Party* (Tatas Kustība Latvijai–Zigerista Partija, TKL–ZP). Led by German-born Joachim Siegerist, expelled from LNNK in 1994 after being convicted in Germany for inciting racial hatred. 1995–98

13 *Latvian Unity Party* (Latvijas Vienības Partija, LVP). Offshoot of the orthodox wing of Latvian Communist Party. Led by Albert Kauls. 1995–98

14 *United List* (Apvienotais Sarakst). Combines Latvian Farmers' Union, Latvian Christian Democratic Union, and Latgale Democratic Party (LDP). 1995

15 *Latvian National Conservative Party/Latvian Green Party* (Latvijas Nacionāli Konservatīvā Partija/Latvijas Zaļā Partija, LNNK/LZP). Alliance of eponymous parties. 1995

16 *Latvian Social Democratic Workers' Party* (Latvijas Sociāldemokrātiska Stradnieku Partija, LSDSP). In 1995 the LSDSP, initially revived in 1989 as successor of a party founded in 1904, and the Latvian Democratic Labour Party

(Latvijas Demokrātiskā Darba Partija, LDDP), a 1990 splinter of the Latvian Communist Party, fought as an alliance, *Labour and Justice Coalition* (Koalīija Darbs un Taisnī, KDT), and in 1998 as the *Latvian Social Democratic Alliance* (Latvijas Sociāldemokrātu Apvienība, LSDA). In 1999 they merged under the LSDSP label. 1995–

17 *Political Union of Economists* (Tautsaimnieku Politiskā Apvienība, TPA). Founded 1994 as splinter from National Harmony Party. 1995

18 *Union of Latvian Farmers* (Latviešu Zemnieku Savienība). Nationalist splinter of Latvian Farmers' Union/LZS. 1995

19 *Political Association of the Underprivileged and Latvian Independence Party* (Maznodrošināto Politiskā Apvienība/Latviešu Neatkarības Partija, MPA/LNP). Both founded to fight 1995 election. 1995

20 *People's Party* (Tautas Partija, TP). Pro-business party established in May 1998 by Andris Šķēle, prime minister (1995–97, 1999–2000).Endorses ethnic Latvian population growth. Led by Prime Minister Aigars Kalvītis (2004–). 1998–

21 *For Fatherland and Freedom/LNNK* (Tēzvemei un Brīvībai/LNNK, TB/LNNK). Merger of nationalist parties. Party of Prime Minister Guntar Krasts (1997–98). 1998–

22 *New Party* (Jaunā Partija, JP). Party led by former Latvian Popular Front politician and composer Raimonds Pauls. 1998

23 *Labour, Christian Democrats, and Greens* (Darba Partijas, Kristīgi Demokrātiskās Savienības, Latvijas Zaīas Partijas Apvienība, DP–KDS–LZPA). Alliance of Latvian Christian Democratic Union, Latvian Green Party, and Labour Party, founded by MPs who broke with Saimnieks. 1998

24 *New Era* (Jaunas Laiks, JL). Founded by Einars Repše, former governor of Bank of Latvia (1991-2001) and prime minister (2002–04), to campaign against corruption. Co-led by Arturs Karins, a US citizen. 2002–

25 *For Human Rights in a United Latvia* (Par Cilvēka Tiesībām Vienotā Latvijā, PCTVL). In 1998 TSP, Equality, and LSP sought to form an alliance, PCTVL, but failed to register in time, and so fought under the TSP label. PCTVL did register as a party for the 2002 election. In 2003 TSP broke away, forming Harmony Centre, later joined by LSP. PCTVL was then led by MEP Tatyana Zhdanok, banned from standing for election in 1998 and 2002 because active in the Latvian Communist Party after 13 January 1991. 2002–

26 *Latvia's First Party* (Latvijas Pirmaā Partija, LPP). Christian Democratic group that absorbed part of membership of New Party and Latvian Christian Democratic Union. Fought 2006 on joint list with Latvia's Way. 2002

27 *Green and Farmers' Union* (Zaļo un Zemnieku Savienība, ZZS). Alliance formed by Green Party and Latvian Farmers' Union. One of its leaders, Indulis Emsis, was prime minister (March–December 2004). 2002–

28 *Life of Latgale* (Latgales Gaisma). Regional party. 2002–

29 *Social Democratic Union–SDS* (Sociāldemokrātu Savienība–SDS). Splinter of Latvian Social Democratic Workers' Party. 2002–

30 *Motherland (Dzimtene).* Founded as Social Democratic Welfare Party (Sociāldemokrātiskā Labklājības Partija, SDLP). In 2004 allied with For Freedom, Justice and Social Rights; in Russian, acronym is 'For the USSR'. 2002–

31 *Harmony Centre* (Saskaņas Centrs). Formed by 2005 merger of TSP and Latvian Socialist Party after withdrawal from PCTVL with New Centre. Promotes Russian minority. Led by journalist Nil Ushakov. 2006–

32 *Latvia's First Party and Latvia's Way* (Latvijas Pirmaā Partija–Latvijas Ceļš, LPP–LC). Joint list of two eponymous parties. 2006–

33 *All for Latvia* (Visu Latvijai). Conservative party for youth. 2006–

34 *New Democrats* (Jaunie Demokrāti). A splinter party of New Era. Formed in 2004. 2006–

Table 12.2a LATVIA: Votes for the *Saeima*

	1993	1995	1998	2002	2006
Electorate	1,243,956	1,328,779	1,341,942	1,395,287	1,448,039
Valid Votes	1,118,316	951,007	955,581	990,249	901,665
Invalid Votes	15,888	14,332	9,086	7,505	5,795
Total Votes	1,134,204	965,339	964,667	997,754	907,460
1 Latvia's Way	362,473	139,929	173,420	48,430	—
32 Latvian First Party and Latvia's Way	—	—	—	—	77,869
26 Latvian First Party	—	—	—	94,752	—
2 LNNK–National Conservative Party	149,347	—	—	—	—
15 LNNK/Latvian Greens	—	60,352	—	—	—
10 Latvian Greens	13,362	—	—	—	—
6 For Fatherland and Freedom	59,855	114,050	—	—	—
21 For Fatherland and Freedom/LNNK	—	—	140,773	53,396	62,989
3 National Harmony Party	134,289	53,041	135,700	—	—
25 For Human Rights in United Latvia	—	—	—	189,088	54,684
4 Equality/LSP	64,444	53,325	—	—	—
31 Harmony Centre	—	—	—	—	130,887
5 Latvian Farmers' Union	119,116	—[1]	23,732	—	—
27 Green and Farmers' Union	—	—	—	93,759	151,595
7 Latvian Christian Democratic Union	56,057	—	—	—	—
14 United List	—	60,498	—	—	—
23 Labour, Christian Democrats & Greens	—	—	22,018	—	—
8 Democratic Party–Saimnieks	53,303	144,758	15,410	—	—
9 Latvian Popular Front	29,396	11,090	—	—	—
11 Russian Citizens of Latvia	13,006	11,924	—	—	—

12 Popular Movement–Siegerists	—	142,324	16,647	—	—
13 Latvian Unity Party	—	68,305	4,445	—	—
16 Latvian Social Democratic Workers	—	43,599	123,056	39,837	31,728
17 Political Union of Economists	—	14,209	—	—	—
18 Union of Latvian Farmers	—	13,009	—	—	—
19 Underprivileged & Independence	—	9,468	—	—	—
20 People's Party	—	—	203,585	165,246	177,481
22 New Party	—	—	70,214	—	—
24 New Era	—	—	—	237,452	148,602
28 Life of Latgale	—	—	—	15,948	—
29 Social Democratic Union–SDS	—	—	—	15,162	—
30 Motherland	—	—	—	13,234	18,860
33 All for Latvia	—	—	—	—	13,469
34 New Democrats	—	—	—	—	11,505
Others[2]	63,668	11,126	26,581	23,945	21,996

Sources: Pujāte, 1997; Central Electoral Commission, 2007.

[1] Part of United List in 1995.

[2] Includes 1993: 12 minor parties winning less than 1.0 per cent of the vote; 1995: 4 parties; 1998: 10 parties; 2002: 9 parties; 2007: 8 parties.

Table 12.2b LATVIA: Percentage of Votes for the *Saeima*

	1993	1995	1998	2002	2006
Valid Votes	89.9	71.6	71.2	71.0	62.3
Invalid Votes	1.3	1.1	0.7	0.5	0.4
Total Votes	91.2	72.7	71.9	71.5	62.7
1 Latvia's Way	32.4	14.7	18.1	4.9	—
32 Latvian First Party and Latvia's Way	—	—	—	—	8.6
26 Latvian First Party	—	—	—	9.6	—
2 LNNK–National Conservative Party	13.4	—	—	—	—
15 LNNK/Latvian Greens	—	6.3	—	—	—
10 Latvian Greens	1.2	—	—	—	—
6 For Fatherland and Freedom	5.4	12.0	—	—	—
21 For Fatherland and Freedom/LNNK	—	—	14.7	5.4	7.0
3 National Harmony Party	12.0	5.6	14.2	—	—
25 For Human Rights in United Latvia	—	—	—	19.1	6.1
4 Equality/LSP	5.8	5.6	—	—	—
31 Harmony Centre	—	—	—	—	14.5
5 Latvian Farmers' Union	10.7	—	2.5	—	—
27 Green and Farmers' Union	—	—	—	9.5	16.8
7 Latvian Christian Democratic Union	5.0	—	—	—	—
14 United List	—	6.4	—	—	—
23 Labour, Christian Democrats & Greens	—	—	2.3	—	—
8 Democratic Party–Saimnieks	4.8	15.2	1.6	—	—
9 Latvian Popular Front	2.6	1.2	—	—	—
11 Russian Citizens of Latvia	1.2	1.3	—	—	—
12 Popular Movement–Siegerists	—	15.0	1.7	—	—

3 Latvian Unity Party	—	7.2	0.5	—	—
16 Latvian Social Democratic Workers	—	4.6	12.9	4	3.5
17 Political Union of Economists	—	1.5	—	—	—
18 Union of Latvian Farmers	—	1.4	—	—	—
19 Underprivileged & Independence	—	1.0	—	—	—
20 People's Party	—	—	21.3	16.7	19.7
22 New Party	—	—	7.3	—	—
24 New Era	—	—	—	24.0	16.5
28 Life of Latgale	—	—	—	1.6	—
29 Social Democratic Union–SDS	—	—	—	1.5	—
30 Motherland	—	—	—	1.3	2.1
33 All for Latvia	—	—	—	—	1.5
34 New Democrats	—	—	—	—	1.3
Others	5.7	1.2	2.8	2.4	2.4

Table 12.2c LATVIA: Number of Seats in the *Saeima*

	1993	1995	1998	2002	2006
1 Latvia's Way	36	17	21	0	—
32 Latvian First Party and Latvia's Way	—	—	—	—	10
26 Latvian First Party	—	—	—	10	—
2 LNNK–National Conservative Party	15	—	—	—	—
15 LNNK/Latvian Greens	—	8	—	—	—
10 Latvian Greens	0	—	—	—	—
6 For Fatherland and Freedom	6	14	—	—	—
21 For Fatherland and Freedom/LNNK	—	—	17	7	8
3 National Harmony Party	13	6	16	—	—
25 For Human Rights in United Latvia	—	—	—	25[1]	6
4 Equality/LSP	7	5	—	—	—
31 Harmony Centre	—	—	—	—	17
5 Latvian Farmers' Union	12	—	0	—	—
27 Green and Farmers' Union	—	—	—	12	18
7 Latvian Christian Democratic Union	6	—	—	—	—
14 United List	—	8	—	—	—
23 Labour, Christian Democrats & Greens	—	—	0	—	—
8 Democratic Party–Saimnieks	5	18	0	—	—
9 Latvian Popular Front	0	0	—	—	—
11 Russian Citizens of Latvia	0	0	—	—	—
12 Popular Movement–Siegerists	—	16	0	—	—
13 Latvian Unity Party	—	8	0	—	—
16 Latvian Social Democratic Workers	—	0	14	0	0
17 Political Union of Economists	—	0	—	—	—
18 Union of Latvian Farmers	—	0	—	—	—

19 Underprivileged & Independence	—	0	—	—	—
20 People's Party	—	—	24	20	23
22 New Party	—	—	8	—	—
24 New Era	—	—	—	26	18
28 Life of Latgale	—	—	—	0	—
29 Social Democratic Union–SDS	—	—	—	0	—
30 Motherland	—	—	—	0	0
33 All for Latvia	—	—	—	—	0
34 New Democrats	—	—	—	—	0
Others	0	0	0	0	0
Total	100	100	100	100	100

Sources: Pujāte, 1997; Central Electoral Commission, 2007.

[1] By the end of 2003, PCTVL's 25 seats were divided: Equality, 6; LSP, 5; National Harmony, 14.

Table 12.2d LATVIA: Percentage of Seats in the *Saeima*

	1993	1995	1998	2002	2006
1 Latvia's Way	36.0	17.0	21.0	0	—
32 Latvian First Party and Latvia's Way	—	—	—	—	10.0
26 Latvian First Party	—	—	—	10.0	—
2 LNNK–National Conservative Party	15.0	—	—	—	—
15 LNNK/Latvian Greens	—	8.0	—	—	—
10 Latvian Greens	0	—	—	—	—
6 For Fatherland and Freedom	6.0	14.0	—	—	—
21 For Fatherland and Freedom/LNNK	—	—	17.0	7.0	8.0
3 National Harmony Party	13.0	6.0	16.0	—	—
25 For Human Rights in United Latvia	—	—	—	25.0	6.0
4 Equality/LSP	7.0	5.0	—	—	—
31 Harmony Centre	—	—	—	—	17.0
5 Latvian Farmers' Union	12.0	—	0	—	—
27 Green and Farmers' Union	—	—	—	12.0	18.0
7 Latvian Christian Democratic Union	6.0	—	—	—	—
14 United List	—	8.0	—	—	—
23 Labour, Christian Democrats & Greens	—	—	0	—	—
8 Democratic Party–Saimnieks	5.0	18.0	0	—	—
9 Latvian Popular Front	0	0	—	—	—
11 Russian Citizens of Latvia	0	0	—	—	—
12 Popular Movement–Siegerists	—	16.0	0	—	—
13 Latvian Unity Party	—	8.0	0	—	—
16 Latvian Social Democratic Workers	—	0	14.0	0	0
17 Political Union of Economists	—	0	—	—	—
18 Union of Latvian Farmers	—	0	—	—	—

19 Underprivileged & Independence	—	0	—	—	—
20 People's Party	—	—	24.0	20.0	23.0
22 New Party	—	—	8.0	—	—
24 New Era	—	—	—	26.0	18.0
28 Life of Latgale	—	—	—	0	—
29 Social Democratic Union–SDS	—	—	—	0	—
30 Motherland	—	—	—	0	0
33 All for Latvia	—	—	—	—	0
34 New Democrats	—	—	—	—	0
Others	0	0	0	0	0

13

LITHUANIA

The thirteenth-century Kingdom of Lithuania was united dynastically with Poland in 1386. Following the partition of Poland in 1795, most of today's territory became part of the Russian Empire. After the First World War Lithuania declared its independence; however, Vilnius was incorporated into the Polish state. In ethnic terms, the inter-war population was 84 per cent Lithuanian; minorities included Jews, Poles, Russians, and Germans. Four proportional representation elections with universal suffrage were held between 1920 and 1926 for the Constitutional Assembly and the unicameral *Seimas* (parliament). Twelve different parties or coalitions held seats, including minorities. Government was in the hands of the clerical and nationalist Christian Democratic Party and its offshoots, the Peasant Union and the Federation of Labour. In December 1926 a military coup established an authoritarian regime under Antanas Smetona.

Under the Nazi–Soviet Pact of August 1939, Soviet troops occupied Lithuania in October. Following unfree elections in July 1940, Lithuania was annexed as a Soviet republic. When Germany invaded the USSR the following year, it conquered Lithuania. Soviet forces returned in early autumn 1944. Civil administration was given to a republic-level committee of the Communist Party of the Soviet Union and Soviet-style elections were held (Misiunas and Taagepera, 1993). Lithuanian guerrilla forces resisted Soviet annexation until 1953. The Holocaust during the Nazi occupation and limited Russian immigration made Lithuania among the most ethnically homogeneous republics of the Soviet Union.

Mikhail Gorbachev's glasnost policy enabled Lithuanians to make explicit protests and form political associations whilst the Latvian Republic was part of the Soviet Union. In June 1988 Sajudis (Lithuanian Reform Movement) was organized to demand fundamental political reform. The Lithuanian branch of the All-Union Communist Party then split; a majority, under Algirdas Brazauskas, advocated pro-independence and democratic views.

Competitive elections to the Lithuanian Supreme Soviet took place on 24 February 1990. Voters chose 141 deputies in single-member districts. An absolute majority was required. In the absence of a majority in the first round, a second-round vote was required between the two leading candidates. Sajudis won 92 seats, including: 17 nationally oriented Communists; 9 Social Democrats; 4 Green Party; and 2 Christian Democratic Party. The Independent Lithuanian Communist Party won 32 seats, the pro-Soviet Lithuanian Communists 7, and 10 went to independents (Taagepera, 1990). On 11 March 1990 the new assembly proclaimed independence, but this was not recognized by the Soviet Union. In January 1991 Soviet forces sought to occupy public buildings in Vilnius; 14 Lithuanians died. In a referendum on 9 February 1991, 90.5 per cent of voters endorsed independence; turnout was 84.7 per cent. Moscow recognized independence on 6 September 1991 (Senn, 1995).

Citizenship is granted to legal residents without a language test. The election law of 4 August 1992 gives all citizens age 18 or over the right to vote, subject to minor legal incapacities. Lithuanians constituted 83.4 per cent of the population in 2001; the remainder were 6.7 per cent Polish, 6.3 per cent Russians, and 3.6 per cent others. Lithuanian citizens in the diaspora are eligible to vote, but in the 1993 presidential election constituted only 0.3 per cent of the electorate (Krickus, 1997: 305).

A year was required to prepare a new constitution. Under Sajudis leader Vytautas Landsbergis, the government held a referendum on 23 May 1992 proposing a strong French-style presidency. Under Lithuanian law a binding referendum required endorsement by an absolute majority of the electorate. Although the proposal was endorsed by 69.3 per cent of those who voted, given a turnout of 59.2 per cent, this was only 41.0 of the electorate. The proposal failed. On 25 October 1992, a new constitution was put to a referendum and was endorsed by 75.4 per cent of voters, 56.8 percent of the electorate on a turnout of 75.3 per cent. Under the constitution, the president is directly elected for a five-year term. If no candidate secures an absolute majority in the first round, there is a run-off between the two leading candidates.

The constitution established a single-chamber parliament, the *Seimas*, with 141 members elected for a four-year term. A referendum on 20 October 1996 proposed reducing its size to 111 seats. While endorsed by 65.0 per cent of those voting, because turnout was 52.1 per cent, the proposal failed to get the necessary endorsement of half the electorate. Of the *Seimas* members, 70 are elected by nationwide proportional representation and 71 in single-member districts. The PR ballot offers closed party lists, and seats are allocated by the Hare method to all parties with more than five per cent of the national vote for a single party or seven per cent for a coalition. There is a turnout requirement of 25 per cent for the PR vote to be valid. An absolute majority was initially required to win a single-member district in the first round, with a second-round run-off if needed between the two leading candidates. Since the 2000 election a plurality is sufficient to win a seat. In single-member districts, the turnout requirement is 40 per cent. In the 1996 election, after two rounds of voting, two seats remained vacant due to low turnout, and were filled in follow-up ballots. Vote totals in Tables 13.3a and 13.3b are for the list ballot and for the first round of voting in single-member districts. Seat totals in Tables 13.3c and 13.3d include the results of follow-up ballots in those single-member districts where such votes were held.

In April 2004, President Rolandas Paksas was impeached on corruption charges by a vote of the *Seimas* and a ruling of the Constitutional Court. This triggered an early presidential election in June 2004, in which Paksas was barred from running.

DATES OF ELECTIONS

President	*Seimas* (parliament)
14 February 1993	25 October, 15 November 1992
21 December 1997, 4 January 1998	20 October, 10 November 1996
22 December 2002, 5 January 2003	8 October 2000
13, 27 June 2004	10 October 2004
	12, 26 October 2008

REFERENCES

Central Electoral Committee, 2008. "Lietuvos Respublikos vyriausioji rinkimų komisija", http://www.vrk.lt.

Krickus, Richard J., 1997. "Democratization in Lithuania". In K. Dawisha and B. Parrott, eds., *The Consolidation of Democracy in East-Central Europe*. Cambridge: Cambridge University Press, 290–333.

Krupavičius, Algis, ed., 2001. *Lithuania's Seimas Elections 1996: The Third Turnover*. Berlin: Sigma.

Lithuanian Department of Statistics, 1997. *Statistical Yearbook of Lithuania, 1997*. Vilnius: Methodical Publishing Centre.

Misiunas, Romuald, and Rein Taagepera, 1993. *The Baltic States: Years of Dependence 1940–1990*. London: C. Hurst, 2nd edition.

Senn, Alfred Eric, 1995. *Gorbachev's Failure in Lithuania*. New York: St Martin's.

Taagepera, Rein, 1990. "The Baltic States", *Electoral Studies* 9, 4, 303–11.

Table 13.1 LITHUANIAN POLITICAL PARTIES

1 *Lithuanian Democratic Labour Party* (Lietuvos Demokratinė Darbo Partija, LDDP). Successor to Independent Lithuanian Communist Party which broke away from CPSU in 1989, and subsequently endorsed independence. Party of Algirdas

Brazauskas, president (1993–98) and prime minister (2001–06). Contested 2000 election as part of A. Brazauskas Social Democratic Coalition. In January 2001 merged into Lithuanian Social Democratic Party. 1992–96

2 *Sajudis/Lithuanian Restructuring Movement* (Lietuvos Persitvarkymo Sąjūdis, LPS). Nationalist movement founded in 1988 to promote Lithuanian independence. Party of Vytautas Landsbergis, chair of Lithuanian government (1990–92); he later established Homeland Union–Lithuanian Conservatives. 1992

3 *Lithuanian Christian Democratic Party* (Lietuvos Krikščionių Demokratų Partija, LKDP). Catholic conservative party founded in 1989 in tradition of party formed in 1904. Contested in 1992 with Lithuanian Democratic Party and Union of Political Prisoners and Deportees. In 2001 merged with Christian Democratic Union/KDS to form Lithuanian Christian Democrats/LKD. Member of Christian Democrat International. 1992–2000

4 *Lithuanian Social Democratic Party* (Lietuvos Socialdemokratų Partija, LSDP). Revived in 1989 in tradition of party formed in 1896. Contested in 2000 as part of A. Brazauskas Social Democratic Coalition. Member of Socialist International. In 2001 merged with LDDP to form LSdP. 1992–96

5 *Coalition for a United Lithuania* (Už Vieningą Lietuvą, UVL). Alliance of Christian Democratic Union and Young Lithuanians. 1992

6 *Lithuanian Centre Union* (Lietuvos Centro Sąjunga, LCS). Contested in 1992 as the Lithuanian Centre Movement. In 2003, merged into Liberal and Centre Union/ LbCS. 1992–2000

7 *Electoral Action for Lithuania's Poles* (Lietuvos Lenkų Rinkimų Akcija, LLRA). Seeks to represent Polish minority. 1992–

8 *Lithuanian Nationalist Union* (Lietuvių Tautinikų Sąjunga, LTS). A revival in 1989 of a party governing 1926 to 1940. Contested 1992 election with smaller parties including Lithuanian Independence Party and in 1996 Lithuanian Democratic Party. In 2000 contested as part of People's Front and separately in 2004. In March 2008 merged into Homeland Union–Lithuanian Conservatives. 1992–2004

9 *Lithuanian Liberal Union* (Lietuvos Liberalų Sąjunga, LLS). Established in 1990. From 1999 to 2001, party of Rolandas Paksas, prime minister (1999, 2000–01) and president (2003–04). In December 2001 Paksas left to form Liberal Democratic Party/LbDP. LLS joined LCS and part of LKDP to form Liberal and Centre Union in 2003. 1992–2000

10 *Lithuanian Liberty Union* (Lietuvos Laisvės Sąjunga, LLaS). Populist, anti-Semitic party led by 2002 presidential candidate Vytautas Sustauskas. 1992–2004

11 *Lithuanian Freedom League* (Lietuvos Laisvės Lyga, LLL). Nationalist

movement formed in 1981and legalized in 1988. Led by Antanas Terleckas. In 2000 part of the People's Front and in 2001 of Lithuanian Rightist Union. 1992–96

12 *National Progress Movement* (Tautos Pažangos Judejimas, TPJ). Splinter of Sajudis. 1992

13 *Moderates' Movement* (Nuosaikiųjų Judejimas, NJ). 1992

14 *Lithuanian Chernobyl Movement* (Lietuvos Judėjimas Černobylis, LJC). Campaigned for victims of 1986 nuclear accident. 1992

15 *Homeland Union–Lithuanian Conservatives* (Tėvynės Sąjunga–Lietuvos Konservatoriai, TS–LK). Founded in 1993 by Vytautas Landsbergis, previously leader of Sajudis. Members included former prime ministers Gediminas Vagnorius (1996–99), Rolandas Paksas (1999, 2000–01) and Andrius Kubilius (1999–2000, 2008–). Before the 2000 election Vagnorius joined the Moderate Conservative Union and Paksas the Lithuanian Liberal Union/LLS. TS–LK absorbed LPKTS before the 2004 election. In spring 2008 TS–LK merged with LKD and LTS to form TS–LKD. 1996–2004

16 *'Young Lithuanians', New Nationalists Union* ('Jaunosios Lietuvos' ir Naujųjų Tautininku Sąjunga, JL–NTS). Historical party re-established in 1988. In 1992 part of UVL. Part of Christian Conservative Social Union in 2004. 1996–

17 *Lithuanian Women's Party* (Lietuvos Moterų Partija, LMP). Launched in 1995 by Kazimiera Prunskienė, prime minister (1990–91). Renamed New Democracy Party (Naujosios Demokratijos Partija, NDP) after 1996 election. In 2000 part of A. Brazauskas Social Democratic Coalition. In 2001 merged with Lithuanian Peasants' Party/LVP to form Union of Peasants' and New Democracy Parties/VNDPS.1996

18 *Christian Democratic Union* (Krikščionių Demokratų Sąjunga, KDS). Led by Kazys Bobelis, presidential candidate in 1997. In 1992 part of UVL. In 2001 merged into Lithuanian Christian Democrats. 1996–2000

19 *Alliance of Lithuania's Ethnic Minorities* (Lietuvos Tautinių Mažumų Aljansas, LTMA). Led by R. Litvinovič. 1996

20 *Lithuanian Peasants' Party* (Lietuvos Valstiečių Partija, LVP). Nominally based on party founded in 1905. Against joining EU and World Trade Organization. In 2001 merged with New Democracy Party to form VNPDS. 1996–2000

21 *Lithuanian Russian Union* (Lietuvos Rusu Sąjunga, LRS). Contested 2000 as part of A. Brazauaskas Social Democratic Coalition. Fielded only single-member district candidates in 2004. 1996–

22 *Union of Political Prisoners and Deportees* (Lietuvos Politiniu Kaliniu ir Tremtinių Sąjunga, LPKTS). Presented only single-member district candidates in 2000. Merged into TS–LK before 2004 election. 1996–2000

23 *Lithuanian Economy Party* (Lietuvos Ukio Partija, LUP). Favours welfare state policies. 1996

24 *A. Brazauskas Social Democratic Coalition* (A. Brazausko Social-Demokratinė Koalicija, AB–SDK). Alliance of LDDP, LSDP, NDP, and LRS. Led by former president (1993–98) and prime minister (2001–06) Brazauskas. 2000

25 *New Union–Social Liberals* (Naujoji Sąjunga-Socialliberalai, NS–SL). Led by Arturas Paulauskas, acting president (April–July 2004). In 2004, joined LSdP in Working for Lithuania alliance, but contested 2008 independently. 2000–

26 *Moderate Conservative Union* (Nuosaikiųjų Konservatorių Sąjunga, NKS). A splinter of Homeland Union led by former prime minister (1991–92, 1996–99) Gediminas Vagnorius. In 2004 contested as Christian Conservative Social Union (Krikščionių Konservatoriu Socialinė Sąjunga, KKSS). 2000–04

27 *Lithuanian People's Union for a Fair Lithuania* (Lietuvos Liaudies Sąjunga 'Už Teisinga Lietuva', LLS–UTL). Formed in 2000 by Julius Veselka, presidential candidate in 2000. Before 2004 election joined For Order and Justice alliance. Contested single-member districts only in 2008. 2000–

28 *Labour Party* (Darbo Partija, DP). Populist party formed in 2003 by ethnic Russian businessman Viktor Uspaskich, who fled Lithuania in 2006 amidst corruption allegations, but returned to lead party in September 2008. 2004–

29 *Liberal and Centre Union* (Liberalųir Centro Sąjunga, LbCS). A 2003 merger of LLS, LCS, and Modern Christian Democratic Union splinter of LKDP.2004–

30 *Union of Peasants' and New Democracy Parties* (Valstiečių ir Naujosios Demokratijos Partijų Sąjunga, VNDPS). Formed in 2001 by merger of LVP and NDP. Led by Kazimiera Prunskienė, former prime minister (1990–91) and presidential candidate (2002, 2004). In 2005 adopted name of historical party Lithuanian Peasants' People's Union (Lietuvos Valstiečių Liaudininkų Sąjunga, LVLS). 2004–

31 *Coalition of Algirdas Brazauskas and Arturas Paulauskas 'Working for Lithuania'* (A.Brazausko ir A.Paulausko Koalicija 'Už Darba Lietuvai', BPK–UDL). Joint list formed for 2004 election by Lithuanian Social Democratic Party/LSdP and NS–SL. Latter left alliance in 2006. 2004

32 *Coalition of Rolandas Paksas for Order and Justice* (Rolando Pakso Koalicija Už Tvarka ir Teisinguma, PK–UTT). Joint electoral list of Liberal Democratic Party/LbDP and LLS–UTL. Led by former president impeached in 2004.2004–

33 *Lithuanian Christian Democrats* (Lietuvos Krikšcionys Demokratai, LKD). Formed 2001 by merger of LKDP and KDS. In May 2008 merged into Homeland Union–Lithuanian Christian Democrats. 2004

34 *Homeland Union–Lithuanian Christian Democrats (conservatives, political prisoners and deportees, nationalists)* (Tėvynės Sąjunga – Lietuvos Krikščionys Demokratai (konservatoriai, politiniai kaliniai ir tremtiniai, tautininkai), TS–LKD). Spring 2008 merger of TS–LK with LKD and LTS. Led by Andrius Kubilius, prime minister (1999–2000; 2008–). 2008–

35 *Nation's Resurrection Party* (Tautos Prisikėlimo Partija, TPP). Populist party formed by TVand pop-music personalities. Led by Arūnas Valinskas, speaker of the *Seimas* after the 2008 election. 2008–

36 *Lithuanian Social Democratic Party* (Lietuvos Socialdemokratu Partija, LSdP) Formed in 2001 by merger of LDDP and LSDP, keeping latter's name. Here abbreviated as LSdP here to distinguish it from LSDP before merger. In 2004 contested as part of Working for Lithuania Coalition (BPK–UDL). Party of Gediminas Kirkilas, prime minister (2006–08). 2008–

37 *Liberal Movement of the Republic of Lithuania* (Lietuvos Respublikos Liberalų Sąjunga, LRLS). 2006 splinter of LbCS. 2008–

38 *'Frontas' Party* ('Fronto' Partija, FP). 2008 splinter of LSdP. 2008–

39 *Party of Civic Democracy* (Pilietinės Demokratijos Partija, PDP). 2006 splinter of Labour Party (DP). 2008–

40 *Labourist Party* (Leiboristų Partija, LP). A 2008 satellite of the Labour Party (DP). 2008–

Table 13.2a PRESIDENTIAL VOTE: 14 February 1993

		%
Electorate	2,586,015	
Valid Votes	1,984,997	76.8
Invalid Votes	34,016	1.3
Total Votes	2,019,013	78.1
Algirdas Brazauskas, LDDP	1,212,075	61.1
Stasys Lozoraitis, Sajudis	772,922	38.9

Source: Lithuanian Department of Statistics, 1997.

Table 13.2b PRESIDENTIAL VOTE: 21 December 1997, 4 January 1998

	1st Round	%	2nd Round	%
Electorate	2,624,312		2,630,681	
Valid Votes	1,852,468	70.6	1,921,806	73.1
Invalid Votes	22,680	0.9	15,980	0.6
Total Votes	1,875,148	71.5	1,937,786	73.7
Valdas Adamkus, Independent	516,798	27.9	968,031	50.4
Arturas Paulauskas, Independent	838,819	45.3	953,775	49.6
Vytautas Landsbergis, TS–LK	294,881	15.9	—	—
Vytenis Andriukaitis, LSDP	105,916	5.7	—	—
Kazys Bobelis, LKDU	73,287	4.0	—	—
Rolandas Pavilionis	16,070	0.9	—	—
Rimantas Smetona	6,697	0.4	—	—

Source: Central Electoral Commission, 2008.

Table 13.2c PRESIDENTIAL VOTE: 22 December 2002, 5 January 2003

	1st Round	%	2nd Round	%
Electorate	2,719,608		2,727,805	
Valid Votes	1,447,117	53.2	1,421,639	52.1
Invalid Votes	19,419	0.7	14,683	0.5
Total Votes	1,466,536	53.9	1,436,322	52.6
Valdas Adamkus	514,154	35.5	643,870	45.3
Rolandas Paksas, LbDP[1]	284,559	19.7	777,769	54.7
Arturas Palauskas, NS–SL	120,238	8.3	—	—
Vytautas Serenas	112,215	7.8	—	—
Vytenis Andriukaitis, LSdP	105,584	7.3	—	—
Kazimira Prunskienė, VNDPS	72,925	5.0	—	—
Juozas Petraitis	54,139	3.7	—	—
Eugenijas Gentvilas, LLS	44,562	3.1	—	—
Julius Veselka	32,293	2.2	—	—
Algimantas Matulevicius	32,137	2.2	—	—
Kazys Bobelis	27,613	1.9	—	—
Vytautas Matulevicius	26,888	1.9	—	—
Kestutis Glaveckas	7,554	0.5	—	—
Vytautas Sustauskas, LLaS	5,372	0.4	—	—
Vytautas Bernatonis	3,546	0.2	—	—
Algirdas Pilvelis	2,074	0.1	—	—
Rimantas Dagys	1,264	0.1	—	—

Source: Central Electoral Commission, 2008.

[1] *Liberal Democratic Party* (Liberalų Demokratų Partija, LbDP).

Table 13.2d PRESIDENTIAL VOTE: 3, 27 June 2004

	1st Round	%	2nd Round	%
Electorate	2,655,309		2,659,211	
Valid Votes	1,245,360	46.9	1,374,915	51.7
Invalid Votes	39,707	1.5	20,188	0.8
Total Votes	1,285,067	48.4	1,395,103	52.5
Valdas Adamkus, Independent	387,837	31.1	723,891	52.7
Kazimira Prunskienė, VNDPS	264,681	21.2	651,024	47.3
Petras Austrevicius, Independent[1]	240,413	19.3	—	—
Vilija Blinkeviciute, NS–SL	204,819	16.5	—	—
Ceslovas Jursenas, LSdP	147,610	11.8	—	—

Source: Central Electoral Commission, 2008.

[1] Independent backed by Homeland Union.

Table 13.3a LITHUANIA: Votes for the *Seimas*

	1992		1996		2000		2004		2008	
	List	SMD[1]	List	SMD[1]	List	SMD[1]	List	SMD[1]	List	SMD[1]
Electorate	2,549,952		2,597,530	2,597,714	2,626,321	2,626,349	2,666,196	2,666,199	2,696,090	2,696,075
Valid Votes	1,858,586	1,877,669	1,306,922	1,312,658	1,471,247	1,466,214	1,195,655	1,160,499	1,236,716	1,228,199
Invalid Votes	59,441	no data	67,751	60,494	68,496	72,585	32,998	67,149	73,239	81,581
Total Votes	1,918,027	no data	1,374,673	1,373,152	1,539,743	1,538,799	1,228,653	1,227,648	1,309,955	1,309,780
2 Sajudis	393,502	345,182	—	—	—	—	—	—	—	—
15 Homeland Union	—	—	409,585	376,081	126,850	104,631	176,409	167,220	—	—
34 Homeland Union LKD	—	—	—	—	—	—	—	—	243,823	240,408
3 Christ'n Dem. LKDP	234,368	222,183	136,259	173,761	45,227	69,827	—	—	—	—
33 Christ'n Dem. LKD	—	—	—	—	—	—	16,362	29,375	—	—
18 Christ'n Dem. KDS	—	—	42,346	20,711	61,583	33,221	—	—	—	—
4 Social Dem. LSDP	112,410	166,277	90,756	95,499	—	—	—	—	—	—
24 Brazauskas SDK	—	—	—	—	457,294	293,926	—	—	—	—
1 Dem. Labour LDDP	817,332	642,423	130,837	146,006	—	—	—	—	—	—
31 Working BPK–UDL	—	—	—	—	—	—	246,852	204,470[2]	—	—
36 Social Dem. LSdP	—	—	—	—	—	—	—	—	144,890	175,023
25 New Union NS–SL	—	—	—	—	288,895	225,878	—[3]	—[3]	46,061	54,502
5 United Lith. UVL	66,027	24,363	—	—	—	—	—	—	—	—
7 Lithuania's Poles	39,773	35,191	40,941	36,434	28,641	40,376	45,302	52,763	59,237	58,883
8 Nationalist Union	36,916	95,228	28,744	49,808	—[4]	—[4]	2,482	5,904	—	—
9 Lith. Liberal Union	28,091	48,120	25,279	34,842	253,823	229,438	—	—	—	—
29 Lib. Centre Union	—	—	—	—	—	—	109,872	143,658	66,078	94,585
6 Lith. Centre Union	46,910	45,652	113,333	89,452	42,030	89,837	—	—	—	—
10 Lith. Liberty Union	7,760	5,752	20,511	12,456	18,622	23,202	3,337	2,841	—	—
11 Lith. Freedom League	22,034	11,616	12,562	6,557	—	—	—	—	—	—

12 Nat'l Progress TPJ	19,835	59,496	—	—	—	—	—	—	—	—
13 Moderates NJ	13,002	41,223	—	—	—	—	—	—	—	—
14 Chernobyl Move't	4,827	—	—	—	—	—	—	—	—	—
16 Young Lithuania	—	—	52,423	22,052	16,941	16,729	—	2,252	21,589	7,080
19 National Minorities	—	—	33,389	22,252	—	—	—	—	—	—
20 Lith. Peasants' Party	—	—	22,826	29,135	60,040	96,853	—	—	—	—
30 Peasants' Union	—	—	—	—	—	—	78,902	89,006	46,162	61,222
17 Lith. Women's Party	—	—	50,494	36,453	—	—	—	—	—	—
21 Lith. Russian Union	—	—	22,395	11,437	—[5]	—[5]	—	2,107	11,357	3,654
22 Prisoners & Deportees	—	—	20,580	24,797	—	8,495	—	—	—	—
23 Lith. Economy Party	—	—	16,475	26,609	—	—	—	—	—	—
26 Christ'n Con. KKSS	—	—	—	—	29,615	42,116	23,426	21,695	—	—
27 For a Fair Lithuania	—	—	—	—	21583	5,323	—[6]	—[6]	—	993
32 Order and Justice	—	—	—	—	—	—	135,807	97,539	156,777	147,656
28 Labour Party DP	—	—	—	—	—	—	340,035	248,214	111,149	59,961
35 Nation's Resurrection	—	—	—	—	—	—	—	—	186,629	116,728
37 Liberals' Movement	—	—	—	—	—	—	—	—	70,862	77,344
38 Frontas	—	—	—	—	—	—	—	—	40,016	38,192
39 Civic Democracy	—	—	—	—	—	—	—	—	13,775	8,568
40 Labourists' Party	—	—	—	—	—	—	—	—	—	32,224
Others[7]	15,799	134,963	37,187	98,316	20,103	186,362	16,869	93,455	19,311	51,176

Sources: Central Electoral Commission, 2008; Lithuanian Department of Statistics, 1997: 64–66.

[1] In single-member districts, first-round votes. [2] Includes 152,698 votes for LSDP and 51,772 for NS–SL candidates. [3] Part of BPK–UDL in 2004. [4] Part of a bloc called People's Front with less than 1.0 per cent of the vote. [5] Part of Brazauskas SDK in 2000. [6] Part of Order and Justice in 2004. [7] Includes 1992: list, 3 parties with less than 1.0 per cent of the vote; SMD, 4 parties and 74,004 votes for independents. 1996: list, 6 parties; SMD, 9 parties and 45,595 votes for independents. 2000: list: 2 parties; SMD, 9 parties, 106,806 votes for independents. 2004: list, 4 parties; SMD, 3 parties and 76,838 votes for independents; 2008: list, 2 parties; SMD, 2 parties and 33,156 votes for independents.

Table 13.3b LITHUANIA: Percentage of Votes for the *Seimas*

	1992		1996		2000		2004		2008	
	List	SMD	List	SMD	List	SMD	List	SMD	List	SMD
Valid Votes	72.9	73.6	50.3	50.5	56.0	55.8	44.8	43.5	45.9	45.6
Invalid Votes	2.3		2.6	2.3	2.6	2.8	1.2	2.5	2.7	3.0
Total Votes	75.2		52.9	52.8	58.6	58.6	46.0	46.0	48.6	48.6
2 Sajudis	21.2	18.4	—	—	—	—	—	—	—	—
15 Homeland Union	—	—	31.3	28.7	8.6	7.1	14.8	14.4	—	—
34 Homeland Union LKD	—	—	—	—	—	—	—	—	19.7	19.6
3 Christian Democratic Party	12.6	11.8	10.4	13.2	3.1	4.8	—	—	—	—
33 Lithuanian Christian Democrats	—	—	—	—	—	—	1.4	2.5	—	—
18 Christian Democratic Union	—	—	3.2	1.6	4.2	2.3	—	—	—	—
4 Social Democratic Party LSDP	6.0	8.9	6.9	7.3	—	—	—	—	—	—
24 A. Brazauskas Coalition	—	—	—	—	31.1	20.0	—	—	—	—
1 Democratic Labour Party	44.0	34.2	10.0	11.1	—	—	—	—	—	—
31 Working for Lithuania	—	—	—	—	—	—	20.6	17.6	—	—
36 Social Democrats LSdP	—	—	—	—	—	—	—	—	11.7	14.3
25 New Union–Social Liberals	—	—	—	—	19.6	15.4	—	—	3.6	4.4
5 Coalition for a United Lithuania	3.6	1.3	—	—	—	—	—	—	—	—
7 Lithuania's Poles	2.1	1.9	3.1	2.8	1.9	2.8	3.8	4.5	4.8	4.8
8 Lith. Nationalist Union	2.0	5.1	2.2	3.8	—	—	0.2	0.5	—	—
9 Lith. Liberal Union	1.5	2.6	1.9	2.7	17.3	15.6	—	—	—	—
29 Liberal and Centre Union	—	—	—	—	—	—	9.2	12.4	5.3	7.7
6 Lith. Centre Union	2.5	2.4	8.7	6.8	2.9	6.1	—	—	—	—
10 Lith. Liberty Union	0.4	0.3	1.6	0.9	1.3	1.6	0.3	0.2	—	—
11 Lith. Freedom League	1.2	0.6	1.0	0.5	—	—	—	—	—	—

12 National Progress Movement	1.1	3.2	—	—	—	—	—	—	—	—
13 Moderates' Movement	0.7	2.2	—	—	—	—	—	—	—	—
14 Chernobyl Movement	0.3	—	—	—	—	—	—	—	—	—
16 Young Lithuania	—	—	4.0	1.7	1.2	1.1	—	0.2	1.7	0.6
19 Alliance National Minorities	—	—	2.6	1.7	—	—	—	—	—	—
20 Lith. Peasants' Party	—	—	1.7	2.2	4.1	6.6	—	—	—	—
30 Peasants' Union	—	—	—	—	—	—	6.6	7.7	3.7	5.0
17 Lith. Women's Party	—	—	3.9	2.8	—	—	—	—	—	—
21 Lith. Russian Union	—	—	1.7	0.9	—	—	—	0.2	0.9	0.3
22 Prisoners & Deportees	—	—	1.6	1.9	—	0.6	—	—	—	—
23 Lith Economy Party	—	—	1.3	2.0	—	—	—	—	—	—
26 Christian Conservatives KKSS	—	—	—	—	2.0	2.9	2.0	1.9	—	—
27 For a Fair Lithuania	—	—	—	—	1.5	0.4	—	—	—	0.1
32 For Order and Justice	—	—	—	—	—	—	11.4	8.4	12.7	12.0
28 Labour Party DP	—	—	—	—	—	—	28.4	21.4	9.0	4.9
35 Nation's Resurrection	—	—	—	—	—	—	—	—	15.1	9.5
37 Liberals' Movement	—	—	—	—	—	—	—	—	5.7	6.3
38 Frontas	—	—	—	—	—	—	—	—	3.2	3.1
39 Civic Democracy	—	—	—	—	—	—	—	—	1.1	0.7
40 Labourists' Party	—	—	—	—	—	—	—	—	—	2.6
Others	0.9	7.2	2.8	7.5	1.4	12.7	1.4	8.1	1.6	4.2

Table 13.3c LITHUANIA: Number of Seats in the *Seimas*

	1992			1996			2000			2004			2008		
	List	SMD	Total	List	SMD	Total	List	SMD	Total	List	SMD	Total	List	SMD	Total
2 Sajudis	17	13	30	—	—	—	—	—	—	—	—	—	—	—	—
15 Homeland Union	—	—	—	33	37	70	8	1	9	11	14	25	—	—	—
34 Homeland Union LKD	—	—	—	—	—	—	—	—	—	—	—	—	18	27	45
3 Christian Democratic Party	10	8	18	11	5	16	0	2	2	—	—	—	—	—	—
33 Lithuanian Christian Democrats	—	—	—	—	—	—	—	—	—	0	0	0	—	—	—
18 Christian Democratic Union	—	—	—	0	1	1	0	1	1	—	—	—	—	—	—
4 Social Democratic Party LSDP	5	3	8	7	5	12	—	—	—	—	—	—	—	—	—
24 A. Brazauskas Coalition	—	—	—	—	—	—	28[1]	23[2]	51[1,2]	—	—	—	—	—	—
1 Democratic Labour Party	36	37	73	10	2	12	—	—	—	—	—	—	—	—	—
31 Working for Lithuania	—	—	—	—	—	—	—	—	—	16[3]	15[4]	31[3,4]	—	—	—
36 Social Democrats LSdP	—	—	—	—	—	—	—	—	—	—	—	—	10	15	25
25 New Union–Social Liberals	—	—	—	—	—	—	18	11	29	—	—	—	0	1	1
5 Coalition for a United Lithuania	0	1	1	—	—	—	—	—	—	—	—	—	—	—	—
7 Lithuania's Poles	2	2	4	0	2	2	—	2	2	0	2	2	0	3	3
8 Lithuanian Nationalist Union	0	4	4	0	3	3	—	—	—	0	0	0	—	—	—
9 Lithuanian Liberal Union	0	0	0	0	1	1	16	18	34	—	—	—	—	—	—
29 Liberal and Centre Union	—	—	—	—	—	—	—	—	—	7	11	18	5	3	8
6 Lithuanian Centre Union	0	2	2	9	6	15	0	2	2	—	—	—	—	—	—
10 Lithuanian Liberty Union	0	0	0	0	0	0	—	1	1	0	0	0	—	—	—
11 Lithuanian Freedom League	0	0	0	0	0	0	—	—	—	—	—	—	—	—	—
12 National Progress Movement	0	0	0	—	—	—	—	—	—	—	—	—	—	—	—
13 Moderates' Movement	0	0	0	—	—	—	—	—	—	—	—	—	—	—	—
14 Chernobyl Movement	0	—	0	—	—	—	—	—	—	—	—	—	—	—	—
16 Young Lithuania	—	—	—	0	1	1	0	1	1	—	0	0	0	0	0

19 Alliance National Minorities	—	—	—	0	0	0	—	—	—	—	—	—	—	—	—
20 Lithuanian Peasants' Party	—	—	—	0	1	1	0	4	4	—	—	—	—	—	—
30 Peasants' Union	—	—	—	—	—	—	—	—	—	5	5	10	0	3	3
17 Lithuanian Women's Party	—	—	—	0	1	1	—	—	—	—	—	—	—	—	
21 Lithuanian Russian Union	—	—	—	0	0	0	—	—	—	—	—	0	0	0	0
22 Prisoners & Deportees	—	—	—	0	1	1	—	0	0	—	—	—	—	—	—
23 Lithuanian Economy Party	—	—	—	0	0	0	—	—	—	—	—	—	—	—	—
26 Christian Conservatives KKSS	—	—	—	—	—	—	0	1	1	0	0	0	—	—	—
27 For a Fair Lithuania	—	—	—	—	—	—	0	0	0	—	—	—	—	0	0
32 For Order and Justice	—	—	—	—	—	—	—	—	—	9[5]	2[6]	11[5,6]	11	4	15
28 Labour Party DP	—	—	—	—	—	—	—	—	—	22	17	39	8	2	10
35 Nation's Resurrection	—	—	—	—	—	—	—	—	—	—	—	—	13	3	16
37 Liberals' Movement	—	—	—	—	—	—	—	—	—	—	—	—	5	6	11
38 Frontas	—	—	—	—	—	—	—	—	—	—	—	—	0	0	0
39 Civic Democracy	—	—	—	—	—	—	—	—	—	—	—	—	0	0	0
40 Labourists' Party	—	—	—	—	—	—	—	—	—	—	—	—	—	0	0
Others	0	1[7]	1[7]	0	5[7]	5[7]	0	4[8]	4[8]	0	5[7]	5[7]	0	4[7]	4[7]
Total	70	71	141	70	71	141	70	71	141	70	71	141	70	71	141

Sources: Central Electoral Commission, 2008; Lithuanian Department of Statistics, 1997: 64–66.

[1] Includes LDDP 14 seats, LSDP 9 seats, Russian Union 3 seats, and New Democracy Party 2 seats. [2] Includes LDDP 14 seats, LSDP 7 seats, and New Democracy Party 2 seats. [3] Includes LSdP 9 seats, NS–SL 7 seats. [4] Includes LSdP 10 seats, NS–SL 5 seats. [5] All 9 seats won by Liberal Democratic Party. [6] Includes Liberal Democratic Party, For a Fair Lithuania 1 seat each. [7] All won by independents. [8] Includes Modern Christian Democratic Union 1 seat, independents 3 seats.

Table 13.3d LITHUANIA: Percentage of Seats in the *Seimas*

	1992			1996			2000			2004			2008		
	List	SMD	Total	List	SMD	Total	List	SMD	Total	List	SMD	Total	List	SMD	Total
2 Sajudis	24.3	18.3	21.3	—	—	—	—	—	—	—	—	—	—	—	—
15 Homeland Union	—	—	—	47.1	52.1	49.6	11.4	1.4	6.4	15.7	19.7	17.7	—	—	—
34 Homeland Union LKD	—	—	—	—	—	—	—	—	—	—	—	—	25.7	38.0	31.9
3 Christian Democratic Party	14.3	11.3	12.8	15.7	7.0	11.3	0	2.8	1.4	—	—	—	—	—	—
33 Lithuanian Christian Democrats	—	—	—	—	—	—	—	—	—	0	0	0	—	—	—
18 Christian Democratic Union	—	—	—	0	1.4	0.7	0	1.4	0.7	—	—	—	—	—	—
4 Social Democratic Party	7.1	4.2	5.7	10.0	7.0	8.5	—	—	—	—	—	—	—	—	—
24 A. Brazauskas Coalition	—	—	—	—	—	—	40.0	32.4	36.2	—	—	—	—	—	—
1 Democratic Labour Party	51.4	52.1	51.8	14.3	2.8	8.5	—	—	—	—	—	—	—	—	—
31 Working for Lithuania	—	—	—	—	—	—	—	—	—	22.9	21.1	22.0	—	—	—
36 Social Democrats LSdP	—	—	—	—	—	—	—	—	—	—	—	—	14.3	21.1	17.7
25 New Union–Social Liberals	—	—	—	—	—	—	25.7	15.5	20.6	—	—	—	0	1.7	0.7
5 Coalition for a United Lithuania	0	1.4	0.7	—	—	—	—	—	—	—	—	—	—	—	—
7 Lithuania's Poles	2.9	2.8	2.8	0	2.8	1.4	—	2.8	1.4	0	2.8	1.4	0	4.2	2.1
8 Lithuanian Nationalist Union	0	5.6	2.8	0	4.2	2.1	—	—	—	0	0	0	—	—	—
9 Lithuanian Liberal Union	0	0	0	0	1.4	0.7	22.9	25.4	24.1	—	—	—	—	—	—
29 Liberal and Centre Union	—	—	—	—	—	—	—	—	—	10.0	15.5	12.8	7.1	4.2	5.7
6 Lithuanian Centre Union	0	2.8	1.4	12.9	8.5	10.6	0	2.8	1.4	—	—	—	—	—	—
10 Lithuanian Liberty Union	0	0	0	0	0	0	—	1.4	0.7	0	0	0	—	—	—
11 Lithuanian Freedom League	0	0	0	0	0	0	—	—	—	—	—	—	—	—	—
12 National Progress Movement	0	0	0	—	—	—	—	—	—	—	—	—	—	—	—
13 Moderates' Movement	0	0	0	—	—	—	—	—	—	—	—	—	—	—	—
14 Chernobyl Movement	0	—	0	—	—	—	—	—	—	—	—	—	—	—	—
16 Young Lithuania	—	—	—	0	1.4	0.7	0	1.4	0.7	—	0	0	0	0	0

19 Alliance National Minorities	—	—	—	0	0	0	—	—	—	—	—	—	—	—	—
20 Lithuanian Peasants' Party	—	—	—	0	1.4	0.7	0	5.6	2.8	—	—	—	—	—	—
30 Peasants' Union	—	—	—	—	—	—	—	—	—	7.1	7.0	7.1	0	4.2	2.1
17 Lithuanian Women's Party	—	—	—	0	1.4	0.7	—	—	—	—	—	—	—	—	—
21 Lithuanian Russian Union	—	—	—	0	0	0	—	—	—	—	0	0	0	0	0
22 Prisoners & Deportees	—	—	—	0	1.4	0.7	—	0	0	—	—	—	—	—	—
23 Lithuanian Economy Party	—	—	—	0	0	0	—	—	—	—	—	—	—	—	—
26 Christian Conservatives KKSS	—	—	—	—	—	—	0	1.4	0.7	0	0	0	—	—	—
27 For a Fair Lithuania	—	—	—	—	—	—	0	0	0	—	—	—	—	0	0
32 For Order and Justice	—	—	—	—	—	—	—	—	—	12.9	2.8	7.8	15.7	5.6	10.6
28 Labour Party DP	—	—	—	—	—	—	—	—	—	31.4	23.9	27.7	11.4	2.8	7.1
35 Nation's Resurrection	—	—	—	—	—	—	—	—	—	—	—	—	18.6	4.2	11.3
37 Liberals' Movement	—	—	—	—	—	—	—	—	—	—	—	—	7.1	8.5	7.8
38 Frontas	—	—	—	—	—	—	—	—	—	—	—	—	0	0	0
39 Civic Democracy	—	—	—	—	—	—	—	—	—	—	—	—	0	0	0
40 Labourists' Party	—	—	—	—	—	—	—	—	—	—	—	—	—	0	0
Others	0	1.4	0.7	0	7.0	3.5	0	5.6	2.8	0	7.0	3.5	0	5.6	2.8

14

POLAND

Between 1795 and 1918 Poland was divided among three imperial powers: Russia, Prussia, and the Habsburg monarchy. At the end of the First World War a new Polish state was constituted on boundaries substantially to the east of today's Poland. Its population was two-thirds Polish; the remainder were Ukrainians, Jews, Belarusians, Germans, and other nationalities. A constitution was adopted in 1921 and an election with universal suffrage held on 5 November 1922. The 444 seats in the *Sejm* (parliament) were allocated by the d'Hondt method of proportional representation; 85 seats went to a bloc of six minority parties. In May 1926, Marshall Piłsudski led a successful military coup. Elections held in 1930, 1935, and 1938 did not determine control of government (Groth, 1964; Schrode, 1969).

In 1939 Poland was invaded by both the Nazi and the Soviet armies, and a government-in-exile was established in London. In July 1944, a Soviet-backed Polish Committee of National Liberation proclaimed itself the government of Poland. In August, the Polish Home Army, loyal to the exiled government in London, rose against German forces in Warsaw. Soviet troops halted nearby and the Germans crushed the uprising. In a proportional representation election to a constituent assembly on 19 January 1947, the right to vote was denied to those described as linked to 'anti-democratic' forces. The Communist list, an amalgam of separately named parties, took 394 of the 444 seats in a campaign marked by fraud, intimidation, and the arrest of opposition leaders (Raina, 1990). Adoption of the constitution of the Polish People's Republic in 1952 was followed by a *Sejm* election controlled by the Polish United Workers' Party (Starr, 1962: 58, 62).

Opposition to the Polish government was repeatedly expressed by popular demonstrations beginning in 1956, and by trade unions that coalesced into the Solidarity movement. In round-table talks early in 1989, the Communist government agreed with opposition groups and the Catholic Church to a compartmentalized election of the 460 members of the *Sejm* and of a new 100-member Senate (Olson, 1993). For 35 national list seats in the *Sejm*, members of the governing Workers' Party and its satellites, including peasant and Catholic groups, ran unopposed. Negative voting was allowed and candidates had to win half the votes to win a seat.

The remaining 425 *Sejm* seats were divided into five separate compartments in four of which competition was allowed amongst multiple candidates, provided each was endorsed by one of the partners in the government's bloc. One compartment with 156 seats was reserved for the ruling Workers' Party, another with 67 seats was for peasants, one with 24 seats was for "democratic" satellite parties, and one with 17 seats was for Catholic groups. With the addition of the 35 national list seats the governing Communist bloc was assured of 65 per cent of the membership of the *Sejm*. In the fifth compartment, comprising the remaining 161 seats, multiple candidates of all types, including those of Solidarity, could compete freely.

The 425 contested seats were divided into 108 multi-member districts with two to five deputies each. To be elected, a candidate had to win an absolute majority of votes in the district, and if this was not achieved a second-round run-off ballot was held between the two leading candidates. Voters were issued separate ballots for the national list and the Senate, and one ballot for each *Sejm* seat in their district.

The election of 100 members of the Senate from two- or three-member districts was open to all types of candidates, including those from the opposition. To win a Senate seat, a candidate required an absolute majority of district votes. If this was not achieved, a second-round ballot was required. The Communist bloc nominated multiple candidates for every seat. The opposition Solidarity bloc nominated one candidate per seat.

The first-round ballot of 4 June 1989 shocked the government. With a turnout of 62.1 percent, candidates of the Workers' Party and its allies failed to win any of the 161 freely contested seats in the *Sejm*. Solidarity-backed candidates won 160 of these seats with a majority in the first ballot, and their share of the popular vote was estimated as between 70 and 72 per cent. Negative voting on the national list led to the rejection of all but two of the unopposed, government-supported candidates. In the rest of the *Sejm* seats, where candidates of the Workers' Party and its allies competed amongst themselves, only three candidates managed to win a majority in the first round. In the second-round ballot, the Communist-endorsed candidates won their 299 reserved *Sejm* seats, and Solidarity won one additional seat in open contest. In the Senate election, Solidarity won 92 seats with more than half the vote in the first round and seven more seats in the second round of voting on 18 June (Pelcyznski and Kowalski, 1990: 350). Only one Communist-endorsed candidate claimed a Senate seat. On 12 September a Solidarity leader, Tadeusz Mazowiecki, became prime minister. The Communist Party disbanded on 29 January 1990. General Wojciech Jaruzelski, chosen as president by the Communist-dominated *Sejm* and Senate, agreed to a free presidential election.

The autumn 1990 presidential election was the first completely free Polish election. In the first round, an absolute majority of votes cast was required to win a five-year term; failing this, a second ballot was required with the top two first-round candidates. The Solidarity leader, Lech Wałęsa, won two-fifths of the vote in the first round; the runner-up was a politically unknown Canadian emigrant, Stanisław Tyminski. Wałęsa won easily in the second round. In the 1995 presidential election Wałęsa lost to former Communist Aleksander Kwaśniewski.

A law of 28 June 1991 authorized the election of a two-chamber parliament. The *Sejm* and the Senate constitute the National Assembly (*Zgromadzenie Narodowe*) only when they meet in a joint session to debate constitutional matters. The lower house, the Diet (*Sejm*), has 460 deputies elected by proportional representation, and the Senate (*Senat*) has 100 members elected by plurality in 40 constituencies with two to four seats each. All citizens age 18 and above have the right to vote. Electors endorse a party by voting for an individual candidate, and parties can form blocs to increase their share of the PR vote. The 1991 law provided for 391 deputies elected by the Hare–Niemeyer formula in 37 districts of 7 to 17 seats, without any threshold beyond that required for district quota, and 69 deputies elected on a national list by a modified Sainte-Laguë formula with a threshold of five per cent of the national vote or winning seats in at least five districts (Jasiewicz, 1992: 497ff.). Ethnic minority parties were exempt from the threshold requirements. Of the 111 parties contesting at least one district, 29 parties won seats in the *Sejm*.

The election law was changed in 1993 to reduce the number of parties winning seats. In multi-member districts, the threshold was raised to five per cent for parties and eight per cent for alliances, and in the national list the threshold was raised to seven per cent. The number of multi-member districts was increased from 37 to 52, creating more districts with just three seats, effectively raising the quota required to win a seat. The d'Hondt formula was introduced for all seat allocations. The number of parties winning seats fell to seven and the outcome was very disproportional; no seats were awarded to 28 parties winning 35 per cent of the vote. In 1997 six parties won seats and 12 per cent of the vote was taken by parties gaining no seats.

A law adopted prior to the 2001 election made it easier for smaller parties to win seats by reducing the number of multi-member districts from 52 to 41 with 7 to 19 seats. The allocation of additional seats to a national list was abolished. In 2001 seats were distributed by a modified Sainte-Laguë formula, with an initial divisor of 1.4. The thresholds required to win a seat remained five per cent for parties and eight per cent for alliances. The number of parties winning seats rose from six to seven. Before the 2005 election the d'Hondt formula replaced the Sainte-Laguë formula.

The new regime amended the 1952 Stalinist constitution in the 1992 'little constitution'. The Constitutional Committee of the *Sejm* elected in 1993 drafted a new constitution, which required a two-thirds' vote there to secure approval. After various compromises, this occurred in April 1997. In a referendum the following month, both Solidarity and Catholic groups campaigned against the document. The new constitution was approved (Table 14.1).

Table 14.1 CONSTITUTIONAL REFERENDUM: 25 May 1997

	Votes	%
Electorate	28,319,650	
Valid Votes	11,967,134	42.3
Invalid Votes	170,002	0.6
Total Votes	12,137,136	42.9
Yes	6,396,641	53.5
No	5,570,493	46.5

Source: Jasiewicz and Gebethner, 1998: 495.

DATES OF ELECTIONS

President	*Sejm* (parliament)
25 November, 9 December 1990	27 October 1991
5, 19 November 1995	19 September 1993
8 October 2000	21 September 1997
9, 23 October 2005	23 September 2001
	25 September 2005
	21 October 2007

REFERENCES

Groth, Alexander, 1964. "Proportional Representation in Prewar Poland", *Slavic Review* 23, 1, 103–16.

Jasiewicz, Krzysztof, 1992. "Poland", *European Journal of Political Research* 22, 4, 489–504.

———, 1994. "Poland", *European Journal of Political Research* 26, 3–4, 397–408.

———, 1996. "Poland", *European Journal of Political Research* 30, 3–4, 433–44.

Jasiewicz, Krzysztof, and Stanisław Gebethner, 1998. "Poland", *European Journal of Political Research* 34, 3–4, 493–506.

National Electoral Commission, 1990. *Wyniki wyborów Prezydent Rzeczypospolitej Polskiej, 25.11.1990–9.12.1990.* Warsaw: National Electoral Commission.

———, 2000. "Wirtualna Polska–Wybory Prezydenckie–Wyniki oficialne", http://pkw.wp.pl.

———, 2001. "Państwowa Komisja Wyborcza: Obwieszczenie Państwowej Komisji Wyborczej z dnia 26 września 2001 r.", http://pkw.gov.pl.

———, 2005. "Elections 2005", http://wybory2005.pkw.gov.pl.

———, 2007. "Elections 2007", http://wybory2007.pkw.gov.pl.

Olson, David M., 1993. "Compartmentalized Competition: The Managed Transitional Election System of Poland", *Journal of Politics* 55, 2, 415–41.

Pelczynski, Z., and S. Kowalski, 1990. "Poland", *Electoral Studies* 9, 4, 346–54.

Raina, Peter, 1990. "Elections in Poland". In R. Furtak, ed., *Elections in Socialist States*. London: Harvester, 98–118.

Schrode, K., 1969. "Polen". In D. Sternberger and B. Vogel, eds., *Die Wahl der Parlamente und anderer Staatsorgane: ein Handbuch*, I:ii, *Europa*. Berlin: Walter de Gruyter, 971–1009.

Starr, Richard F., 1962. *Poland, 1944–1962: The Sovietization of a Captive People*. Baton Rouge: Louisiana State University Press.

Szczerbiak, Aleks, 2001. *Poles Together? Emergence and Development of Political Parties in Post-Communist Poland*. Budapest: Central European University Press.

Table 14.2 POLISH POLITICAL PARTIES

1 *Democratic Union* (Unia Demokratyczna, UD). Launched in 1990 to support Prime Minister (1989–90) Tadeusz Mazowiecki's presidential bid. In 1994 merged with Liberal Democratic Congress to form Freedom Union. 1991–93

2 *Democratic Left Alliance* (Sojusz Lewicy Demokratycznej, SLD). Formed in 1991 by Social Democracy for the Republic of Poland (SDRP), successor to Communist-era Polish United Workers' Party, All-Poland Alliance of Trade Unions, and others. In 1999 registered as a single party. Party of president Aleksander Kwaśniewski (1995–2005). In 2001 SLD presented a joint list with Union of Labour, in 2005 fought independently, and in 2007 as part of Left and Democrats electoral alliance. 1991–

3 *Christian National Union* (Zjednoczenie Chrześcijańsko-Narodowe, ZChN). Conservative Catholic party formed in 1989. In 1991 core of alliance Catholic Electoral Action (Wyborcza Akcja Katolicka, WAK) and in 1993 of Homeland (Ojczyzna) alliance. In 1997 joined Solidarity Electoral Action. 1991–93

4 *Centre Alliance* (Porozumienie Centrum, PC/POC). Originally Centre Citizen's Alliance (Porozumienie Obywatelskie Centrum). Formed in 1991. Part of Solidarity Electoral Action in 1997. 1991–93

5 *Polish Peasant Party* (Polskie Stronnictwo Ludowe, PSL). Heir of agrarian wing

of Communist-era National Unity Front. Leader, Waldemar Pawlak, served as prime minister (1993–95) supported by Democratic Left Alliance. 1991–

6 *Confederation for an Independent Poland* (Konfederacja Polski Niepodleglej, KPN). Anti-Communist and nationalist party led by former dissident Leszek Moczulski. Joined Solidarity Electoral Action of the Right in 2001. 1991–93

7 *Liberal Democratic Congress* (Kongres Liberalno-Demokratyczny, KLD). Launched in 1990 and led by Donald Tusk. In 1994 KLD joined with Democratic Union to form Freedom Union. 1991–93

8 *Peasant Alliance* (Porozumienie Ludowe, PL). Formed in 1991 by ex-Solidarity members and anti-Communist PSL splinters. In 1997 PL joined Solidarity Electoral Action. 1991–93

9 *Solidarity* (Solidarność). Political arm of trade union movement banned by Communist regime. Led by Lech Wałęsa until his election as president in 1990. Dominant partner in Solidarity Electoral Action in 1997. In 2001, Solidarity trade union withdrew from active involvement in party politics. 1991–93

10 *Polish Beer-Lovers' Party* (Polska Partia Przyjaciol Piwa, PPPP). Founded by a comedian with support of pro-market businessmen. After winning 16 seats in 1991, 12 deputies broke away to form Polish Economic Program. 1991–93

11 *Christian Democratic Labour Party* (Chrześcijańsko-Demokratyczne Stronnictwo Pracy, ChDSP). Founded 1989 as a continuation of the Labour Party suspended in 1946. 1991

12 *Union of Labour* (Unia Pracy, UP). Known as Labour Solidarity in 1991. Social democratic outgrowth of Solidarity movement. In 2001 in electoral alliance with Democratic Left; in 2005 joined electoral list of SDPL, and in 2007 joined Left and Democrats. 1991–97

13 *German Minority in Opole Silesia* (Mniejszość Niemiecka Slaska Opolskiego, MNSO). Seeks to represents ethnic Germans in south-west Poland. 1991–

14 *Realpolitik Union* (Unia Polityki Realnej, UPR). Libertarian nationalist party founded in 1990 by Janusz Korwin-Mikke, thrice a presidential candidate. Contested 1997 election as part of Union of Republic's Rightists (Unia Prawicy Rzeczypospolitej) alliance. In 2001 UPR candidates were included in lists of Civic Platform, but did not win any seats. In 2005, Korwin-Mikke broke away to form Platform of Janusz Korwin-Mikke. In 2007 UPR joined contested with the League of the Right of the Republic. 1991–97

15 *Democratic Party: SD* (Stronnictwo Democratyczne, SD). Successor to party co-opted by Communist regime. 1991

16 *Christian Democratic Party* (Partia Chrześcijańskich Demokratow, PChD).

Moderate Catholic party allied with Christian Democracy, ChD. 1991

17 *Party X* (Partia X). Led by presidential candidate Stanisław Tyminski. 1991–93

18 *Movement for Autonomy of Silesia* (Ruch Autonomii Slaska). Regional party in south-west Poland. 1991–93

19 *Non-Partisan Bloc in Support of Reforms* (Bezpartyjny Blok Wspierania Reform, BBWR). Created before 1993 election at urging of President Lech Wałęsa. Its initials are the same as a group formed in 1928 to support Marshal Piłsudski. Part of Solidarity Electoral Action in 1997. 1993

20 *Self-Defence of the Republic of Poland* (Samoobrona Rzeczypospolitej Polskiej, SRP). Established in 1992 by Andrzej Lepper, thrice a presidential candidate. Joined by Leszek Miller, prime minister (2001–04), before 2007 election. 1993–

21 *Movement for the Republic* (Ruch dla Rzeczypospolitej, RdR). Founded as Christian Democratic Forum in 1992 by Jan Olszewski, prime minister (1991–92) and presidential candidate in 1995, after his expulsion from Centre Alliance. In 1997 RdR joined Solidarity Electoral Action. 1993

22 *Democratic Party: PD* (Partia Demokratyczna, PD). Formerly Freedom Union (Unia Wolności, UW), formed in 1994 by merger of Democratic Union with Liberal Democratic Congress. Prime Minister Tadeusz Mazowiecki (1989–90) a member. Led from 1995 to 2000 by Leszek Balcerowicz and for 2001 election by Bronisław Geremek. In January 2001 Donald Tusk and others left to form Citizens' Platform. UW re-launched as Democratic Party before the 2005 election and attracted ex-SLD prime minister Marek Belka (2004–05). In 2007 PD joined Left and Democrats electoral alliance. 1997–

23 *Movement for the Reconstruction of Poland* (Ruch Odrodzenia Polski, ROP). Led by ex-prime minister Jan Olszewski, former leader of RdR. In 2001 joined the League of Polish Families. 1997

24 *Solidarity Electoral Action* (Akcja Wyborcza Solidarność, AWS). Formed in 1996 by 35 organizations including: Solidarity, which was guaranteed half the places on the party list, Christian National Union, Centre Alliance, BBWR, KPN, and Movement for the Republic. Party of Prime Minister Jerzy Buzek (1997–2001). After 1997 election Solidarity was a single party, Social Movement Solidarity Electoral Action (Ruch Społeczny Akcja Wyborcza Solidarność, Rs-AWS) but only about half the members of AWS parliamentary group joined. Before 2001 election trade union Solidarity group withdrew and splits occurred. Solidarity and Christian National Union contested 2001 election as Solidarity Electoral Action of the Right (Akcja Wyborcza Solidarność Prawicy, AWSP). 1997–2001

25 *National Party of the Retired and Pensioners* (Krajowa Partia Emerytów i

Rencistów, KPEiR). Formed in 1994 to lobby for pensioners. 1997

26 *National Alliance of the Retired and Pensioners of the Polish Republic* (Krajowe Porozumienie Emerytów i Rencistów Rzeczpospolita Polska, KPEiRRP). Established to confuse voters by similarity of name to KPEiR. 1997

27 *Bloc for Poland* (Blok dla Polski, BdP). Offshoot of Christian National Union and BBWR. Endorses family values and a strong state. 1997

28 *Democratic Left Alliance–Union of Labour* (Sojusz Lewicy Demokratycznej–Unia Pracy, SLD+UP). Electoral alliance of eponymous parties formed for 2001 election. 2001

29 *Citizens' Platform* (Platforma Obywatelska, PO). Pro-European party created by former members of Solidarity Electoral Action and of Freedom Union, including Donald Tusk, prime minister (2007–). 2001–

30 *Law and Justice* (Prawo i Sprawiedliwość, PiS). Emerged from Solidarity Electoral Action. Includes parts of Christian National Union, PChD, and Centre Alliance. Led by former Solidarity activist Lech Kaczyński, president of Poland (2005–) and his twin Jarosław, prime minister (2006–07). 2001–

31 *League of Polish Families* (Liga Polskich Rodzin, LPR). Opposes abortion and EU membership. In 2007 joined League of the Right of the Republic. 2001–

32 *Social Democracy of Poland* (Socjaldemokracja Polska, SDPL). Splinter of Democratic Left formed in 2004. Contested in 2005 in alliance with Union of Labour and 2007 as part of Left and Democrats electoral alliance. 2005–

33 *Platform of Janusz Korwin-Mikke* (Platforma Janusza Korwin-Mikke). Splinter of UPR led by eponymous three-time presidential candidate. 2005

34 *Patriotic Movement* (Ruch Patriotyczny). Splinter of LPR led by Jan Olszewski, former prime minister (1991–92). 2005

35 *Left and Democrats* (Lewica i Demokraci). Alliance formed in 2006 to contest local elections. Includes Democratic Left Alliance, Social Democracy of Poland, Democratic Party: PD, and Union of Labour. Led by ex-president Aleksander Kwaśniewski (1995–2005). 2007

36 *League of the Right of the Republic* (Liga Prawicy Rzeczypospolitej, LPrR). Alliance of League of Polish Families, UPR and Right of the Republic, splinter of PiS. 2007

Table 14.3a PRESIDENTIAL VOTE: 25 November, 9 December 1990

	1st Round	%	2nd Round	%
Electorate	27,545,625		27,436,078	
Valid Votes	16,442,474	59.7	14,305,794	52.1
Invalid Votes	259,526	0.9	344,243	1.3
Total Votes	16,702,000	60.6	14,650,037	53.4
Lech Wałęsa, Solidarity	6,569,889	40.0	10,622,696	74.3
Stanisław Tyminski, Independent	3,797,605	23.1	3,683,098	25.7
Tadeusz Mazowiecki, UD	2,973,264	18.1	—	—
Włodzimierz Cimoscewicz, SLD	1,514,025	9.2	—	—
Roman Bartosczcze, PSL	1,176,175	7.2	—	—
Leszek Moczulski, KPN	411,516	2.5	—	—

Source: National Electoral Commission, 1990.

Table 14.3b PRESIDENTIAL VOTE: 5, 19 November 1995

	1st Round	%	2nd Round	%
Electorate	28,136,332		28,062,409	
Valid Votes	17,872,350	63.5	18,762,615	66.9
Invalid Votes	330,868	1.2	383,881	1.4
Total Votes	18,203,218	64.7	19,146,496	68.3
Aleksander Kwaśniewski, SLD	6,275,670	35.1	9,704,439	51.7
Lech Wałęsa, Independent	5,917,328	33.1	9,058,176	48.3
Jacek Kuroń, UW	1,646,946	9.2	—	—
Jan Olszewski, Independent	1,225,453	6.9	—	—
Waldemar Pawlak, PSL	770,419	4.3	—	—
Tadeusz Zieliński, Independent	631,432	3.5	—	—
Hanna Gronkiewicz-Waltz, Independent	492,628	2.8	—	—
Janusz Korwin-Mikke, UPR	428,969	2.4	—	—
Andrzej Lepper, Self-Defence	235,797	1.3	—	—
Jan Pietrzak, Independent	201,033	1.1	—	—
Tadeusz Koźluk, Independent	27,259	0.2	—	—
Kazimierz Piotrowicz, Independent	12,591	0.1	—	—
Leszek Bubel, PPPP	6,825	0	—	—

Source: Jasiewicz, 1996: 433.

Table 14.3c PRESIDENTIAL VOTE: 8 October 2000

		%
Electorate	29,122,304	
Valid Votes	17,598,919	60.4
Invalid Votes	190,312	0.7
Total Votes	17,798,791	61.1
Aleksander Kwaśniewski, Independent[1]	9,485,224	53.9
Andrzej Olechowski, Independent	3,044,141	17.3
Marian Krzaklewski, AWS	2,739,621	15.6
Jaroslaw Kalinowski, PSL	1,047,949	6.0
Andrzej Lepper, Samoobrona	537,570	3.1
Janusz Korwin-Mikke, UPR	252,499	1.4
Lech Wałęsa, ChDRP[2]	178,590	1.0
Jan Łopuszański, Independent	139,682	0.8
Dariusz Grabowski, Independent	89,002	0.5
Piotr Ikonowicz, PPS[3]	38,672	0.2
Tadeusz Wilecki, Independent	28,805	0.2
Bogdan Pawlowski, Independent	17,164	0.1

Source: National Electoral Commission, 2000.

[1] Endorsed by SLD.

[2] Christian Democracy of the Third Republic of Poland (Chrześciańska Demokracja III Rzeczypospolitej Polskiej, ChDRP), founded on the fringes of AWS by Lech Wałęsa's supporters.

[3] Polish Socialist Party (Polska Partia Socjalistyczna, PPS), a revived version of the pre-war party of the same name, which broke up in 1948.

Table 14.3d PRESIDENTIAL VOTE: 9, 23 October 2005

	1st Round	%	2nd Round	%
Electorate	30,260,027		30,279,209	
Valid Votes	14,946,689	49.4	15,279,787	50.5
Invalid Votes	99,661	0.3	155,233	0.5
Total Votes	15,046,350	49.7	15,435,020	51.0
Donald Tusk, PO	5,429,666	36.3	7,022,319	46.0
Lech Kaczynski, PiS	4,947,927	33.1	8,257,468	54.0
Andrzej Lepper, Samoobrona	2,259,094	15.1	-	-
Marek Borowski, SDPL	1,544,642	10.3	-	-
Jaroslaw Kalinowski, PSL	269,316	1.8	-	-
Janusz Korwin-Mikke, UPR	214,116	1.4	-	-
Henryka Bochniarz, PD	188,598	1.3	-	-
Liwiusz Ilasz, Independent	31,691	0.2	-	-
Stanisław Tyminski, Independent	23,545	0.2	-	-
Leszek Bubel, Independent	18,828	0.1	-	-
Jan Pyszko, Independent	10,371	0.1	-	-
Adam Slomka, Independent	8,895	0.1	-	-

Source: National Electoral Commission, 2005.

Table 14.4a POLAND: Votes for the *Sejm*

	1991	1993	1997	2001	2005	2007
Electorate	27,517,280	27,677,302	28,409,054	29,364,455	30,229,031	30,615,471
Valid Votes	11,218,602	13,796,227	13,088,231	13,017,929	11,804,676	16,142,202
Invalid Votes	669,347	619,359	528,147	541,483	440,227	335,532
Total Votes	11,887,949	14,415,586	13,616,378	13,559,412	12,244,903	16,477,734
1 Democratic Union	1,382,051	1,460,957	—	—	—	—
2 Democratic Left: SLD	1,344,820	2,815,169	3,551,224	—[1]	1,335,257	—[2]
28 Democratic Left Alliance: SLD+UP	—	—	—	5,342,519	—	—
12 Union of Labour: UP	230,975	1,005,004	620,611	—[1]	—	—[2]
35 Left and Democrats: SLD+SDPL+PD+UP	—	—	—	—	—	2,122,981
22 Democratic Party: PD[3]	—	—	1,749,518	404,074	289,276	—[2]
32 Social Democracy of Poland: SDPL+UP	—	—	—	—	459,380	—[2]
9 Solidarity	566,553	676,334	—[4]	—	—	—
24 Solidarity Electoral Action–AWS	—	—	4,427,373	729,207	—	—
3 Christian National Union	980,304	878,445	—[4]	—	—	—
4 Centre Alliance	977,344	609,973	—[4]	—	—	—
11 Christian Democracy	265,179	—	—[4]	—	—	—
19 Non-Party Reform Bloc BBWR	—	746,653	—[4]	—	—	—
21 Movement for the Republic	—	371,923	—[4]	—	—	—
5 Polish Peasant Party	972,952	2,124,367	956,184	1,168,659	821,656	1,437,638
6 Confederation Independent Poland	841,738	795,487	—	—	—	—
7 Liberal-Democratic Congress	839,978	550,578	—	—	—	—
8 Peasant Alliance	613,626	327,085	—	—	—	—
10 Polish Beer-Lovers' Party	367,106	14,382	—	—	—	—
13 German Minority	132,059	60,770	51,027	47,230	34,469	32,462

15 Democratic Party: SD	159,017	—	—	—	—	—
16 Christian Democratic Party	125,314	—	—	—	—	—
17 Party X	52,735	377,480	—	—	—	—
18 Movement for Autonomy of Silesia	40,061	26,357	—	—	—	—
20 Samoobrona: Self-Defence	—	383,967	10,073	1,327,624	1,347,355	247,335
23 Move't for Reconstruction of Poland	—	—	727,072	—	—	—
25 National Pensioners' Party	—	—	284,826	—	—	—
26 National Alliance of Pensioners	—	—	212,826	—	—	—
27 Bloc for Poland	—	—	178,395	—	—	—
29 Citizens' Platform	—	—	—	1,651,099	2,849,259	6,701,010
30 Law and Justice	—	—	—	1,236,787	3,185,714	5,183,477
31 League of Polish Families	—	—	—	1,025,148	940,762	—
36 League of the Right of the Republic	—	—	—	—	—	209,171
14 Realpolitik Union	253,024	438,559	266,317	—	—	—
33 Platform of Janusz Korwin-Mikke	—	—	—	—	185,885	—
34 Patriotic Movement	—	—	—	—	124,038	—
Others[5]	1,073,766	132,737	52,785	85,582	231,625	208,128

Sources: Jasiewicz, 1992: 489–90; 1994: 397–99; Jasiewicz and Gebethner, 1998: 493–94; National Electoral Commission, 2001, 2005, 2007.

[1] SLD led an electoral alliance with Union of Labour in 2001.

[2] Left and Democrats alliance included SLD, SDPL, PD, and UP.

[3] Prior to 2005 known as Freedom Union.

[4] Members of Solidarity Electoral Action in 1997.

[5] Includes: 1991: 94 parties each winning less than 1.0 per cent of the vote; 1993: 17 parties; 1997: 9 parties; 2001: 5 parties; 2005: 11 parties; 2007: 3 parties.

Table 14.4b POLAND: Percentage of Votes for the *Sejm*

	1991	1993	1997	2001	2005	2007
Valid Votes	40.8	49.8	46.1	44.3	39.1	52.7
Invalid Votes	2.4	2.2	1.9	1.8	1.5	1.1
Total Votes	43.2	52	48	46.2	40.5	53.8
1 Democratic Union	12.3	10.6	—	—	—	—
2 Democratic Left: SLD	12.0	20.4	27.1	—	11.3	—
28 Democratic Left Alliance: SLD+UP	—	—	—	41.0	—	—
12 Union of Labour: UP	2.1	7.3	4.7	—	—	—
35 Left and Democrats: SLD+SDPL+PD+UP	—	—	—	—	—	13.2
22 Democratic Party: PD	—	—	13.4	3.1	2.5	—
32 Social Democracy of Poland: SDPL+UP	—	—	—	—	3.9	—
9 Solidarity	5.1	4.9	—	—	—	—
24 Solidarity Electoral Action–AWS	—	—	33.8	5.6	—	—
3 Christian National Union	8.7	6.4	—	—	—	—
4 Centre Alliance	8.7	4.4	—	—	—	—
11 Christian Democracy	2.4	—	—	—	—	—
19 Non-Party Reform Bloc BBWR	—	5.4	—	—	—	—
21 Movement for the Republic	—	2.7	—	—	—	—
5 Polish Peasant Party	8.7	15.4	7.3	9.0	7.0	8.9
6 Confederation Independent Poland	7.5	5.8	—	—	—	—
7 Liberal-Democratic Congress	7.5	4.0	—	—	—	—
8 Peasant Alliance	5.5	2.4	—	—	—	—
10 Polish Beer-Lovers' Party	3.3	0.1	—	—	—	—
13 German Minority	1.2	0.4	0.4	0.4	0.3	0.2
15 Democratic Party: SD	1.4	—	—	—	—	—

16 Christian Democratic Party	1.1	—	—	—	—	—
17 Party X	0.5	2.7	—	—	—	—
18 Movement for Autonomy of Silesia	0.4	0.2	—	—	—	—
20 Samoobrona: Self-Defence	—	2.8	0.1	10.2	11.4	1.5
23 Move't Reconstruction of Poland	—	—	5.6	—	—	—
25 National Pensioners' Party	—	—	2.2	—	—	—
26 National Alliance of Pensioners	—	—	1.6	—	—	—
27 Bloc for Poland	—	—	1.4	—	—	—
29 Citizens' Platform	—	—	—	12.7	24.1	41.5
30 Law and Justice	—	—	—	9.5	27.0	32.1
31 League of Polish Families	—	—	—	7.9	8.0	—
36 League of the Right of the Republic	—	—	—	—	—	1.3
14 Realpolitik Union	2.3	3.2	2.0	—	—	—
33 Platform of Janusz Korwin-Mikke	—	—	—	—	1.6	—
34 Patriotic Movement	—	—	—	—	1.1	—
Others	9.6	1.0	0.4	0.7	2	1.3

Table 14.4c POLAND: Number of Seats in the *Sejm*

	1991	1993	1997	2001	2005	2007
1 Democratic Union	62	74	—	—	—	—
2 Democratic Left: SLD	60	171	164	—	55	—
28 Democratic Left Alliance: SLD+UP	—	—	—	216[1]	—	—
12 Union of Labour: UP	4	41	0	—	—	—
35 Left and Democrats: SLD+SDPL+PD+UP	—	—	—	—	—	53[2]
22 Democratic Party: PD	—	—	60	0	0	—
32 Social Democracy of Poland: SDPL+UP	—	—	—	—	0	—
9 Solidarity	27	0	—[3]	—	—	—
24 Solidarity Electoral Action–AWS	—	—	201[3]	0	—	—
3 Christian National Union	49	0	—[3]	—	—	—
4 Centre Alliance	44	0	—[3]	—	—	—
11 Christian Democracy	5	—	—[3]	—	—	—
19 Non-Party Reform Bloc BBWR	—	16	—[3]	—	—	—
21 Movement for the Republic	—	0	—[3]	—	—	—
5 Polish Peasant Party	48	132	27	42	25	31
6 Confederation Independent Poland	46	22	—	—	—	—
7 Liberal-Democratic Congress	37	0	—	—	—	—
8 Peasant Alliance	28	0	—	—	—	—
10 Polish Beer-Lovers' Party	16	0	—	—	—	—
13 German Minority	7	4	2	2	2	1
15 Democratic Party: SD	1	—	—	—	—	—
16 Christian Democratic Party	4	—	—	—	—	—
17 Party X	3	0	—	—	—	—
18 Movement for Autonomy of Silesia	2	0	—	—	—	—
20 Samoobrona: Self-Defence	—	0	0	53	56	0

23 Move't Reconstruction of Poland	—	—	6	—	—	—
25 National Pensioners' Party	—	—	0	—	—	—
26 National Alliance of Pensioners	—	—	0	—	—	—
27 Bloc for Poland	—	—	0	—	—	—
29 Citizens' Platform	—	—	—	65	133	209
30 Law and Justice	—	—	—	44	155	166
31 League of Polish Families	—	—	—	38	34	—
36 League of the Right of the Republic	—	—	—	—	—	0
14 Realpolitik Union	3	0	0	—	—	—
33 Platform of Janusz Korwin-Mikke	—	—	—	—	0	—
34 Patriotic Movement	—	—	—	—	0	—
Others	14	0	0	0	0	0
Total	460	460	460	460	460	460

Sources: Jasiewicz, 1992: 489–90; 1994: 397–99; Jasiewicz and Gebethner, 1998: 493–94; National Electoral Commission, 2001, 2005, 2007.

[1] Includes: SLD 200 seats; UP 16 seats.

[2] Includes: SLD 37 seats; Social Democracy of Poland: 10 seats; non-party candidates: 5 seats; Democratic Party PD: 1 seat; UP: no seats.

[3] Members of Solidarity Electoral Action in 1997. All sat together at the opening of the parliament elected in 1997.

Table 14.4d POLAND: Percentage of Seats in the *Sejm*

	1991	1993	1997	2001	2005	2007
1 Democratic Union	13.5	16.1	—	—	—	—
2 Democratic Left: SLD	13.0	37.2	35.7	—	12.0	—
28 Democratic Left Alliance: SLD+UP	—	—	—	47.0	—	—
12 Union of Labour: UP	0.9	8.9	0	—	—	—
35 Left and Democrats: SLD+SDPL+PD+UP	—	—	—	—	—	11.5
22 Democratic Party: PD	—	—	13.0	0	0	—
32 Social Democracy of Poland: SDPL+UP	—	—	—	—	0	—
9 Solidarity	5.9	0	—	—	—	—
24 Solidarity Electoral Action–AWS	—	—	43.7	0	—	—
3 Christian National Union	10.7	0	—	—	—	—
4 Centre Alliance	9.6	0	—	—	—	—
11 Christian Democracy	1.1	—	—	—	—	—
19 Non-Party Reform Bloc BBWR	—	3.5	—	—	—	—
21 Movement for the Republic	—	0	—	—	—	—
5 Polish Peasant Party	10.4	28.7	5.9	9.1	5.4	6.7
6 Confederation Independent Poland	10.0	4.8	—	—	—	—
7 Liberal-Democratic Congress	8.0	0	—	—	—	—
8 Peasant Alliance	6.1	0	—	—	—	—
10 Polish Beer-Lovers' Party	3.5	0	—	—	—	—
13 German Minority	1.5	0.9	0.4	0.4	0.4	0.2
15 Democratic Party	0.2	—	—	—	—	—
16 Christian Democratic Party	0.9	—	—	—	—	—
17 Party X	0.7	0	—	—	—	—
18 Movement for Autonomy of Silesia	0.4	0	—	—	—	—

20 Samoobrona: Self-Defence	—	0	0	11.5	12.2	0
23 Move't Reconstruction of Poland	—	—	1.3	—	—	—
25 National Pensioners' Party	—	—	0	—	—	—
26 National Alliance of Pensioners	—	—	0	—	—	—
27 Bloc for Poland	—	—	0	—	—	—
29 Citizens' Platform	—	—	—	14.1	28.9	45.4
30 Law and Justice	—	—	—	9.6	33.7	36.1
31 League of Polish Families	—	—	—	8.3	7.4	—
36 League of the Right of the Republic	—	—	—	—	—	0
14 Realpolitik Union	0.7	0	0	—	—	—
33 Platform of Janusz Korwin-Mikke	—	—	—	—	0	—
34 Patriotic Movement	—	—	—	—	0	—
Others	3.0	0	0	0	0	0

15

ROMANIA

Romania's independence was recognized by the 1878 Congress of Berlin. Prior to 1914 a curia system of electoral colleges gave representation to different elites in society. Representation was not given to individuals but to estates of the realm, principally landowners and wealthy city dwellers (Ziemer, 1969: 1031ff.).

At the end of the First World War the territory of Romania was substantially expanded and the population became much more multi-ethnic. In November 1918 an election law authorized the election of a *Camera Deputaţilor* (Chamber of Deputies) by proportional representation (PR); three elections were held on that basis. In March 1926 a new election law was enacted, based on an Italian fascist model. If any one party won at least 40 per cent of the total vote, it received half the seats in the assembly. The other half were distributed proportionately among all parties. Thus, a party winning 40 per cent of the vote was assured of receiving at least 70 per cent of the seats. The governing party on election day invariably won the election, using a variety of means to influence voters, including fraud and physical intimidation. However, since control of government changed hands between elections, unfair elections were combined with an alternation of governors (Dogan, 1987: 370ff.). In the December 1937 election no party won two-fifths of the vote. Because of the rise of nationalist, anti-Semitic, anti-democratic movements led by the fascist Iron Guard, the king suspended the constitution and sought to introduce a corporatist regime.

During the Second World War Romania was subject to military pressure from both Nazi Germany and the Soviet Union. In 1940 King Carol II went into exile, and General Ion Antonescu took power. Nazi Germany pushed Romania to join in the war against the Soviet Union, but later in the war it switched to the Allied side (Hitchins, 1994).

The Soviet army occupied Romania at the end of the Second World War and imposed a coalition government on King Michael, who had replaced his father as head of state. The Communist Party was so weak that the major government leaders were initially non-Communist politicians subject to Soviet influence. In November 1946 an election was held in which the government coalition won 376 of the 414 seats in the *Camera Deputaţilor*. The following year King Michael abdicated, and a Communist regime was established with Gheorghe Gheorghiu-Dej as leader of the

People's Democratic Front. In the election of 28 March 1948 the Front claimed 93 per cent of the vote and 405 of the 414 seats in the national assembly. In 1965 Nicolae Ceauşescu became party leader. Ceauşescu ruled in a highly personalistic way, relying heavily on the secret police, the *Securitate*, and the personal authority of himself and his wife Elena. In December 1989 popular protests against the regime by ethnic Hungarians and Romanians in Timişoara were suppressed by gunfire, and this sparked off demonstrations in Bucharest and other large cities. The army mutinied, and many hundreds were killed in fighting against the loyalist *Securitate*. A hastily created National Salvation Front (FSN) seized power. On 25 December 1989 Ceauşescu and his wife were summarily tried and executed.

On 14 March 1990 the Provisional Council of National Unity approved a law valid only for an election on 20 May of a president and a bicameral parliament (*Parlamentul României*), with a 396-seat Chamber of Deputies (*Camera Deputaţilor*) and a 119-member Senate (*Senatul*). The president required an absolute majority to win on the first round; failing that, a run-off ballot between the two leading candidates decided the result. The right to vote was given all citizens age 18 or over, except for persons legally incapacitated. The Chamber of Deputies was to be elected by proportional representation from 41 multi-member districts, the 40 counties (*judeţe*), and Bucharest. The number of seats in a district ranged from 4 to 15, and there were 39 in Bucharest. In the Senate, the range was two to four, with 14 senators from Bucharest. A valid vote in a district required a turnout of at least half the electorate. In the Chamber of Deputies, district seats were initially allotted to closed party lists by the Hare quota. In addition, seats were allocated at the national level by the d'Hondt method, using the remainder of votes from the initial allocation. No minimum share of the vote was required to qualify for PR seats. Nine seats were reserved for national minority organizations that failed to win representation through the PR system: Armenians, Bulgarians, Greeks, Lipovans, Poles, Serbs, Slovaks, Turks, and Ukrainians. The Senate election system was similar.

In May 1990 both presidential and parliamentary elections were held on the same day. The interim president, Ion Iliescu, was the candidate of the National Salvation Front. He had been secretary of the Romanian Communist Party's central committee in 1971, but lost the job after six months for criticizing the Ceauşescu regime's policies. Thereafter he served in a variety of low-profile administrative positions. He won the presidency on the first ballot, with 85.1 per cent of the reported vote.

In the Chamber of Deputies ballot, the National Salvation Front was credited with 66.3 per cent of the vote, confirming the prime minister, Petre Roman, in office. Shortly before election day the number of eligible electors was increased from 15,936,000 to 17,200,000. The number of votes declared invalid was abnormally high, 6.5 per cent. Foreign observers witnessed numerous voting irregularities. The American Commission on Security and Cooperation in Europe (1990: 97) reported both spontaneous and planned violent intimidation of the government's opponents creating 'an uneven field with unequal access ... and inconsistent and faulty application of electoral procedures on election day' (see also Nelson, 1990: 357ff.). Nonetheless, it concluded that the National Salvation Front would probably have won a free and fair election.

The new parliament drafted a constitution proposing a strong presidential system. A constitutional referendum was hurriedly called for 8 December 1991. After the opposition recommended a boycott of the referendum, the number of registered electors dropped by more than one million. According to the official report, on a turnout of 69.1 per cent 77.3 per cent favoured the constitution, and 20.4 per cent were against; 2.7 per cent of votes were invalid. Districts with large Hungarian populations voted overwhelmingly against the constitution (Eyal, 1993: 132ff.).

A new electoral law adopted in July 1992 confirmed the use of proportional representation. The law introduced a threshold of three per cent for a party to qualify for the distribution of seats, with the threshold rising by one per cent for each additional party joining an alliance, up to a maximum of eight per cent. The number of seats in the Chamber of Deputies was reduced to 328, based on a representation norm of one deputy per 70,000 inhabitants, plus seats for ethnic minorities. In the Senate, the representation norm was one deputy per 160,000 inhabitants. Every officially recognized minority presenting a list or forming joint ethnic lists was entitled to one seat, if it had not won a seat in either the Chamber or the Senate, providing its total national vote was at least five per cent of the national average vote required to elect a deputy (Shafir, 1992). The number of seats for minorities thus varied from one election to the next; in 1992 it was 13. There were 42 multi-member districts (MMDs) returning from 4 to 29 deputies. The initial seat distribution at district level used a Hare quota; a second distribution at the national level applied the d'Hondt formula to allocate any remaining seats on the basis of votes wasted at the regional level. Independent candidates were elected if they won a Hare quota in their district. An election was held under this law on 27 September 1992. Prior to the election, more than 250 nominal parties were registered and 82 parties and alliances appeared on the ballot. Although the PR ballot for the Chamber was the same as two years earlier, the number of votes declared invalid was very high, 9.7 per cent.

In March 1996, a law tightened the rules for the registration of parties, reducing their number to 57 before the November 1996 election. The total number of presidential candidates rose from 5 to 16, each of whom was required to secure 100,000 signatures to qualify. The number of seats allocated to minorities rose to 15.

The OSCE Observer Mission judged that the administration of the election showed a discernible improvement, while noting minor irregularities. It concluded that the results 'reflect the will of the voters' (OSCE, 1996: 16).

Prior to the 2000 election, legislation increased the threshold for representation to five per cent, or eight per cent for alliances of two parties, rising by one per cent for each additional party up to a maximum of ten per cent. There were 327 ordinary seats, and 19 seats were allocated to minorities. Before the 2004 election, the threshold for minority parties to win a seat was raised to ten per cent of the national average vote required to elect a deputy. In the 2004 election, there were 314 ordinary seats, and 18 were allocated to minorities.

In March 2008, parliament passed legislation designed to increase individual accountability of members of parliament by changing the form of PR ballot. In the Chamber of Deputies, a voter states a preference for an individual candidate, who is linked with a particular single-member district (SMD) as well as a party. Each vote is counted twice, once for the candidate and once for the party's list in a multi-member region. The number of SMDs varies with the population of the region from 4 to 28 for Bucharest. In total, there are 315 SMDs from 43 regions, including one for Romanians living abroad. For the election of the Senate, the 137 seats are divided into multi-member regions with from 2 to 12 SMDs. The threshold to win seats is five per cent of the nationwide vote or winning a plurality in at least six SMDs for the Chamber of Deputies or three SMDs for the Senate.

There are three stages to the distribution of seats. First, candidates of parties above the threshold who win an absolute majority of the vote in an SMD are allocated seats. In the November 2008 election 85 seats in the Chamber of Deputies were won in this way. Secondly, the rest of the seats are allocated to parties winning a Hare quota, calculated by dividing the total valid votes in a multi-member region by the total number of SMDs within it. Thirdly, any remaining unallocated seats are distributed at national level by the d'Hondt formula on the basis of wasted votes at the regional level. PR seats are allocated to individual candidates within parties in descending order of votes, ensuring that each SMD has only one MP. If the candidate coming first in an SMD does not win an absolute majority of the vote, it is possible for the candidate coming second there to win it through the PR allocation. If a party wins more seats by absolute majority in SMDs than it is entitled to by PR, the size of the Chamber of Deputies is increased. In 2008 the Democratic Liberal Party won one seat this way, bringing the total number of Chamber seats up to 316. Every officially recognized minority presenting a list or joint ethnic lists is entitled to one seat, if it has not won a seat in either the Chamber or the Senate, providing its total national vote is at least ten per cent of the national average vote required to elect a deputy. In the 2008 election national minorities were given 18 seats, making a total of 334 seats in the Chamber of Deputies. Independent candidates can win a seat by gaining either an absolute majority in their SMD or a Hare quota in their MMD; none did so in 2008.

In 2004, Romania adopted a constitutional amendment extending the presidential term to five years and applicable to the incumbent president. Thus, presidential elections will no longer be held at the same time as the election of parliament.

DATES OF ELECTIONS

President	*Camera Deputaţilor* (Lower House)
20 May 1990	20 May 1990
27 September 1992	27 September 1992
3, 17 November 1996	3 November 1996
26 November, 10 December 2000	26 November 2000
28 November, 12 December 2004	28 November 2004
	30 November 2008

REFERENCES

Alvarez-Rivera, Manuel, 2008. "Romania Votes Under a New Electoral System", http://globaleconomydoesmatter.blogspot.com/2008/11/romania-votes-under-new-electoral.html.

Carey, Henry F., 1995. "Irregularities or Rigging: The 1992 Romanian Parliamentary Elections", *East European Quarterly* 29, 1, 43–66.

Central Electoral Bureau, 1992. "Proces Verbal privind alegerile generale pentru Camera Deputaţilor 27 septembrie 1992", Bucharest.

———, 1992a. "Proces Verbal privind rezultatul alegerilor pentru Preşedintele României", Bucharest.

———, 1996. "Proces Verbal privind rezultatul alegerilor pentru Camera Deputaţilor 3 noiembrie 1996", Bucharest.

———, 1996a. "Proces Verbal privind rezultatul pentru alegerea Preşedintelui României", Bucharest.

———, 2002. "Alegeri parlamentare şi prezidenţiale (26 noiembrie si 10 decembrie 2000)", http://domino.kappa.ro/election/election2000.nsf.

———, 2004. "Alegeri pentru Camera Deputatilor, Senat si Presedintele României – anul 2004", http://www.bec2004.ro/rezultate.htm.

———, 2008. "Parlamentare 2008", http://www.roaep.ro/ro/section.php?id=atasamentescrutin&ids=43.

CSCE (Commission on Security and Cooperation in Europe), 1990. *Elections in Central and Eastern Europe*. Washington, DC: US Government Printing Office.

Deletant, Dennis, 1990. "The Romanian Elections of May 1990", *Representation* 29, 108, 23–26.

Dogan, Mattei, 1987. "Mimic Democracy in Romania". In M. Weiner and E. Ozbudun, eds., *Competitive Elections in Developing Countries*. Washington, DC: American Enterprise Institute, 369–89.

Eyal, Jonathan, 1993. "Romania". In S. Whitefield, ed., *The New Institutional Architecture of Eastern Europe*. London: Macmillan, 121–42.

Hitchins, K., 1994. *Romania, 1866–1947*. Oxford: Clarendon Press.

Mackie, Thomas T., 1992. "General Elections in Western Nations During 1990", *European Journal of Political Research* 21, 317–32.

Nelson, Daniel N., 1990. "Romania", *Electoral Studies* 9, 4, 355–66.

OSCE (Organization for Security and Cooperation in Europe), 1996. "Final Report: Romanian Parliamentary and Presidential Elections 3rd and 17th November 1996", http://www.osce.org/odihr/documents/reports/election_reports/ro/rom2-3.pdf.

Shafir, Michael, 1992. "Romania: Main Candidates in the Presidential Election", *Radio Free Europe/RL Research Report* 1, 35, 11–18.

Stan, Lavinia, and Ravzan Zaharia, 2007. "Romania", *European Journal of Political Research* 47, 1082–95.

Ziemer, K., 1969. "Rümanien". In D. Sternberger and B. Vogel, eds., *Die Wahl der Parlamente und anderer Staatsorgane: ein Handbüch*, I:ii, *Europa*. Berlin: Walter de Gruyter, 1031–74.

Table 15.1 ROMANIAN POLITICAL PARTIES

1 *National Salvation Front* (Frontul Salvării Naţionale, FSN). Break-away of Romanian Communist Party formed in December 1989 to overthrow Ceauşescu regime. Led by Ion Iliescu, president, and Petre Roman, prime minister. After Iliescu dismissed Roman in October 1991, FSN split into Democratic National Salvation Front/FDSN and Democratic Party–National Salvation Front/PD–FSN. 1990

2 *Hungarian Democratic Union of Romania* (Uniunea Democrată Maghiară din România, UDMR). Ethnic party. 1990–

3 *National Liberal Party* (Partidul National Liberal, PNL). Revival of pre-war party

of same name. Fought in 1996 as part of Democratic Convention of Romania, in 2000 independently, in 2004 as part of Justice and Truth Alliance, and in 2008 independently. Led 2002–03 by Theodor Stolojan, prime minister (1991–92), and then by Călin Popescu-Tăriceanu, prime minister (2004–08). Stolojan was expelled in 2006. 1990–

4 *Ecological Movement of Romania* (Mişcarea Ecologistă din România, MER). One of two large ecology parties of early 1990s, the other being PER. In 1996 became part of Democratic Convention of Romania. 1990–92

5 *Christian Democratic National Peasants' Party* (Partidul National Ţărănesc-Creştin şi Democrat, PNŢCD). Based on pre-war National Peasants' Party. In 1992 became leading party in Democratic Convention of Romania. After the Convention won no seats in 2000, PNŢCD contested in 2004 alone. 1990–2004

6 *Romanian Unity Alliance* (Alianţa pentru Unitatea Românilor, AUR). Alliance of Romanian National Unity Party and Republican Party. 1990

7 *Agrarian Democratic Party of Romania* (Partidul Democrat Agrar din România, PDAR). Agricultural workers' party. 1990–92

8 *Romanian Ecologist Party* (Partidul Ecologist Român, PER). Founded in 1978 and legalized in December 1989. In 1992–96 part of Democratic Convention of Romania. 1990–2004

9 *Romanian Socialist Democratic Party* (Partidul Socialist Democrat Român, PStDR). Closely allied to FSN. In 1993 merged into Democratic National Salvation Front. 1990–92

10 *Romanian Social Democratic Party* (Partidul Social Democrat Român, PSDR). Claimed continuity with socialist parties dating from 1893. In 1992 joined Democratic Convention of Romania. Fought 1996 election as member of Social Democratic Union. Before 2000 election joined Social Democratic Pole of Romania, and in 2001 formally merged with Social Democracy Party of Romania/PDSR to form Social Democratic Party (Partidul Social Democrat, PSD). 1990

11 *Democratic Group of the Centre* (Gruparea Democrată Centristă, GDC). Alliance of minor parties. 1990

12 *Democratic National Salvation Front* (Frontul Democratic al Salvarii Naţionale, FDSN). Formed in 1992 under the aegis of President Ion Iliescu following split in FSN. In 1993 merged with PStDR and Republican Party to form Social Democracy Party of Romania/PDSR. 1992

13 *Democratic Convention of Romania* (Convenţia Democrata din România, CDR). Anti-FSN alliance formed in 1992 by 18 organizations, including Christian and

Democratic National Peasants' Party, PSDR, Romanian Ecologist Party, National Liberal Party–Democratic Convention/PNL-CD, and part of National Liberal Party. Party of Emil Constantinescu, president (1996–2000). After splits in 1998 and 1999, re-named CDR-2000. 1992–2000

14 *Democratic Liberal Party* (Partidul Democrat Liberal, PDL). Originated as wing of FSN led by Petre Roman, prime minister (December 1989–October 1991). Fought 1992 election as Democratic Party–National Salvation Front (Partidul Democrat–Frontul Salvării Naţionale, PD–FSN). Contested in 1996 as part of Social Democratic Union, in 2000 independently as Democratic Party (Partidul Democrat, PD), in 2004 with National Liberal Party as part of Justice and Truth Alliance, and in 2008 independently under present name. Since 2001 led by Traian Băsescu, president (2004–). In January 2008 joined by Theodor Stolojan. 1992–

15 *Romanian National Unity Party* (Partidul Unităţii Naţionale Române, PUNR). Organized in 1990 as electoral wing of nationalist and anti-Hungarian group Romanian Hearth (Vatra Româneasca), which seeks to recover pre-war Romanian territory. Led until 1997 by Gheorghe Funar, presidential candidate in 1992 and 1996. Contested 2000 election with Romanian National Party as National Alliance Party (Partidul Alianţa Naţională, PAN); fought 2004 election separately. 1992–2004

16 *Greater Romania Party* (Partidul România Măre, PRM). Nationalist and anti-Hungarian party formed in 1991; electoral wing of Greater Romania movement, which endorses recovery of Romanian territories lost during Second World War. Praises both Ceauşescu regime and wartime Antonescu dictatorship. Led by Corneliu Vadim Tudor, presidential candidate in 1996, 2000, and 2004. 1992–

17 *Socialist Labour Party* (Partidul Socialist al Muncii, PSM). Neo-Communist party founded in 1990 by former prime minister (1979–82) Ilie Verdeţ. 1992–2000

18 *Republican Party* (Partidul Republican, PR). Formed in 1991 by Professor Ioan Manzatu, protégé of Elena Ceauşescu. In 1993 merged into Social Democracy Party/PDSR but re-emerged as an independent party in 2000. 1992–2000

19 *Social Democracy Party of Romania* (Partidul Democraţiei Sociale din România, PDSR). Formed in 1993 by merger of President Iliescu's Democratic National Salvation Front with Romanian Socialist Democratic Party and Republican Party. For 2000 election PDSR formed Social Democratic Pole alliance with PSDR. In 2001 the two merged as Social Democratic Party (Partidul Social Democrat, PSD). 1996

20 *Social Democratic Union* (Uniunea Social Democrată, USD). Alliance of Democratic Party–National Salvation Front and Romanian Social Democratic Party/PSDR. 1996

21 *Socialist Party* (Partidul Socialist, PS). Founded by Tudor Mohora, presidential

candidate (1996). Merged into Romanian Social Democratic Party/PSDR before the 2000 election. 1996

22 *Romanian Socialist Workers' Party* (Partidul Socialist Muncitoresc Român, PSMR). Launched 1995 by defenders of Ceauşescus. 1996

23 *National Liberal Alliance* (Alianţa National Liberal, ANL). Splinter of National Liberal Party. 1996

24 *Pensioners' Party in Romania* (Partidul Pensionarilor din România, PPR). Seeks to represent senior citizens. 1996–2000

25 *Social Democratic Pole of Romania* (Polul Democrat Social din România, PDSdR). Alliance comprising PDSR, PSDR, and Humanist Party of Romania (Partidul Umanist din România, PUR). In 2001 PDSR and PSDR merged to form Social Democratic Party (Partidul Social Democrat, PSD). Led by Ion Iliescu, president (1989–96, 2000–04). 2000

26 *Alliance for Romania* (Alianţa pentru România, ApR). Splinter group of Social Democracy Party of Romania/PDSR. In 2002 merged with National Liberal Party/PNL. 2000

27 *National Liberal Party–Campeanu* (Partidul Naţional Liberal–Câmpeanu, PNL–C). Splinter PNL led by ex-political prisoner Radu Câmpeanu, PNL presidential candidate in 1990 and 1996. 2000

28 *Alliance of the Social Democratic Party and the Conservative Party* (Alianţa Politică Partidul Social Democrat + Partidul Conservator, PSD+PC). Social Democratic Party (Partidul Social Democrat, PSD) formed in 2001 by merger of PDSR and PSDR. Led by Adrian Năstase, prime minister (2000–04). In 2004, PSD formed alliance with Humanist Party of Romania (Partidul Umanist din România, PUR), contesting as National Union: PSD+PUR (Uniunea Naţională PSD+PUR). Afterwards PUR co-operated with Justice and Truth Alliance. In 2005 re-named itself Conservative Party (Partidul Conservator, PC), claiming continuity with party active before 1914. It rejoined the PSD-led alliance in January 2008. 2004–

29 *Justice and Truth Alliance: PNL+PD* (Alianţa Dreptate şi Adevăr, ADA). Alliance of PNL and PD formed November 2003. Backed former mayor of Bucharest and PD leader Traian Băsescu, president (2004–). 2004

30 *Party of the New Generation–Christian Democrat* (Partidul Noua Generaţie–Creştin Democrat, PNG–CD). Party of George Becali, football club owner and presidential candidate in 2004. In 2004 contested as Party of the New Generation (Partidul Noua Generaţie, PNG). 2004–

Table 15.2a PRESIDENTIAL VOTE: 20 May 1990[1]

		%
Electorate	17,200,722	
Valid Votes	14,378,693	83.6
Invalid Votes	447,923	2.6
Total Votes	14,826,616	86.2
Ion Iliescu, FSN	12,232,498	85.1
Radu Câmpeanu, PNL	1,529,188	10.6
Ion Ratiu, PNŢCD	617,007	4.3

Source: Deletant, 1990: 25.

[1] For qualifications on the integrity of the vote, see text above.

Table 15.2b PRESIDENTIAL VOTE: 27 September 1992

	1st Round	%	2nd Round	%
Electorate	16,380,663		16,597,508	
Valid Votes	11,898,856	72.6	12,034,636	72.5
Invalid Votes	580,617	3.6	116,092	0.7
Total Votes	12,479,473	76.2	12,150,728	73.2
Ion Iliescu, FDSN	5,633,456	47.3	7,393,429	61.4
Emil Constantinescu, PNŢCD	3,717,006	31.2	4,641,207	38.6
Gheorghe Funar, PUNR	1,294,388	10.9	—	—
Caius Traian Dragomir, PD–FSN	564,655	4.7	—	—
Ioan Manzatu, PR	362,485	3.0	—	—
Mircea Druc, POD[1]	326,866	2.7	—	—

Source: Central Electoral Bureau, 1992a.

[1] Reunification Party of the Daco-Latin Choice (Partidul Reîntregirii Opţiunea Dacolatină, POD). Seeks recovery of pre-Second World War Romanian territory.

Table 15.2c PRESIDENTIAL VOTE: 3 and 17 November 1996

	1st Round	%	2nd Round	%
Electorate	17,218,654		17,230,654	
Valid Votes	12,652,900	73.5	12,972,485	75.3
Invalid Votes	426,545	2.5	102,579	0.6
Total Votes	13,079,445	76.0	13,075,064	75.9
Ion Iliescu, PDSR	4,081,093	32.3	5,914,579	45.6
Emil Constantinescu, PNŢCD	3,569,941	28.2	7,057,906	54.4
Petre Roman, USD	2,598,545	20.5	—	—
Gyorgy Frunda, UDMR	761,411	6.0	—	—
Corneliu Vadim Tudor, PRM	597,508	4.7	—	—
Gheorghe Funar, PUNR	407,828	3.2	—	—
Tudor Mohora, PS	160,387	1.3	—	—
Nicolae Manolescu	90,122	0.7	—	—
Adrian Păunescu	87,163	0.7	—	—
Ioan Pop de Popa	59,752	0.5	—	—
George Muntean	54,218	0.4	—	—
Radu Câmpeanu, PNL	43,780	0.3	—	—
Nutu Anghelina	43,319	0.3	—	—
Constantin Mudava	39,477	0.3	—	—
Constantin Niculescu	30,045	0.2	—	—
Nicolae Militaru	28,311	0.2	—	—

Source: Central Electoral Bureau, 1996a.

Table 15.2d PRESIDENTIAL VOTE: 26 November, 10 December 2000

	1st Round	%	2nd Round	%
Electorate	17,699,727		17,711,757	
Valid Votes	11,087,378	62.6	10,020,870	56.6
Invalid Votes	336,507	1.9	160,264	0.9
Total Votes	11,423,885	64.5	10,181,134	57.5
Ion Iliescu, PDSdR	4,076,273	36.4	6,696,623	66.8
Corneliu Vadim Tudor, PRM	3,178,293	28.3	3,324,247	33.2
Theodor Stolojan, PNL	1,321,420	11.8	—	—
Constantin Isarescu, PNŢCD	1,069,463	9.5	—	—
Gyorgy Frunda, UDMR	696,989	6.2	—	—
Petre Roman, PD	334,852	3.0	—	—
Teodor Viorel Meleşcanu	214,642	1.9	—	—
Eduard Gheorghe Manole	133,991	1.2	—	—
Graziela-Elena Barla	61,455	0.5	—	—

Source: Central Electoral Bureau, 2002.

TABLE 15.2e PRESIDENTIAL VOTE: 28 November, 12 December 2004

	1st Round	%	2nd Round	%
Electorate	18,449,344		18,316,104	
Valid Votes	10,452,205	56.7	10,008,314	54.6
Invalid Votes	339,010	1.8	103,245	0.6
Total Votes	10,791,215	58.5	10,111,559	55.2
Adrian Năstase, PSD	4,278,864	40.9	4,881,520	48.8
Traian Băsescu, ADA[1]	3,545,236	33.9	5,126,794	51.2
Corneliu Vadim Tudor, PRM	1,313,714	12.6	—	—
Marko Bela, UDMR	533,446	5.1	—	—
Gheorghe Ciuhandu, PNŢCD	198,394	1.9	—	—
George Becali, PNG	184,560	1.8	—	—
Petre Roman, FD[2]	140,702	1.3	—	—
Gheorghe Dinu, Independent	113,321	1.1	—	—
Marian Petre Milut, AP[3]	43,378	0.4	—	—
Ovidiu Tudorici, URR[4]	37,910	0.4	—	—
Aurel Rădulescu	35,455	0.3	—	—
Alexandru Raj Tunaru	27,225	0.3	—	—

Sources: Central Electoral Bureau, 2004.

[1] Replacing Theodor Stolojan, leader of PNL and the original ADA candidate who withdrew in October 2004.

[2] Democratic Force (Forţa Democrată), founded in 2003 by former prime minister (1989–91) Petre Roman.

[3] People's Action (Actiunea Populară), founded and led by former president Emil Constantinescu (1996–2000).

[4] Union for Romanian Reconstruction (Uniunea pentru Reconstrucţia României, URR). Formed in December 2000 by supporters of Emil Constantinescu.

Table 15.3a ROMANIA: Votes for the *Camera Deputaților*

	1990	1992	1996	2000	2004	2008
Electorate	17,200,722	16,380,663	17,218,654	17,699,727	18,449,344	18,464,274
Valid Votes	13,707,159	10,880,252	12,238,746	10,839,424	10,188,106	6,886,794
Invalid Votes	1,117,858	1,591,071	834,687	706,761	599,641	350,133
Total Votes[1]	14,825,017	12,471,323	13,073,433	11,546,185	10,787,747	7,236,927
1 National Salvation Front	9,089,659	—	—	—	—	—
2 Hungarian Democratic Union	991,601	811,290	812,628	736,863	628,125	425,008
3 National Liberal Party: PNL	879,290	286,467	—[2]	747,263	—[3]	1,279,063
29 Justice and Truth: PNL+PD	—	—	—	—	3,191,546	—
14 Democratic Liberal Party: PDL	—	1,108,500	—[4]	762,365	—[3]	2,228,860
20 Social Democratic Union: PD+PSDR	—	—	1,582,231	—	—	—
10 Romanian Social Democrats: PSDR	73,014	—	—	—	—	—
5 Christian Dem. Nat'l Peasants: PNŢCD	351,357	—[2]	—[2]	—[2]	188,268	—
13 Democratic Convention of Romania: CDR	—	2,177,144	3,692,321	546,135	—	—
8 Romanian Ecologist Party: PER	232,212	—[2]	—[2]	101,256	73,001	—
4 Ecological Movement: MER	358,864	245,194	—[2]	—	—	—
6 Romanian Unity Alliance	290,875	—	—	—	—	—
7 Agrarian Democratic Party	250,403	326,289	—	—	—	—
9 Romanian Socialist Democratic Party	143,393	95,041	—	—	—	—
11 Democratic Group of the Centre	65,914	—	—	—	—	—
12 Democratic National Salvation Front	—	3,015,708	—	—	—	—
19 Social Democracy Party: PDSR	—	—	2,633,860	—	—	—
25 Social Democratic Pole	—	—	—	3,968,464	—	—
28 Soc. Dem.–Conservative Alliance PSD+PC	—	—	—	—	3,730,352	2,279,449
15 Romanian National Unity Party	—	839,586	533,348	149,525	53,222	—
16 Greater Romania Party	—	424,061	546,430	2,112,027	1,316,751	217,595

17 Socialist Labour Party	—	330,378	262,563	91,027	—	—
18 Republican Party	—	178,355	—[5]	10,840	—	—
21 Socialist Party	—	—	280,364	—	—	—
22 Romanian Socialist Workers' Party	—	—	212,303	—	—	—
23 National Liberal Alliance	—	—	192,495	—	—	—
24 Pensioners' Party in Romania	—	—	175,676	76,704	—	—
26 Alliance for Romania	—	—	—	441,228	—	—
27 National Liberal Party–Campeanu	—	—	—	151,518	—	—
30 Party of the New Generation: PNG–CD	—	—	—	—	227,443	156,901
Others[6]	980,577	1,042,239	1,314,527	944,209	779,398	299,918

Sources: Mackie, 1992: 331; Central Electoral Bureau, 1992, 1996, 2002, 2004, 2008.

[1] The sum of valid and invalid ballots. Official results also include missing ballots in the reported turnout.

[2] Part of Democratic Convention of Romania.

[3] Part of Justice and Truth in 2004.

[4] Part of Social Democratic Union in 1996.

[5] Part of PDSR in 1996.

[6] Includes: 1990: 51 minor parties winning less than 1.0 per cent of the vote and 217,929 votes for independents; 1992: 70 parties and 58,347 votes for independents; 1996: 43 parties and 248,825 votes for independents; 2000: 56 parties and 137,561 votes for independents; 2004: 44 parties and 51,646 votes for independents; 2008: 23 parties and 28,355 votes for independents.

Table 15.3b ROMANIA: Percentage of Votes for the *Camera Deputaților*

	1990	1992	1996	2000	2004	2008
Valid Votes	79.7	66.4	71.1	61.3	55.2	37.3
Invalid Votes	6.5	9.7	4.8	4.0	3.3	1.9
Total Votes	86.2	76.1	75.9	65.3	58.5	39.2
1 National Salvation Front	66.3	—	—	—	—	—
2 Hungarian Democratic Union	7.2	7.5	6.6	6.8	6.2	6.2
3 National Liberal Party: PNL	6.4	2.6	—	6.9	—	18.6
29 Justice and Truth: PNL+PD	—	—	—	—	31.3	—
14 Democratic Liberal Party: PDL	—	10.2	—	7.0	—	32.4
20 Social Democratic Union: PD+PSDR	—	—	12.9	—	—	—
10 Romanian Social Democrats: PSDR	0.5	—	—	—	—	—
5 Christian Dem. Nat'l Peasants: PNȚCD	2.6	—	—	—	1.8	—
13 Democratic Convention of Romania: CDR	—	20.0	30.2	5.0	—	—
8 Romanian Ecologist Party: PER	1.7	—	—	0.9	0.7	—
4 Ecological Movement: MER	2.6	2.3	—	—	—	—
6 Romanian Unity Alliance	2.1	—	—	—	—	—
7 Agrarian Democratic Party	1.8	3.0	—	—	—	—
9 Romanian Socialist Democratic Party	1.0	0.9	—	—	—	—
11 Democratic Group of the Centre	0.5	—	—	—	—	—
12 Democratic National Salvation Front	—	27.7	—	—	—	—
19 Social Democracy Party of Romania: PDSR	—	—	21.5	—	—	—
25 Social Democratic Pole	—	—	—	36.6	—	—
28 Soc. Dem.–Conservative Alliance PSD+PC	—	—	—	—	36.6	33.1
15 Romanian National Unity Party	—	7.7	4.4	1.4	0.5	—

16 Greater Romania Party	—	3.9	4.5	19.5	12.9	3.2
17 Socialist Labour Party	—	3.0	2.1	0.8	—	—
18 Republican Party	—	1.6	—	0.1	—	—
21 Socialist Party	—	—	2.3	—	—	—
22 Romanian Socialist Workers' Party	—	—	1.7	—	—	—
23 National Liberal Alliance	—	—	1.6	—	—	—
24 Pensioners' Party in Romania	—	—	1.4	0.7	—	—
26 Alliance for Romania	—	—	—	4.1	—	—
27 National Liberal Party–Campeanu	—	—	—	1.4	—	—
30 Party of the New Generation: PNG–CD	—	—	—	—	2.2	2.3
Others	7.2	9.6	10.7	8.7	7.7	4.4

Table 15.3c ROMANIA: Number of Seats in the *Camera Deputaţilor*

	1990	1992	1996	2000	2004	2008
1 National Salvation Front	263	—	—	—	—	—
2 Hungarian Democratic Union	29	27	25	27	22	22[1]
3 National Liberal Party: PNL	29	0	—	30	—	65[2]
29 Justice and Truth: PNL+PD	—	—	—	—	112[3]	—
14 Democratic Liberal Party: PDL	—	43	—[4]	31	—[3]	115[5]
20 Social Democratic Union: PD+PSDR	—	—	53[4]	—	—	—
10 Romanian Social Democrats: PSDR	2	—	—	—	—	—
5 Christian Dem. Nat'l Peasants: PNŢCD	12	—[6]	—[7]	—[8]	0	—
13 Democratic Convention of Romania: CDR	—	82[6]	122[7]	0	—	—
8 Romanian Ecologist Party: PER	8	—[6]	—[7]	0	0	—
4 Ecological Movement: MER	12	0	—	—	—	—
6 Romanian Unity Alliance	9	—	—	—	—	—
7 Agrarian Democratic Party	9	0	—	—	—	—
9 Romanian Socialist Democratic Party	5	0	—	—	—	—
11 Democratic Group of the Centre	2	—	—	—	—	—
12 Democratic National Salvation Front	—	117	—	—	—	—
19 Social Democracy Party: PDSR	—	—	91	—	—	—
25 Social Democratic Pole	—	—	—	155	—	—
28 Soc. Dem.–Conservative Alliance PSD+PC	—	—	—	—	132[9]	114[10]
15 Romanian National Unity Party	—	30	18	0	0	—
16 Greater Romania Party	—	16	19	84	48	0
17 Socialist Labour Party	—	13	0	0	—	—
18 Republican Party	—	0	—	0	—	—
21 Socialist Party	—	—	0	—	—	—

22 Romanian Socialist Workers' Party	—	—	0	—	—	—
23 National Liberal Alliance	—	—	0	—	—	—
24 Pensioners' Party in Romania	—	—	0	0	—	—
26 Alliance for Romania	—	—	—	0	—	—
27 National Liberal Party–Campeanu	—	—	—	0	—	—
30 Party of the New Generation: PNG–CD	—	—	—	—	0	0
Minority organizations[11]	9	13	15	19	18	18
Others	7[12]	0	0	0	0	0
Total	396	341	343	346	332	334

Sources: Mackie, 1992: 331; Central Electoral Bureau, 1992, 1996, 2002, 2004, 2008.

[1] Includes 14 seats won by absolute majority in SMDs.

[2] Includes 4 seats won by absolute majority in SMDs.

[3] Justice and Truth includes 64 seats for PNL and 48 seats for PD, now known as PDL.

[4] Social Democratic Union includes 43 seats for PD, now known as PDL, and 10 seats for PSDR.

[5] Includes 27 seats won by absolute majority in SMDs.

[6] CDR in 1992 includes 42 seats for PNŢCD, 10 for PSDR, 4 for PER, and 26 spread amongst more than a dozen other parties.

[7] CDR in 1996 includes 88 seats for PNŢCD, 25 for PNL, 5 for PER, 4 for others.

[8] Part of CDR in 2000, with no seats.

[9] Includes 113 seats for PSD and 19 seats for PUR, now known as PC.

[10] Includes 111 seats for PSD and 3 seats for PC; 40 seats were won by absolute majority in SMDs, all by PSD.

[11] All seats allocated under special guarantees for minorities, except for 3 seats won in 1992 in open contest.

[12] Seven separate parties, each winning less than 0.5 per cent of the vote.

Table 15.3d ROMANIA: Percentage of Seats in the *Camera Deputaţilor*

	1990	1992	1996	2000	2004	2008
1 National Salvation Front	66.4	—	—	—	—	—
2 Hungarian Democratic Union	7.3	7.9	7.3	7.8	6.6	6.6
3 National Liberal Party	7.3	0	—	8.7	—	19.5
29 Justice and Truth: PNL+PD	—	—	—	—	33.7	—
14 Democratic Liberal Party: PDL	—	12.6	—	9.0	—	34.4
20 Social Democratic Union: PD+PSDR	—	—	15.5	—	—	—
10 Romanian Social Democrats: PSDR	0.5	—	—	—	—	—
5 Christian Dem. Nat'l Peasants: PNŢCD	3.0	—	—	—	0	—
13 Democratic Convention of Romania: CDR	—	24.0	35.6	0	—	—
8 Romanian Ecologist Party: PER	2.0	—	—	0	0	—
4 Ecological Movement: MER	3.0	0	—	—	—	—
6 Romanian Unity Alliance	2.3	—	—	—	—	—
7 Agrarian Democratic Party	2.3	0	—	—	—	—
9 Romanian Socialist Democratic Party	1.3	0	—	—	—	—
11 Democratic Group of the Centre	0.5	—	—	—	—	—
12 Democratic National Salvation Front	—	34.3	—	—	—	—
19 Social Democracy Party of Romania	—	—	26.5	—	—	—
25 Social Democratic Pole	—	—	—	44.9	—	—
28 Soc. Dem.–Conservative Alliance PSD+PC	—	—	—	—	39.8	34.1
15 Romanian National Unity Party	—	8.8	5.2	0	0	—
16 Greater Romania Party	—	4.7	5.5	24.3	14.5	0
17 Socialist Labour Party	—	3.8	0	0	—	—
18 Republican Party	—	0	—	0	—	—
21 Socialist Party	—	—	0	—	—	—

22 Romanian Socialist Workers' Party	—	—	0	—	—	—
23 National Liberal Alliance	—	—	0	—	—	—
24 Pensioners' Party in Romania	—	—	0	0	—	—
26 Alliance for Romania	—	—	—	0	—	—
27 National Liberal Party–Campeanu	—	—	—	0	—	—
30 Party of the New Generation: PNG–CD	—	—	—	—	0	0
Minority organizations	2.3	3.8	4.4	5.5	5.4	5.4
Others	1.8	0	0	0	0	0

16

SLOVENIA

Until 1918 Slovenia was part of Cisleithanian Austria and participated in elections to its *Reichsrat* on a restricted franchise. It then joined the Kingdom of Serbs, Croats, and Slovenes, contributing about eight per cent of its population. Four elections were held between 1920 and 1927 to the parliament (*Skupščina*) with a system of universal suffrage and proportional representation. Parties tended to compete within one region rather than across the whole kingdom. In Slovenia the leading party was the Slovenian Populist Party, a Catholic party that had sat in the Vienna parliament. On 6 January 1929 King Alexander suspended the constitution and dismissed parliament. The 1931 constitution formally banned political organizations based on ethnic or religious criteria. The king was assassinated in 1934 and a regency established. Three elections were held; the government claimed an overwhelming majority in each (Franke and Ziemer, 1969). The Axis invasion of Yugoslavia in April 1941 divided Slovenia among German, Italian, and Hungarian forces.

At the end of the Second World War, Yugoslavia was established as a Federation by Communist partisans; Slovenia was one of its constituent republics. An election in November 1945 was, in the words of Milovan Djilas, a 'people's plebiscite' to endorse one-party rule by the Communist Party of Yugoslavia. A total of 90.5 per cent of valid votes favoured the new regime; in Slovenia 83.5 per cent did so (Höpken, 1990: 119ff.; Franke and Ziemer, 1969). The Yugoslav Communist regime was independent of Moscow. It experimented with elections but, since nominations were controlled by the Communist Party, elections were not free. The Slovenian Republic had nominally separate party and governmental institutions, but the integrative role of the Communist Party maintained Belgrade's overall authority.

In tandem with changes initiated by Mikhail Gorbachev, groups at the republic level began to demand independence from Belgrade. In December 1989 a new election law allowed opposition parties to organize. A bloc of groups formed the Democratic Opposition of Slovenia (*Demokratična Opozicija Slovenije*, DEMOS) and competitive elections were authorized. The first free elections in Slovenia were held on 8 and 22 April 1990, for the president and four more seats in the presidential council, and for two of the three chambers in the Slovenian National Assembly (*Skupščina Republike Slovenije*), the Sociopolitical Chamber, and the Chamber of

Municipalities, each with 80 seats. Another ballot for 80 seats in the Chamber of Labour was held on 12 April. For the post of president, an absolute majority was required to win, failing which a run-off was held between the two leading candidates. For the four seats in the presidential council, the four candidates with the most votes won seats. Election to the Sociopolitical Chamber was by proportional representation in 14 districts with three to seven seats, which were distributed to all parties with a full Hare quota. At the national level, unallocated seats were given parties with at least 2.5 per cent of the national vote, using the d'Hondt formula. Electors had as many votes as there were seats in their constituency and could either vote for a party list or cast preference votes for individual candidates. To vote in the Sociopolitical Chamber and the Chamber of Municipalities, electors had to be at least 18 years old and for the Chamber of Labour at least 15 years old and in employment.

Fifteen parties competed in the April 1990 elections; they defined themselves as Slovene but differed in their relationship with the League of Communists of Yugoslavia. Of the 240 seats, 124 were won by the pro-independence DEMOS bloc of parties. The new president, Milan Kučan, was the former head of the League of Communists of Slovenia. After declaring full sovereignty on 2 July, the DEMOS government began negotiating for independence. In a referendum on 23 December 1990 93.2 per cent endorsed independence with a turnout of 88.5 per cent. Independence was unilaterally declared 25 June 1991. Yugoslav troops briefly intervened and negotiations with Belgrade followed. Formal independence was achieved on 8 October 1991. The DEMOS umbrella party dissolved in December 1991. Subsequently, three of its original members, the Christian Democrats, the People's Party, and the Social Democrats, joined together in 1996 in the Slovenian Spring umbrella (*Stranke Slovenske Pomladi*).

Under the constitution adopted on 23 December 1991 Slovenia has a president directly elected for five years by majority vote; if no one achieves this in the first round, a run-off between the two leading candidates is held. The *Državni Zbor* (National Assembly) has 90 members elected for four years; of these 88 are elected by proportional representation in eight 11-member districts. In 1992 and 1996, voters cast a single ballot for a list of candidates. In the districts, seats were allocated to parties for each full Hare quota secured. Unallocated seats were filled at national level using the d'Hondt formula on the basis of remainder votes. Only parties winning at least three seats in two or more districts could take part in the national-level allocation. In 2000 the law was changed so that voters cast a ballot for a single candidate. The votes for all candidates of a party in a district are totalled, and seats are awarded for each full Droop quota secured. Unallocated seats are distributed at national level using the d'Hondt system with a four per cent threshold. In this allocation, each party receives a number of seats equal to the difference between the number it would win on the basis of its nationwide vote total and the number of district seats already awarded to it. One seat each is reserved for Hungarian and Italian ethnic minorities, which together constitute about 0.6 per cent of the population. Each representative is elected by their ethnic group using first-past-the-post with preferential voting and a Borda count. The voting age is 18.

An upper house with limited powers, the *Državni Svet* (National Council), has 22 members directly elected from single-member districts for five years, and 18 chosen by functional interests according to their own rules, four each from associations of employers, employees, and the self-employed, and six from non-commercial groups.

DATES OF ELECTIONS

President	*Državni Zbor* (parliament)
8, 22 April 1990	8 April 1990
6 December 1992	6 December 1992
23 November 1997	10 November 1996
10 November, 1 December 2002	15 October 2000
21 October, 11 November 2007	3 October 2004
	21 September 2008

REFERENCES

Franke, L., and K. Ziemer, 1969. "Jugoslavien". In D. Sternberger and B. Vogel, eds., *Die Wahl der Parlamente und anderer Staatsorgane: ein Handbuch*, I:i, *Europa*. Berlin: Walter de Gruyter, 753–91.

Grad, Franc, et al., 2002. *The Constitutional System of the Republic of Slovenia: Structural Survey*. Ljubljana: SECLI–Zavod, 116–19.

Höpken, W., 1990. "Elections in Yugoslavia". In R. Furtak, ed., *Elections in Socialist States*. London: Harvester Wheatsheaf, 119–42.

National Electoral Commission, 2008. *Republic of Slovenia: Decision-making by Citizens on [sic] Elections and Referendums*, http://www.volitve.gov.si/en/index.html.

Official Gazette of the Republic of Slovenia (Uradni List Republike Slovenije). Ljubljana.

Toš, Niko, and Vlado Miheljak, eds., *Slovenia Between Continuity and Change, 1990–1997: Analyses, Documents and Data*. Berlin: Sigma, 114–18.

Table 16.1 SLOVENIAN POLITICAL PARTIES

1 *Party of Democratic Reform* (Stranka Demokratične Prenove, SDP). Successor to League of Communists of Slovenia, ruling party in Yugoslav state. Backed presidential bid of Milan Kučan in 1990. Later merged into United List of Social Democrats. 1990

2 *Liberal Democratic Party* (Liberalna Demokratična Stranka, LDSt). Successor to Federation of Socialist Youth of Slovenia (Zveza Socialistične Mladine Slovenije, ZSMS). Led by Janez Drnovšek, prime minister (1992–May 2000, November 2000–02) and president (2002–07). In 1994 LDSt merged with Socialist Party and part of Democratic Party of Slovenia and Greens, forming Liberal Democracy of Slovenia (LDS). 1990–92

DEMOS bloc Democratic Opposition of Slovenia (Demokratična Opozicija Slovenije). Founded December 1989; dissolved December 1991. Includes parties 3 to 9.

3 *Slovenian Christian Democrats* (Slovenski Krščanski Demokrati, SKD). Founded 1990 by Catholic intellectuals. Led until 2000 by Lojze Peterle, prime minister (1990–92). Part of 1996 Slovenian Spring umbrella. In mid-2000 merged with Slovenian People's Party (SLSt), and Peterle left to join New Slovenia–Christian People's Party. 1990–96

4 *Slovenian People's Party* (Slovenska Ljudska Stranka, SLSt). Founded in 1988 as non-political Slovenian Peasant League, based on pre-war organization of same name. Adopted present name in 1991. Part of the Slovenian Spring umbrella in 1996. In 2000 merged with Slovenian Christian Democrats in Slovenian People's Party–SLS–SKD. 1990–96

5 *Democratic Party of Slovenia* (Demokratična Stranka Slovenije, DSS). Originally Slovenian Democratic League, member of DEMOS supporting independence from Yugoslavia. Adopted new name after splits in 1991. In 1994 further splits led to loss of three deputies to the restructured LDS. 1990–

6 *Greens of Slovenia* (Zeleni Slovenije, ZS). Environmentalist group launched in June 1989. In 1994 its MPs joined Liberal Democracy of Slovenia. Contested 2000 election jointly with smaller environmental party as United Greens (Združeni Zeleni, ZZ). 1990–

7 *Slovenian Democratic Party* (Slovenska Demokratska Strana, SDS). Founded in 1989 as Social Democratic League of Slovenia (Socialdemokratska Zveza Slovenije, SDZS). Under leadership of former dissident and 1990 presidential candidate Jože Pučnik evolved into Social Democratic Party of Slovenia (Socialdemokratska Stranka Slovenije, SDSS, later shortened to SDS). Part of Slovenian Spring umbrella in 1996.

Adopted present name in 2003. Led by ex-dissident and prime minister (2004–08) Janez Janša. 1990–

8 *Liberal Party* (Liberalna Stranka, LS). Contested in 1990 as Slovenian Craftsmen's Party (Slovenska Obrtniška Stranka, SOS). 1990–96

9 *Democratic Party of Pensioners of Slovenia* (Demokratska Stranka Upokojencev, DeSUS). Also known as Grey Panthers. In 1992 part of United List of Social Democrats. 1996–

10 *Socialist Party of Slovenia* (Socialistična Stranka Slovenije, SSS). Descended from Communist-era front party. In 1994 merged with Liberal Democracy of Slovenia. 1990–92

11 *League for Citizens' Equality* (Zveza za Enakopravnost Občanov, ZEO). Sought to represent Serbian workers in Slovenia. 1990

12 *Civic Green List* (Državljanska Zelena Lista, DZL). 1990

13 *Party of Craftsmen and Entrepreneurs of Slovenia* (Slovenska Obrtno Podjetniška Stranka, SOPS). Party of small business. 1990–96

14 *Social Democrats* (Socialni Demokrati, SD). Until 2005 known as United List of Social Democrats (Združena Lista Socialnih Demokratov, ZLSD). Formed in 1992 as electoral alliance including Party of Democratic Reform, Social Democratic Union, and Democratic Party of Pensioners of Slovenia, which withdrew to fight 1996 election independently. Led by Borut Pahor, prime minister (2008–). Member of Socialist International. 1992–

15 *Slovenian National Party* (Slovenska Nacionalna Stranka, SNS). Against immigrants from other former Yugoslav republics. In 1993 suffered defections after party founder and 2007 presidential candidate Zmago Jelinčič was accused of being Yugoslav agent. 1992–

16 *National Democratic Party* (Nacionalna Demokratska Stranka, NDS). Splinter of Slovenian Christian Democrats. 1992

17 *Liberal Democratic Party of Slovenia* (Liberalna Demokratska Stranka Slovenije, LDSS). Separate from LDS and LDSt parties with similar names. 1992

18 *Party of Independents* (Stranka Neodvisnih, SN). 1992

19 *Christian Socialists* (Krščanski Socialisti, KS). 1992

20 *League for Primorska/League for Gorejnska* (Zveza za Primorsko/Zveza za Gorejnsko, ZP/ZG). Alliance of northern and western Slovenia. 1992–96

21 *Liberal Democracy of Slovenia* (Liberalna Demokracija Slovenije, LDS). Merger of LDSt, Greens of Slovenia, and Socialist Party of Slovenia. Led until 2002 by Janez Drnovšek, prime minister (1992–2000, November 2000–02) and president (2002–07), and Anton Rop, prime minister (2002–04), who joined Social Democrats

(SD) in 2007. 1996–

22 *New Slovenia–Christian People's Party* (Nova Slovenija–Krščanska Ljudska Stranka, NSi–KLS). Founded August 2000 by Andrej Bajuk, prime minister (May–November 2000), formerly of SLS–SKD. 2000–

23 *Party of Slovenian Youth* (Stranka Mladih Slovenije, SMS). Pro-environment party founded in 1999. 2000–

24 *Slovenian People's Party* (Slovenska Ljudska Stranka, SLS). Founded in mid-2000 as Slovenian People's Party–SLS–SKD (Slovenska Ljudska Stranka–SLS–SKD), merging Slovenian People's Party (SLSt) and Slovenian Christian Democrats. 2000–

25 *Active Slovenia* (Aktivna Slovenija). May 2004 splinter of SMS. 2004

26 *Slovenia Is Ours* (Slovenija je Naša, SJN). Nationalist party active in coastal region of western Slovenia. 2004

27 *For Real* (Zares). 2007 splinter of LDS. Led by former LDS secretary General Gregor Golobič. 2008–

28 *Slovenian People's Party* (Slovenska Ljudska Stranka, SLS) and *Party of Slovenian Youth* (Stranka Mladih Slovenije, SMS). Joint list formed for 2008 election. 2008

29 *Lime Tree* (Lipa). 2008 splinter of SNS. 2008–

Table 16.2a PRESIDENTIAL VOTE: 8, 22 April 1990

	1st Round	%	2nd Round	%
Electorate	1,490,136		1,489,822	
Valid Votes	1,211,570	81.3	1,121,631	75.3
Invalid Votes	25,975	1.7	23,354	1.6
Total Votes	1,237,545	83.0	1,144,985	76.9
Milan Kučan, SDP/SSS	538,278	44.4	657,196	58.6
Jože Pučnik, DEMOS	322,706	26.6	464,435	41.4
Ivan Kramberger, Independent	224,162	18.5	—	—
Marko Demsar, LDSt	126,424	10.4	—	—

Source: *Official Gazette of the Republic of Slovenia*, No. 17/90.

Table 16.2b PRESIDENTIAL VOTE: 6 December 1992

		%
Electorate	1,491,374	
Valid Votes	1,242,358	83.3
Invalid Votes	35,797	2.4
Total Votes	1,278,155	85.7
Milan Kučan, Independent	793,851	63.9
Ivo Bizjak, SKD	262,847	21.2
Jelko Kacin, DSS	90,711	7.3
Stanislav Buser, SLSt	24,042	1.9
Darja Lautižar-Bebler, SSS	22,681	1.8
Alenka Žagar-Stana, NDS	21,603	1.7
Ljubo Sirc, LDSt	18,774	1.5
France Tomšič, SDSS	7,849	0.6

Source: *Official Gazette of the Republic of Slovenia*, No. 60/92.

Table 16.2c PRESIDENTIAL VOTE: 23 November 1997

		%
Electorate	1,550,775	
Valid Votes	1,042,344	67.2
Invalid Votes	22,102	1.4
Total Votes	1,064,446	68.6
Milan Kučan, Independent	578,925	55.5
Janez Podobnik, SLS	191,645	18.4
Jožef Bernik, SDSS/SKD	98,996	9.5
Marjan Cerar, Independent	73,439	7.0
Marjan Poljšak	33,477	3.2
Anton Peršak, DSS	32,039	3.1
Bogomir Kovač, LDS	28,110	2.7
Franc Miklavčič, KS	5,713	0.5

Source: *Official Gazette of the Republic of Slovenia*, No. 76/97.

Table 16.2d PRESIDENTIAL VOTE: 10 November, 1 December 2002

	1st Round	%	2nd Round	%
Electorate	1,609,985		1,610,137	
Valid Votes	1,144,472	71.1	1,038,219	64.5
Invalid Votes	15,209	0.9	14,275	0.9
Total Votes	1,159,681	72.0	1,052,494	65.4
Janez Drnovšek, LDS	508,014	44.4	586,847	56.5
Barbara Brezigar, Independent	352,520	30.8	451,372	43.5
Zmago Jelinčič Plemeniti, SNS	97,178	8.5	—	—
Franc Arhar, Independent	86,836	7.6	—	—
Franc Bučar, Independent	37,069	3.2	—	—
Lev Kreft, ZLSD	25,715	2.2	—	—
Anton Bebler, DeSUS	21,165	1.8	—	—
Gorazd Drevenšek	9,791	0.9	—	—
Jure Jurček Cekuta, Independent	6,184	0.5	—	—

Source: National Electoral Commission, 2008.

TABLE 16.2e PRESIDENTIAL VOTE: 21 October, 11 November 2007

	1st Round	%	2nd Round	%
Electorate	1,720,481		1,720,174	
Valid Votes	986,429	57.3	995,621	57.9
Invalid Votes	5,279	0.3	9,738	0.6
Total Votes	991,708	57.6	1,005,359	58.5
Danilo Türk, Independent[1]	241,349	24.5	677,333	68.0
Lojze Peterle, Independent[2]	283,412	28.7	318,288	32.0
Mitja Gaspari, Independent[3]	237,632	24.1	—	—
Zmago Jelinčič Plemeniti, SNS	188,951	19.2	—	—
Darko Krajnc, SMS	21,526	2.2	—	—
Elena Pečarič, Independent	8,830	0.9	—	—
Monika Piberl, Women's Voice	4,729	0.5	—	—

Source: National Electoral Commission, 2008.

[1] Independent but supported by NSi–KLS, SDS, and SLS–SKD.

[2] Independent but supported by Social Democrats (SD), DeSUS, Active Slovenia, and Zares.

[3] Independent but supported by LDS.

Table 16.3a SLOVENIA: Votes for the *Državni Zbor*

	1990[1]	1992	1996	2000	2004	2008
Electorate	1,490,136	1,491,374	1,542,218	1,588,528	1,634,402	1,696,437
Valid Votes	1,082,050	1,188,378	1,069,204	1,076,520	968,772	1,051,827
Invalid Votes	109,754	89,226	67,007	36,904	22,351	18,597
Total Votes[2]	1,191,804	1,277,604	1,136,211	1,113,424	991,123	1,070,424
1 Party of Democratic Reform	186,928	—	—	—	—	—
2 Liberal Democratic Party	156,843	278,851	—	—	—	—
21 Liberal Democracy	—	—	288,783	390,306	220,848	54,771
10 Socialist Party	58,082	32,696	—	—	—	—
3 Slovenian Christian Democrats	140,403	172,424	102,852	—	—	—
24 Slovenian People's Party–SLS–SKD	—	—	—	102,691	66,032	—
4 Slovenian People's Party	135,808	103,300	207,186	—	—	—
28 Joint List: SLS+Slovenian Youth	—	—	—	—	—	54,809
23 Party of Slovenian Youth	—	—	—	46,674	10,174	—
5 Democratic Party	102,931	59,487	28,624	8,079	—	—
6 Greens	95,640	44,019	18,853	9,691	6,703	5,367
7 Slovenian Democratic Party	79,951	39,675	172,470	170,228	281,710	307,735
8 Liberal Party	38,269	18,069	7,972	—	—	—
9 Democratic Party of Pensioners	—	—	46,152	55,634	39,150	78,353
11 League for Citizens' Equality	26,629	—	—	—	—	—
12 Civic Green List	21,583	—	—	—	—	—
13 Party of Small Entrepreneurs	17,021	18,965	12,335	—	—	—
14 Social Democrats	—	161,349	96,597	130,079	98,527	320,248
15 Slovenian National Party	—	119,091	34,422	47,214	60,750	56,832
16 National Democratic Party	—	25,852	—	—	—	—

17 Liberal Democratic Party: LDSS	—	16,892	—	—	—	—
18 Party of Independents	—	16,178	—	—	—	—
19 Christian Socialists	—	13,592	—	—	—	—
20 Leagues for Primorska & Gorejnska	—	10,059	11,383	—	—	—
22 New Slovenia–Christian People's Party	—	—	—	93,247	88,073	35,774
25 Active Slovenia	—	—	—	—	28,767	—
26 Slovenia Is Ours	—	—	—	—	25,343	—
27 Zares	—	—	—	—	—	98,526
29 Lime Tree	—	—	—	—	—	19,068
Others[3]	21,962	57,879	41,575	22,677	32,695	20,344

Sources: *Official Gazette of the Republic of Slovenia,* Nos. 17/90, 60/92, 65/96, 98/2000; National Electoral Commission, 2008.

[1] Votes for the directly elected members of the Sociopolitical Chamber. Total valid votes in 1990 are less than the number of votes counted due to complicated voting procedure involving positional voting with panachage and vote splitting.

[2] Official Slovene election results count missing ballots in the reported turnout, thus varying slightly from our figures for 'total vote' which include only ballots found in the ballot boxes.

[3] Includes: 1990: 4 minor parties winning less than 1.0 per cent of the vote, and 4,714 votes for independents; 1992: 9 minor parties and 11,850 votes for independents; 1996: 10 parties and 7,398 votes for independents; 2000: 7 parties and 1,712 votes for independents; 2004: 9 parties and 859 votes for independents; 2008: 7 minor parties.

Table 16.3b SLOVENIA: Percentage of Votes for the *Državni Zbor*

	1990	1992	1996	2000	2004	2008
Valid Votes	72.6	79.7	69.3	67.8	59.3	62.0
Invalid Votes	7.4	6.0	4.3	2.3	1.4	1.1
Total Votes	80.0	85.7	73.6	70.1	60.7	63.1
1 Party of Democratic Reform	17.3	—	—	—	—	—
2 Liberal Democratic Party	14.5	23.5	—	—	—	—
21 Liberal Democracy	—	—	27.0	36.3	22.8	5.2
10 Socialist Party	5.4	2.8	—	—	—	—
3 Slovenian Christian Democrats	13.0	14.5	9.6	—	—	—
24 Slovenian People's Party–SLS–SKD	—	—	—	9.5	6.8	—
4 Slovenian People's Party	12.6	8.7	19.4	—	—	—
28 Joint list: SLS + Slovenian Youth	—	—	—	—	—	5.2
23 Party of Slovenian Youth	—	—	—	4.3	2.1	—
5 Democratic Party	9.5	5.0	2.7	0.8	—	—
6 Greens	8.8	3.7	1.8	0.9	0.7	0.5
7 Slovenian Democratic Party	7.4	3.3	16.1	15.8	29.1	29.3
8 Liberal Party	3.5	1.5	0.7	—	—	—
9 Democratic Party of Pensioners	—	—	4.3	5.2	4.0	7.4
11 League for Citizens' Equality	2.5	—	—	—	—	—
12 Civic Green List	2.0	—	—	—	—	—
13 Party of Small Entrepreneurs	1.6	1.6	1.2	—	—	—
14 Social Democrats	—	13.6	9.0	12.1	10.2	30.4
15 Slovenian National Party	—	10.0	3.2	4.4	6.3	5.4
16 National Democratic Party	—	2.2	—	—	—	—
17 Liberal Democratic Party: LDSS	—	1.4	—	—	—	—

18 Party of Independents	—	1.4	—	—	—	—
19 Christian Socialists	—	1.1	—	—	—	—
20 Leagues for Primorska & Gorejnska	—	0.8	1.1	—	—	—
22 New Slovenia–Christian People	—	—	—	8.7	9.1	3.4
25 Active Slovenia	—	—	—	—	3.0	—
26 Slovenia Is Ours	—	—	—	—	2.6	—
27 Zares	—	—	—	—	—	9.4
29 Lime Tree	—	—	—	—	—	1.8
Others	2.0	4.9	3.9	2.1	3.4	1.9

Table 16.3c SLOVENIA: Number of Seats in the *Državni Zbor*

	1990[1]	1992	1996	2000	2004	2008
1 Party of Democratic Reform	14	—	—	—	—	—
2 Liberal Democratic Party	12	22	—	—	—	—
21 Liberal Democracy	—	—	25	34	23	5
10 Socialist Party	5	0	—	—	—	—
3 Slovenian Christian Democrats	11	15	10	—	—	—
24 Slovenian People's Party–SLS–SKD	—	—	—	9	7	—
4 Slovenian People's Party	11	10	19	—	—	—
28 Joint list: SLS + Slovenian Youth	—	—	—	—	—	5
23 Party of Slovenian Youth	—	—	—	4	0	—
5 Democratic Party	8	6	0	0	—	—
6 Greens	8	5	0	0	0	0
7 Slovenian Democratic Party	6	4	16	14	29	28
8 Liberal Party	3	0	0	—	—	—
9 Democratic Party of Pensioners	—	—	5	4	4	7
11 League for Citizens' Equality	0	—	—	—	—	—
12 Civic Green List	0	—	—	—	—	—
13 Party of Small Entrepreneurs	0	0	0	—	—	—
14 Social Democrats	—	14	9	11	10	29
15 Slovenian National Party	—	12	4	4	6	5
16 National Democratic Party	—	0	—	—	—	—
17 Liberal Democratic Party: LDSS	—	0	—	—	—	—
18 Party of Independents	—	0	—	—	—	—
19 Christian Socialists	—	0	—	—	—	—
20 Leagues for Primorska & Gorejnska	—	0	0	—	—	—
22 New Slovenia–Christian People	—	—	—	8	9	0

25 Active Slovenia	—	—	—	—	0	—
26 Slovenia Is Ours	—	—	—	—	0	—
27 Zares	—	—	—	—	—	9
29 Lime Tree	—	—	—	—	—	0
Minority organizations[2]	2	2	2	2	2	2
Total	80	90	90	90	90	90

Sources: *Official Gazette of the Republic of Slovenia,* Nos. 17/90, 60/92, 65/96, 98/2000; National Electoral Commission, 2008.

[1] In 1990, seats in the Sociopolitical Chamber.

[2] Hungarian and Italian minorities elect 1 representative each by first-past-the-post preferential vote.

Table 16.3d SLOVENIA: Percentage of Seats in the *Državni Zbor*

	1990	1992	1996	2000	2004	2008
1 Party of Democratic Reform	17.5	—	—	—	—	—
2 Liberal Democratic Party	15.0	24.4	—	—	—	—
21 Liberal Democracy	—	—	27.8	37.8	25.6	5.6
10 Socialist Party	6.3	0	—	—	—	—
3 Slovenian Christian Democrats	13.8	16.7	11.1	—	—	—
24 Slovenian People's Party–SLS–SKD	—	—	—	10.0	7.8	—
4 Slovenian People's Party	13.8	11.1	21.1	—	—	—
28 Joint list: SLS + Slovenian Youth	—	—	—	—	—	5.6
23 Party of Slovenian Youth	—	—	—	4.4	0	—
5 Democratic Party	10.0	6.7	0	0	—	—
6 Greens	10.0	5.6	0	0	0	0
7 Slovenian Democratic Party	7.5	4.4	17.8	15.6	32.2	31.1
8 Liberal Party	3.8	0	0	—	—	—
9 Democratic Party of Pensioners	—	—	5.6	4.4	4.4	7.8
11 League for Citizens' Equality	0	—	—	—	—	—
12 Civic Green List	0	—	—	—	—	—
13 Party of Small Entrepreneurs	0	0	0	—	—	—
14 Social Democrats	—	15.6	10.0	12.2	11.1	32.2
15 Slovenian National Party	—	13.3	4.4	4.4	6.7	5.6
16 National Democratic Party	—	0	—	—	—	—
17 Liberal Democratic Party: LDSS	—	0	—	—	—	—
18 Party of Independents	—	0	—	—	—	—
19 Christian Socialists	—	0	—	—	—	—
20 Leagues for Primorska & Gorejnska	—	0	0	—	—	—
22 New Slovenia–Christian People	—	—	—	8.9	10.0	0

25 Active Slovenia	—	—	—	—	0	—
26 Slovenia Is Ours	—	—	—	—	0	—
27 Zares	—	—	—	—	—	10.0
29 Lime Tree	—	—	—	—	—	0
Minority organizations	2.5	2.2	2.2	2.2	2.2	2.2

17

RUSSIA

Tsarist Russia was an autocracy, and Slavophiles denounced democratic institutions as alien threats to the country's traditional form of government. Following public demonstrations against the regime, in 1905 Tsar Nicholas II authorized the election of a national assembly, the State Duma, whose members represented estates rather than individuals. In the first stage, members were elected in three separate electoral colleges of landowners and nobility; urban residents meeting property or related qualifications; and peasants. The electoral colleges chose Duma members. The government remained accountable to the tsar and the tsar's police infiltrated opposition groups (Emmons, 1983; A. Wilson, 2005: Chapter 1).

The Russian Revolution began in February 1917 and a Constituent Assembly was elected in November 1917 by universal adult suffrage. In competition with a multiplicity of groups supporting the revolution, Bolshevik candidates won about one-quarter of the vote. When the Constituent Assembly opened in January 1918, it rejected by 101 votes a resolution endorsing actions of Bolshevik commissars. The next day Red Guards refused to admit members to the assembly on the grounds that it was assisting the bourgeois counter-revolution (Radkey, 1950). One-party elections became the rule for the next 70 years.

Soviet elections. The Union of Soviet Socialist Republics (USSR) was a notorious example of unfree, non-competitive elections. The leading role assigned the Communist Party of the Soviet Union (CPSU) meant that the only choice individuals had was whether to vote for or against the party's candidates. From 1936 there was universal suffrage with minor exceptions, abolishing provisions in the 1918 constitution which had disfranchised people with property and church officials. Urban areas, where more workers lived, were over-represented in the distribution of seats. At polling stations an elector could vote for the party-approved candidate by dropping an unread and unmarked ballot in the box. To express disapproval involved a request to mark the ballot in secret, an act that invited attention from party officials. Few did so. Officials responsible for mobilizing every elector routinely totalled votes on the assumption that everyone had voted (see Karklins, 1986). In the 4 March 1984 election for the Supreme Soviet, the reported turnout was 99.99 per cent and the official slate received 99.9 per cent of the vote.

When Mikhail Gorbachev introduced multi-candidate elections in 1989, the overwhelming majority of candidates were Communists, since that was the only political party. Within the CPSU there were divisions between those who went along with Gorbachev's perestroika policy, those who opposed it because it went too far, and those who opposed it because it did not go far enough. In 1990 Gorbachev promoted revising the Soviet Constitution to authorize an elected president. However, he claimed that conditions were so unsettled that the law should not apply to him. In a vote of the USSR Congress of People's Deputies, Gorbachev stood as the sole presidential candidate and received the vote of 59 per cent of Congress members.

Elections in early 1990 to the Supreme Soviets of the constituent republics of the federal Soviet Union created an opportunity for winners in the republics to claim popular support for greater freedom from Moscow. Following the re-formulation of Article 6 of the Soviet Constitution in March 1990, the Communist Party no longer had a monopoly on power. However, other parties had no legal status. In the election to the Congress of People's Deputies of the Russian Republic (RSFSR) on 4 March 1990, there was an average of 6.3 candidates per single-member seat and 86 per cent of the candidates were CPSU members (White, Rose, and McAllister, 1997: 31). The Congress, with 1,068 deputies, chose a 252-member Supreme Soviet of the Russian Republic. Boris Yeltsin, a former Politburo member who had fallen out with Gorbachev, was elected its chair.

In the Russian Republic referendum on 17 March 1991, 69.9 per cent endorsed electing a Russian president and a republic-level presidential election was held on 12 June 1991. In a field of six candidates, Boris Yeltsin won almost three-fifths of the vote. Nikolai Ryzhkov, backed by hard-liners within the Communist Party, came second, and Gorbachev's preferred candidate, Vadim Bakatin, finished last (Table 17.1). At the end of 1991, leaders of the republics agreed to dissolve the Soviet Union and the Russian Republic became the independent Russian Federation.

Elections in the Russian Federation. The new Federation government claimed authority from popular elections but both President Yeltsin and the parliament, the Congress of People's Deputies, had been elected in Soviet times. The constitutional status of the government was unclear, particularly the relationship between the president and the parliament. There were acrimonious disputes between them about preparing a new constitution to replace the much amended RSFSR Constitution of 1978 (McFaul, 2001).

In a four-issue referendum on 25 April 1993 there was a turnout of 64 per cent. Two questions sought popular endorsement for President Yeltsin: 58.7 per cent of voters expressed confidence in the president and 53.0 per cent confidence in his

Table 17.1 RSFSR PRESIDENTIAL VOTE: 12 June 1991

	Votes	% Electorate
Electorate	106,484,518	
Valid Votes	77,790,525	73.1
Invalid Votes	1,716,757	1.6
Total Votes	79,507,282	74.7
		% All ballots[1]
Boris Yeltsin	45,552,041	57.3
Nikolai Ryzhkov	13,395,335	16.8
Vladimir Zhirinovsky	6,211,007	7.8
Aman-Geldy Tuleev	5,417,464	6.8
Albert Makashov	2,969,511	3.7
Vadim Bakatin	2,719,757	3.4
Against all candidates	1,525,410	1.9

Source: *Pravda*, 20 June 1991: 1.

[1] In accordance with official Russian practice, percentages in this chapter are calculated on the basis of all votes, including invalid votes and votes against all.

economic and social policies. Two questions proposed early elections of deputies and of the Russian president. The former received a majority of votes, and the second a plurality but not a majority. Under the terms of the October 1990 law on referendums, a majority of the entire electorate was required to make the results binding on an issue of constitutional significance (White, Rose, and McAllister, 1997: Table 4.2). This was not secured.

Following continuing disputes about a new constitution, on 21 September 1993 President Yeltsin decreed the dissolution of the Congress of People's Deputies. The Constitutional Court declared the action unlawful. Deputies impeached President Yeltsin and named the suspended vice president, Aleksandr Rutskoi, in his place. Led by Rutskoi and the speaker of the Supreme Soviet, Ruslan Khasbulatov, the deputies ignored Yeltsin's decree of dissolution and continued their sessions. Government forces surrounded the building and, after armed clashes in which more than 100 people were killed, the Congress surrendered on 4 October. The presidential administration issued a new version of a draft constitution that was already under discussion and it was put to a popular vote on 12 December, the same day as the election of the new Duma. The constitution, endorsed by 56.6 per cent of voters, came into effect on the day of its official publication, 25 December (Table 17.2).

The constitution authorizes a president directly elected by universal suffrage for no more than two consecutive terms. In the event of the president's sustained

Table 17.2 VOTE ON CONSTITUTION: 12 December 1993

Electorate: 106,182,030	Votes	% Vote	% Electorate
Yes	32,937,630	56.6	31.0
No	23,431,333	40.3	22.1
Invalid	1,818,792	3.1	1.7
Total votes	58,187,755	100	54.8

Source: CEC, 1993a.

incapacity or early resignation, as happened at the end of 1999, a new election must take place within three months. The constitution established a bicameral parliament. The lower house, the State Duma, has 450 members. The upper house, the Federation Council, has two representatives from each 'subject' (that is, republic or oblast) of the Federation, one from its legislature and one from the executive. The total number of regions was initially 89 but has been reduced by mergers beginning in 2005; as of January 2009, there are 83 subjects of the Federation.

The 1993 constitution set the term of office of both the president and the Duma at four years. In November 2008 President Dmitry Medvedev proposed lengthening the term of the next president to six years and of the next Duma to five years. The bill was immediately put to the Duma and passed its third reading the same month. In December it received the required approval of the Federation Council, as well as all 83 of the legislative assemblies of the subjects of the Federation and was signed by the president into law.

Administration of elections is the responsibility of the Central Election Commission (CEC). Its membership is determined by the Duma, the Federation Council, and the president, each nominating five members. Both presidential and Duma elections grant all citizens age 18 or above the right to vote, except for prisoners and persons whom a court has deemed mentally incapable. For citizens whose circumstances prevent attendance at the polling station, special arrangements are made and citizens resident abroad can vote at consulates and embassies. Detailed laws governing the election of the president and Duma were first adopted in 1995. Since then these have been amended by new legislation.

Presidential elections. To qualify for the presidential ballot, a candidate must be a Russian citizen, be at least 35 years old, and have lived in the Russian Federation for the ten years preceding the election. A candidate may be nominated by a political party or run as an independent. Party candidates must be selected by secret ballot at a party conference, and the minutes of such conferences form part of their nomination papers. To be elected president, a candidate must secure more than half the total votes, including invalid votes. If no candidate achieves this in the first-round ballot, a second round is held between the two leading candidates. For the first three presidential elections, a turnout of 50 per cent in the first round was required for the election to be valid. This requirement was abolished by an amendment to the law in April 2007.

In 1996, the right to nominate candidates was restricted to parties registered with the Ministry of Justice at least six months before the election and to groups of at least 100 citizens specifically formed to support an independent candidate. All candidates, whether standing for a party or independent, had to present information about their income for the two years preceding the election. In addition, their supporters had to collect at least one million valid signatures endorsing their nomination, of which no more than seven per cent could be from any one subject of the Federation. These signatures formed part of the nomination petition presented to the Central Election Commission (CEC) in order to request registration for a place on the ballot. In total, 17 candidates submitted nomination petitions. The CEC refused six on the grounds that, after exclusion of invalid signatures, the total number of signatures was fewer than one million, and the Supreme Court upheld its decisions (CEC, 1996a: 97, 99). None of these candidates was considered a front-runner. Two candidates, Grigory Yavlinsky of Yabloko and Vladimir Zhirinovsky of the Liberal Democratic Party of Russia (LDPR), successfully registered for a place on the ballot as nominees of their parties. Nine candidates, including the incumbent Boris Yeltsin, successfully registered as independents. Of these, four were also leaders of political parties, including Gennady Zyuganov, head of the largest party in the Duma, the Communists (KPRF). In the tables below, we identify these leaders as party candidates rather than independents. One independent, nominally a KPRF member, withdrew at the last minute in favour of Zyuganov, leaving ten candidates on the election day ballot.

For the 2000 election, income declarations for candidates were extended to cover the property and liabilities of the candidate and his or her spouse and children, and faults in these declarations could justify refusal of a nomination petition. As the 2000 election was held early, the number of valid signatures required for a petition was halved to 500,000. The number of signatures presented could exceed the required number by 15 per cent to allow for invalid signatures. In total, 15 candidates submitted nomination petitions. The CEC refused two because of faults in signatures and two withdrew. Initially, Vladimir Zhirinovsky's petition was rejected because of faults in his property and income declaration, but he successfully appealed to the Supreme Court (CEC, 2000a: 63f.).

In 2004 the right to nominate was restricted to groups of at least 500 citizens supporting an independent candidate and to parties registered with the Ministry of

Justice on the day of the announcement of the election by the Federation Council. Income and property declarations for candidates and their spouses and children were extended to cover the four years preceding the election, but faults in these declarations no longer constituted grounds for rejecting a nomination petition. Instead, the declarations were merely made public by the CEC. The number of valid signatures required was set at two million and the number of signatures presented could exceed the required number by 25 per cent. In total, 11 candidates submitted nomination petitions. Of these, two withdrew, one had his petition rejected for mistakes in documentation, and one was rejected because the nominating bloc, Motherland (*Rodina*), did not follow correct procedures (OSCE/ODIHR, 2004a: 9). The CEC accepted nominations of seven candidates. Ivan Rybkin, who acknowledged financial support from Boris Berezovsky, withdrew his candidacy ten days before the election claiming to have been abducted during the campaign by unidentified persons.

In 2008 parties winning seats in the immediately preceding Duma election were exempt from the requirement to collect signatures as part of their nomination petition. As in 2004, nominations were also open to independent candidates with supporters' groups of 500 or more citizens and to parties registered with the Ministry of Justice when the election was announced. Income and property declarations covering the four years preceding the election were made public by the CEC. The number of valid signatures required for nomination by a non-Duma party or as an independent continued to be two million, but the maximum number of signatures presented in excess of the required number was reduced to five per cent. In total, five candidates submitted nomination petitions. Three Duma parties nominated candidates while Fair Russia endorsed United Russia's, Dmitry Medvedev, who had been hand-picked by Vladimir Putin. Two nominees were independents. The former prime minister, Mikhail Kasyanov, had his petition rejected for having too many invalid signatures, but Democratic Party leader Andrei Bogdanov registered successfully.

Duma elections. The 1993 Duma election was conducted under the terms of a presidential decree issued in November of that year. Detailed laws governing the election of the Duma and the president were first adopted in 1995. Under the system in effect from 1993 to 2003, half the 450 Duma members were elected by a party-list system of proportional representation (PR) and half from single-member districts (SMDs). Every voter therefore received two ballots. To share in the distribution of PR seats, a party had to receive at least five per cent of the total national vote. The Hare method was used to allocate seats. To win an SMD seat, a simple plurality of the vote was sufficient. A turnout of at least 25 per cent in the PR list or in a single-member district was required for the results to be valid.

Changes to the electoral law in 2005 abolished the SMDs. All 450 Duma seats have since been allocated by proportional representation. Before the 2007 election, further amendments eliminated the turnout requirement, raised the PR threshold to seven per cent (K. Wilson, 2006; Moraski, 2007), and removed the option of voting 'against all' parties or candidates (see McAllister and White, 2008).

Single-member districts. The SMD ballot offered a choice of individuals who could stand as independents or be nominated by a registered party. In 1993 any party affiliation of an SMD candidate could not be given on the ballot. In subsequent elections, the party nominating an SMD candidate had to be indicated on the ballot. All candidates, whether nominated by a party or independent, required a petition with signatures of at least one per cent of the electorate in the district. In 1999 candidates were given the option of paying a cash deposit of 83,490 rubles, returnable if the candidate won five per cent of the district vote. In 2003 the deposit was 900,000 rubles. A candidate could run both on a party list and in a single-member district. If seats were won on both ballots, the candidate sat in the Duma for a single-member district and the PR seat went to the next person on the party's list. Candidates were required to submit income and property declarations with their nomination papers.

Single-member districts had many independent candidates (Table 17.5c; Hale, 2007). There were 873 independent candidates in 1993. The number peaked in 1999 with 1,149 candidates, an average of more than five independent candidates in a single-member district. Moreover, major list parties did not nominate candidates in many districts. In half the seats in 1993 none did so. Many parties winning list seats ran candidates in fewer than 100 single-member districts.

In the median district in 1993 there were 7 candidates; in 1995, 11; in 1999, 10; and in 2003, 13 candidates. With so many candidates, the median winner in 1993 received 25.5 per cent of the district vote; in 1995, 26.2 per cent; in 1999, 30.9 per cent; and in 2003, 39.6 per cent. In 1993 and 1995, if 'against all' received the most votes, the runner-up, that is, the individual with the most positive votes, was the winner. In 1993, this occurred in 29 districts, and in 1995 in 3 districts. In 1999 and 2003, if 'against all' won the most votes, a repeat election was held; in 1999 this occurred in eight districts, and in the following election in three districts.

Collectively, independent candidates consistently won a substantial number of the 225 SMD seats. In 1993 independents took more than half; in 1995, 77; in 1999, 114 seats; and 68 in 2003. Since a majority of nominal independents then joined a party bloc on taking their seat in the Duma the following month, this created a disjunction between the seats parties won on election day and their seats in the Duma.

rubles. The deposit is returnable if the party wins four per cent or more of the vote. In January 2009, the Duma abolished deposits for elections at all levels.

The Central Election Commission then checks the validity of signatures collected. If a sample of signatures contains five per cent or more which are false or invalid, the CEC can refuse the party a place on the ballot. It can also do so on procedural grounds or in case of gross violations of election law. Rejected parties have the right of appeal to the Supreme Court, which must consider the appeal within five days.

Under the terms of the law on political parties (2001), public funding is given to parties winning at least three per cent of the list vote in the preceding Duma election or nominating a presidential candidate doing so. In addition, a party may generate income by collecting membership dues and by conducting other legal commercial activities. Maximum permitted campaign expenditure at the federal level is 400 million rubles, of which no more than 50 per cent can come from the party's own resources. The remainder must come from donations made specifically for the given electoral campaign. At the level of subjects of the federation, the maximum expenditure varies from 6 million to 30 million rubles depending on the population of the region. Foreign companies, foreign organizations, and foreign persons and Russian companies with more than 30 per cent foreign capital are not permitted to make campaign donations. The CEC may ask the Supreme Court to annul a party's registration on specified grounds, including exceeding campaign expenditure limits by more than five per cent, calling for violent seizure of power or overthrow of the constitution, or inciting social, racial, national, or religious hatred. The CEC can also use these provisions to exclude individual candidates. If the number of excluded candidates exceeds 25 per cent of the list or if, after exclusions, the number of party regional subdivisions falls below 80, the party's place on the ballot is forfeited.

In 1993 there were 130 electoral associations or parties; of these, 35 certified lists of candidates, 21 submitted nomination petitions, and 8 were disallowed, leaving 13 parties on the ballot (Lentini, 1995). In 1995, of 273 registered electoral associations, 69 certified lists of candidates, 51 submitted nomination petitions, 8 were disallowed, and 43 parties appeared on the ballot. Yabloko and Derzhava were initially disqualified by the CEC, but appeals to the Supreme Court gained each a place on the ballot. In 1999, of 139 eligible parties, 34 certified lists of candidates and 31 submitted formal nominations, of which 17 paid a deposit. Vladimir Zhirinovsky's party, the Liberal Democrats, was disqualified because of faults in the income and property declarations of its candidates, but Zhirinovsky was able to register a list under the name of the Zhirinovsky Bloc, combining several other electoral associations. Twenty-six parties appeared on the ballot (CEC, 2000b: 66, 70). In 2003, 44 associations had the right to nominate candidates; 26 parties or blocs certified lists of candidates, and 23 presented nomination petitions, of which only one paid the deposit. None was disallowed, producing 23 party lists on the ballot (CEC, 2003b). When an election was called in September 2007, only 15 political parties were registered and eligible to nominate candidates. Of these, 14 certified lists of candidates and presented nomination petitions. Three were refused on the basis of insufficient valid signatures, leaving 11 party lists on the ballot.

The requirement to receive at least five per cent of the list vote to qualify for PR seats was an incentive to electoral associations with limited support to combine in an electoral bloc. Of the 43 registered lists on the ballot in 1995, 18 belonged to blocs combining 49 different parties. However, none of the blocs qualified for list seats. Of the 26 lists on the ballot in 1999, 11 were those of electoral blocs containing 36 parties. Four of the six successful lists were electoral blocs: Unity (seven associations), Fatherland–OVR (five), Right Forces (four), and the Zhirinovsky Bloc (two). Of the 23 registered lists on the 2003 ballot, five were electoral blocs containing 13 parties (CEC, 2003b). Only one of the electoral blocs, Motherland, was able to win list seats. Unlike previous elections, in 2007 parties could not form a bloc in order to improve their chances of clearing the seven per cent threshold.

The large number of parties attracting some votes but failing to win enough to pass the PR threshold has resulted in a substantial albeit varying number of wasted votes, that is, votes cast for parties that do not gain any list seats in the Duma. In 1993, 13 per cent of the ballots did not elect any Duma members and in 1995 a total of 49 per cent was wasted. The 1999 election saw 17 per cent of the list votes wasted and the 2003 election 28 per cent. With fewer parties on the ballot and greater support for United Russia in 2007, only seven per cent of votes were wasted.

Wasted votes introduce a degree of disproportionality into a nominally proportional representation system (Figure 17.1). Every party clearing the threshold benefits by receiving a larger percentage of list seats than its share of list votes – and larger parties benefit most. In 1995 the discrepancies were extreme: the Communist Party won 44.0 per cent of the list seats with only 22.3 per cent of the list vote. The discrepancies are also variable. When the wasted vote rose in 2003, United Russia was the big beneficiary; it won 53.3 per cent of the Duma list seats with 37.6 per cent of the vote. The law enacted before the 1999 election stipulated that if parties passing the five per cent threshold collectively won no more than 50 per cent of the vote, parties with at least three per cent of the vote would be allocated seats until the 50 per cent total was achieved, failing which the election was invalid. Before the 2003

Figure 17.1. DISPROPORTIONALITY IN DUMA VOTES AND SEATS

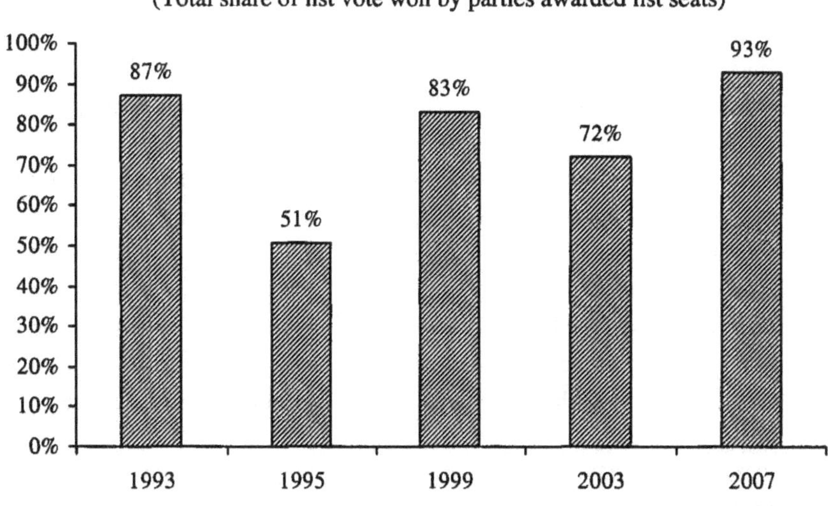

Source: Results reported in this chapter.

election, the law was changed to stipulate that at least three parties should win seats in the Duma. If only two parties passed the five per cent threshold, seats would be allocated to parties until their combined vote exceeded half the total vote. Beginning with the 2007 election, if the total vote for parties passing the seven per cent threshold does not exceed 60 per cent, then parties with less than seven per cent of the total vote also win seats until the combined total exceeds 60 per cent. If one party wins more than 60 per cent of the vote and each of its competitors fails to qualify for seats by passing the seven per cent threshold, then the second 'biggest' party also qualifies for seats. At the 2007 Duma election United Russia won 64.3 per cent of the list vote, but the special provision for ensuring another party in the Duma did not need to be invoked since three other parties cleared the seven per cent threshold.

The tradition of electoral manipulation from previous regimes appears to some extent to have persisted (A. Wilson, 2005; Gel'man, 2007; OSCE/ODIHR, 2000, 2000a, 2004). Before the 2007 Duma and 2008 presidential elections, the OSCE's Office of Democratic Institutions and Human Rights (ODIHR) cited the restrictive terms on election observation proposed by the Russian CEC and did not send international observers (OSCE/ODIHR, 2007, 2008). The CEC rejected these criticisms and called for reform of the ODIHR (CEC, 2007a, 2008b). The Bureau of the Parliamentary Assembly of the Council of Europe (PACE) accepted CEC invitations to observe the elections. Their reports concluded that both elections were not fair, because of aspects of electoral law, media bias, and use of administrative resources for campaigning (PACE/BOA, 2008, 2008a). International observers did not deny that the results broadly reflected popular preferences, a conclusion borne out by independent public opinion polls and by the views of Russian electors (see Rose and Mishler, 2009).

The election results given here are as reported in the official protocols issued to confirm the award of seats in the Duma and the presidency. As the result of subsequent court cases and the discovery of clerical errors by election officials, results may be changed trivially without affecting the award of seats. In the following tables all percentages are based on the total vote, including invalid votes and votes against all. The data on votes in the SMD elections are first-round totals; the data on SMD seats won include the results of follow-up elections in a few districts.

DATES OF ELECTIONS

President	Duma
16 June, 3 July 1996	12 December 1993
26 March 2000	17 December 1995
14 March 2004	19 December 1999
2 March 2008	7 December 2003
	2 December 2007

REFERENCES

CEC (Central Electoral Commission), 1993. "Postanovlenie 'Ob ustanovlenii obshchikh itogov vyborov deputatov Gosudarstvennoi Dumy Federalnogo Sobraniya Rossiiskoi Federatsii'", *Rossiiskaya Gazeta*, 28 December, 2–5.

———, 1993a. "Postanovlenie Tsentralnoi Izbiratelnoi Komissii Rossiiskoi Federatsii 'O rezultatakh vsenarodnogo golosovaniya po proektu Konstitutsii Rossiiskoi Federatsii'", *Byulleten* 10 (December), 4–5.

———, 1994. "Rezultaty vyborov deputatov Gosudarstvennoi Dumy", *Byulleten* 1, 12, 67–80.

———, 1995. "Protokol Tsentralnoi Izbiratelnoi Komissii Rossiiskoi Federatsii o raspredelenii deputatskikh mandatov po obshchefederalnomu okrugu mezhdu izbiratelnymi obedineniyami, izbiratelnymi blokami", http://www.cikrf.ru/vib_arhiv/gosduma/1995/files/1995-Protokol_CIK.doc.

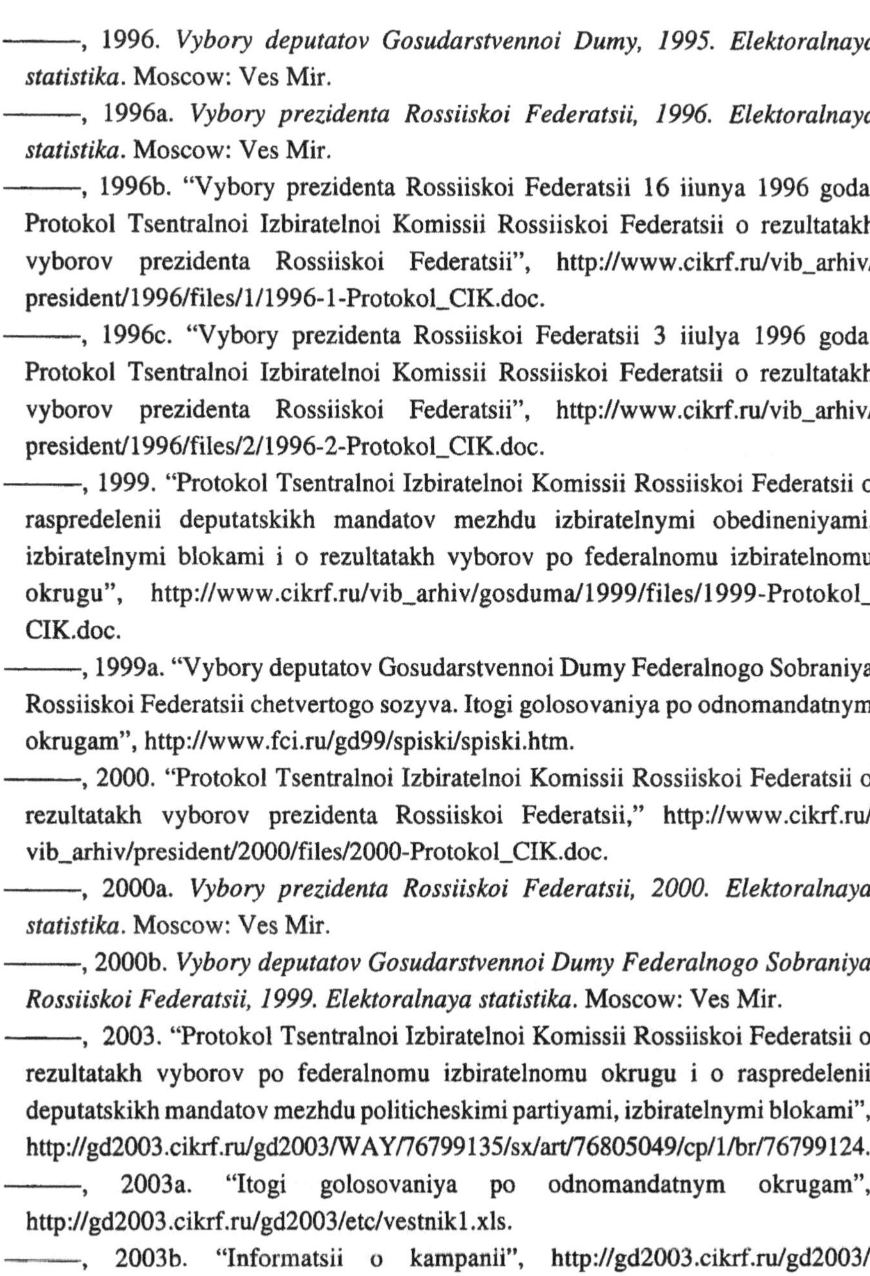

———, 1996. *Vybory deputatov Gosudarstvennoi Dumy, 1995. Elektoralnaya statistika*. Moscow: Ves Mir.

———, 1996a. *Vybory prezidenta Rossiiskoi Federatsii, 1996. Elektoralnaya statistika*. Moscow: Ves Mir.

———, 1996b. "Vybory prezidenta Rossiiskoi Federatsii 16 iiunya 1996 goda. Protokol Tsentralnoi Izbiratelnoi Komissii Rossiiskoi Federatsii o rezultatakh vyborov prezidenta Rossiiskoi Federatsii", http://www.cikrf.ru/vib_arhiv/president/1996/files/1/1996-1-Protokol_CIK.doc.

———, 1996c. "Vybory prezidenta Rossiiskoi Federatsii 3 iiulya 1996 goda. Protokol Tsentralnoi Izbiratelnoi Komissii Rossiiskoi Federatsii o rezultatakh vyborov prezidenta Rossiiskoi Federatsii", http://www.cikrf.ru/vib_arhiv/president/1996/files/2/1996-2-Protokol_CIK.doc.

———, 1999. "Protokol Tsentralnoi Izbiratelnoi Komissii Rossiiskoi Federatsii o raspredelenii deputatskikh mandatov mezhdu izbiratelnymi obedineniyami, izbiratelnymi blokami i o rezultatakh vyborov po federalnomu izbiratelnomu okrugu", http://www.cikrf.ru/vib_arhiv/gosduma/1999/files/1999-Protokol_CIK.doc.

———, 1999a. "Vybory deputatov Gosudarstvennoi Dumy Federalnogo Sobraniya Rossiiskoi Federatsii chetvertogo sozyva. Itogi golosovaniya po odnomandatnym okrugam", http://www.fci.ru/gd99/spiski/spiski.htm.

———, 2000. "Protokol Tsentralnoi Izbiratelnoi Komissii Rossiiskoi Federatsii o rezultatakh vyborov prezidenta Rossiiskoi Federatsii," http://www.cikrf.ru/vib_arhiv/president/2000/files/2000-Protokol_CIK.doc.

———, 2000a. *Vybory prezidenta Rossiiskoi Federatsii, 2000. Elektoralnaya statistika*. Moscow: Ves Mir.

———, 2000b. *Vybory deputatov Gosudarstvennoi Dumy Federalnogo Sobraniya Rossiiskoi Federatsii, 1999. Elektoralnaya statistika*. Moscow: Ves Mir.

———, 2003. "Protokol Tsentralnoi Izbiratelnoi Komissii Rossiiskoi Federatsii o rezultatakh vyborov po federalnomu izbiratelnomu okrugu i o raspredelenii deputatskikh mandatov mezhdu politicheskimi partiyami, izbiratelnymi blokami", http://gd2003.cikrf.ru/gd2003/WAY/76799135/sx/art/76805049/cp/1/br/76799124.

———, 2003a. "Itogi golosovaniya po odnomandatnym okrugam", http://gd2003.cikrf.ru/gd2003/etc/vestnik1.xls.

———, 2003b. "Informatsii o kampanii", http://gd2003.cikrf.ru/gd2003/normat_acts.

———, 2004. "Vybory prezidenta Rossiiskoi Federatsii 14 marta 2004 goda. Protokol Tsentralnoi Izbiratelnoi Komissii Rossiiskoi Federatsii o rezultatakh vyborov prezidenta Rossiiskoi Federatsii", http://pr2004.cikrf.ru/protokol_cik_pr.

———, 2007. "Politicheskie partii, obshcherossiiskie obshchestvennye obedineniya na vyborakh v Gosudarstvennuyu Dumu Federalnogo Sobraniya chetvertogo sozyva", http://www.cikrf.ru/cikrf/ politparty/parties_on_election.jsp.

———, 2007a. "Kommentarii chlena TsIK Rossii I. B. Borisova ob otkaze BDIPCh OBSE prisutstvovat na vyborakh v Rossii", press release, 16 November, http://www.cikrf.ru/aboutcik/activity/int/int_borisov_161107.jsp.

———, 2008. "Dannye protokola TsIK Rossii o rezultatakh vyborov deputatov Gosudarstvennoi Dumy Federalnogo Sobraniya", http://www.vybory.izbirkom.ru.

———, 2008a. "Rezultaty vyborov prezidenta Rossiiskoi Federatsii", http://www.vybory.izbirkom.ru.

———, 2008b. "Press konferentsiya chlena TsIK Rossii I. B. Borisova v informatsionnom agenstve RIA Novosti na temu Prisutstvie mezhdunarodnykh nabliudatelei na vyborakh prezidenta Rossiiskoi Federatsii 08 fevralya 2008".

Emmons, Terence, 1983. *The Formation of Political Parties and the First National Elections in Russia.* Cambridge, MA: Harvard University Press.

Gel'man, Vladimir, ed., 2007. *Tretii elektoralnyi tsikl v Rossii, 2003–2004.* Saint Petersburg: European University at Saint Petersburg Press.

Hale, Henry E., 2007. *Why Not Parties in Russia? Democracy, Federalism, and the State.* New York: Cambridge University Press.

Karklins, Rasma, 1986. "Soviet Elections Revisited: Voter Abstention in Noncompetitive Voting", *American Political Science Review* 80, 449–69.

Lentini, Peter, ed., 1995. *Elections and Political Order in Russia.* Budapest: Central European University Press.

McAllister, Ian, and Stephen White, 2008. "Voting Against All in Post-Communist Russia", *Europe-Asia Studies* 60, 1, 67–87.

McFaul, Michael, 2001. *Russia's Revolution: Political Change from Gorbachev to Putin.* Ithaca: Cornell University Press.

McFaul, Michael, and Nikolai Petrov, eds., 1998. *Politicheskii almanakh Rossii 1997.* Moscow: Carnegie Endowment for International Peace.

Moraski, Bryon, 2007. "Electoral System Reform in Democracy's Grey Zone: Lessons from Putin's Russia", *Government and Opposition* 42, 4, 536–63.

OSCE/ODIHR (Organization for Security and Cooperation in Europe/Office for Democratic Institutions and Human Rights), 2000. *Elections to the State Duma 19 December 1999: Final Report.* Warsaw: ODIHR.

———, 2000a. *Presidential Election 26 March 2000: Final Report.* Warsaw: ODIHR.

———, 2004. *Elections to the State Duma 7 December 2003: Final Report.* Warsaw: ODIHR.

———, 2004a. *Presidential Election 14 March 2004: Final Report.* Warsaw: ODIHR.

———, 2007. "ODIHR Unable to Observe Russian Duma Elections", press release, 16 November, http://www.osce.org/item/27967.html.

———, 2008. "OSCE/ODIHR Regrets that Restrictions Force Cancellation of Election Observation Mission to Russian Federation", press release, 7 February, http://www.osce.org/odihr/item_1_29599.html.

PACE/BOA (Parliamentary Assembly of the Council of Europe/Bureau of the Assembly), 2008. *Observation of the Parliamentary Elections in the Russian Federation (2 December 2007)*, http://assembly.coe.int/main.asp?Link=/documents/workingdocs/doc07/edoc11473.htm.

———, 2008a. *Observation of the Presidential Election in the Russian Federation (2 March 2008)*, Document 11536, http://assembly.coe.int/main.asp?Link=/documents/workingdocs/doc08/edoc11536.htm.

Radkey, Oliver, 1950. *The Election of the Russian Constituent Assembly of 1917.* Cambridge, MA: Harvard University Press.

Rose, Richard and William Mishler, 2009. "How Do Electors Respond to an 'Unfair' Election? The Experience of Russians", *Post-Soviet Affairs* 25.

Rose, Richard and William Mishler, forthcoming. "A Supply–Demand Model of Party-System Institutionalization: The Russian Case", *Party Politics.*

White, Stephen, Richard Rose, and Ian McAllister, 1997. *How Russia Votes.* Chatham, NJ: Chatham House.

Wilson, Andrew, 2005. *Virtual Politics: Faking Democracy in the Post-Soviet World.* New Haven: Yale University Press.

Wilson, Kenneth, 2006. "Party-System Development Under Putin", *Post-Soviet Affairs* 22, 4, 314–48.

Table 17.3 RUSSIAN POLITICAL PARTIES

1 *Liberal Democratic Party of Russia* (Liberalno-Demokraticheskaya Partiya Rossii, LDPR). Founded 1990 under maverick nationalist Vladimir Zhirinovsky as an all-USSR party. In 1999, when LDPR was disqualified from list ballot, candidates were registered in Zhirinovsky Bloc, combining two smaller parties. 1993–

2 *Russia's Choice* (Vybor Rossii). Founded October 1993 as pro-market and pro-Yeltsin party, including part of Democratic Russia movement of 1990. Leaders included Yegor Gaidar, acting prime minister (1992), and Anatoly Chubais, first deputy prime minister (1994–96). Contested 1995 as Democratic Choice of Russia–United Democrats (Demokraticheskii Vybor Rossii–Obedinenye Demokraty,

DVR–OD). 1993–95

3 *Communist Party of the Russian Federation* (Kommunisticheskaya Partiya Rossiiskoi Federatsii, KPRF). Founded late 1992 as successor to Communist Party of the Soviet Union, banned after failed August 1991 coup. Led by Gennady Zyuganov, presidential candidate in 1996, 2000, and 2008. 1993–

4 *Women of Russia* (Zhenshchiny Rossii, ZR). Founded October 1993 by a variety of women's organizations. In 2003 supported United Russia. 1993–99

5 *Agrarian Party of Russia* (Agrarnaya Partiya Rossii, APR). Founded February 1993 by deputies in Agrarian Union of collective and state farm employees. In 1999 failed to contest due to split between allies of Communists and allies of Fatherland–All Russia. 1993–

6 *Yabloko.* Founded October 1993 as Yavlinsky/Boldyrev/Lukin Bloc, which has Russian acronym Yabloko (Apple). Led by Grigory Yavlinsky, deputy premier for economic reform in RSFSR government in 1990, and presidential candidate in 1996 and 2000. In 1999, criticized government over Chechnya. 1993–

7 *Party of Russian Unity and Concord* (Partiya Rossiiskogo Edinstva i Soglasiya, PRES). Regionalist party founded October 1993 by Sergei Shakhrai. 1993–95

8 *Democratic Party of Russia* (Demokraticheskaya Partiya Rossii, DPR). Founded December 1990 under Nikolai Travkin. Part of pre-1992 Democratic Russia movement. Disbanded in 1994; re-organized in 2001. Current leader Andrei Bogdanov, presidential candidate in 2008. 1993–

9 *Russian Movement for Democratic Reforms* (Rossiiskoe Dvizhenie Demokraticheskikh Reform, RDDR). Organization founded 1992 by ex-Moscow mayor Gavriil Popov, St Petersburg mayor Anatoly Sobchak, and eye surgeon Svyatoslav Fedorov. 1993

10 *Civic Union for Stability, Justice, and Progress* (Grazhdanskii Soyuz Stabilnosti, Spravedlivosti i Progresa, GSSSP). Formed October 1993 as alliance of Democratic Party of Russia; People's Party of Free Russia, led by Aleksandr Rutskoi, vice president (1991–93); and industrial groups led by Arkady Volsky. In 1995 succeeded by Union of Labour. 1993

11 *Future of Russia–New Names* (Budushchee Rossii–Novye Imena, BR/NI). Formed October 1993 by the Youth Movement of People's Party of Free Russia and Civic Union. 1993

12 *Cedar* (Kedr). Constructive Ecological Movement (Konstruktivnoe Ekologicheskoe Dvizhenie). Green party founded in 1993. Disqualified in 1999 after withdrawal of two leading candidates. In 2003, contested with other environmental groups as *Russian Ecological Party Greens* (Rossiiskaya Ekologicheskaya Partiya Zelenye). In 2006 allied with Yabloko. 1993–2003

13 *Dignity and Charity* (Dostoinstvo i Miloserdie, DM). Bloc formed in October 1993 by organizations including pensioners, veterans, invalids, and victims of Chernobyl. 1993

14 *Our Home Is Russia* (Nash Dom – Rossiya, NDR). Launched April 1995 on initiative of President Yeltsin and led by Viktor Chernomyrdin, prime minister (1992–98). 1995–99

15 *Communists of the USSR* (Kommunisty SSSR). Full name: Communists–Working Russia–For the Soviet Union (Kommunisty: Trudovaya Rossii: za Sovetskii Soyuz). Favours restoration of Soviet system. 1995–99

16 *Congress of Russian Communities* (Kongres Russkikh Obshchin, KRO). Formed March 1993 under Dmitry Rogozin to promote Russian interests in post-Soviet states. Failed to collect required number of signatures to participate in 1993 election. In 1995 joined by presidential candidate General Aleksandr Lebed. 1995–99

17 *Party of Workers' Self-Government* (Partiya Samoupravleniya Trudyashchikhsya, PST). Founded 1995 by Svyatoslav Fedorov, formerly of RDDR, to represent small and medium-sized businesses. 1995

18 *Great Power* (Derzhava). Full name: Social Patriotic Movement Great Power (Sotsialno-Patrioticheskoe Dvizhenie Derzhava). Founded in 1994 by a Yeltsin opponent, Aleksandr Rutskoi, vice president (1991–93). 1995

19 *Forward Russia!* (Vpered, Rossiya!). Founded 1995 by Boris Fedorov, finance minister (1993–94). 1995

20 *Power to the People!* (Vlast Narodu!). Led by Sergei Baburin, founder of Russian National Union (Rossiiskii Obshchenatsionalnyi Soyuz, RONS), which was banned from contesting 1993 election, and Nikolai Ryzhkov, USSR prime minister (1985–91) and 1991 presidential candidate. 1995

21 *Union of Labour* (Soyuz Truda). Outgrowth of Civic Union (GSSSP) founded in 1995 by industrialist Vladimir Shcherbakov. 1995

22 *Pamfilova–Gurov–Lysenko Bloc*. Led by Ella Pamfilova, ex-minister for social protection (1991–93) and presidential candidate in 2000; Aleksandr Gurov, ex-head of Interior Ministry's Organized Crime Department; and Vladimir Lysenko, opponent of first Chechen war. 1995

23 *Ivan Rybkin Bloc*. Created April 1995 on initiative of President Yeltsin. Eponymous leader was speaker of Russian Duma (1994–95). 1995

24 *Stanislav Govorukhin Bloc*. Eponymous leader, a film director, was formerly leader of Democratic Party of Russia in the Duma. 1995

25 *Unity* (Edinstvo). Full name: Inter-Regional Movement Unity (Mezhregionalnoe Dvizhenie Edinstvo; acronym Medved, Bear). Formed in October 1999 under leadership of Sergei Shoigu, minister in Yeltsin and Putin cabinets. Endorsed by Putin

during 1999 Duma election In 2001, merged with Fatherland–All Russia to form United Russia. 1999

26 *Fatherland–All Russia* (Otechestvo–Vsya Rossiya, OVR). Formed in 1999 as alliance of Fatherland, founded in 1998 by Yuri Luzhkov, mayor of Moscow, and All-Russia movement, led by President Mintimer Shaimiev of Tatarstan. Yevgeny Primakov, prime minister (1998–99), also joined. In 2001 OVR merged into United Russia. 1999

27 *Union of Right Forces* (Soyuz Pravykh Sil, SPS). Pro-market bloc initially including Boris Nemtsov, first deputy prime minister (1997–98); Sergei Kirienko, prime minister (April–August 1998); Irina Khakamada, presidential candidate in 2000; and Yegor Gaidar and Anatoly Chubais, formerly of Russia's Choice. Putin expressed guarded support for SPS before 1999 election. Kirienko left party in 2000 to serve as president's representative in Volga district. After 2003 election, remaining co-chairs resigned. In 2005, Nikita Belykh, regional politician from Perm, was elected chair. He left the party in 2008, and later that year was appointed governor of Kirov Oblast. Chubais remains in the party leadership. 1999–

28 *Party of Pensioners* (Partiya Pensionerov). Founded in 1997. Contested in 2003 in a bloc with Party of Social Fairness (Partiya Sotsialnoi Spravedlivosti, PSS). In 2005 PSS joined Social Democratic Party of Russia. 1999–2003

29 *For Citizens' Dignity* (Za Grazhdanskoe Dostoinstvo, ZGD). Founded 1998 and led by Ella Pamfilova. 1999

30 *Movement in Support of the Army, Defence Industry, and Military Science* (Obshcherossiiskoe Politicheskoe Dvizhenie v Podderzhku Armii, Oboronnoi Promyshlennosti i Voennoi Nauki, DPA). Founded 1997 by Viktor Ilyukhin, formerly of KPRF. 1999

31 *Nikolaev–Fedorov Bloc.* Full name: Bloc of General Andrei Nikolaev and Academician Svyatoslav Fedorov (Blok Generala Andreya Nikolaeva i Akademika Svyatoslava Fedorova). Alliance of a border guards' general and the eye surgeon formerly in RDDR. 1999

32 *Russian People's Union* (Rossiiskii Obshchenarodnyi Soyuz, ROS). Based on Power to the People! and led by Sergei Baburin. Before 2003 election, ROS joined Motherland, but afterwards formed its own faction in Duma. 1999

33 *Russian Socialist Party* (Russkaya Sotsialisticheskaya Partiya, RSP). Founded by entrepreneur Vladimir Bryntsalov. 1999

34 *Spiritual Heritage Movement* (Vserossiiskoe Obshchestvenno-Politicheskoe Dvizhenie Dukhovnoe Nasledie, DN). Led by Aleksei Podberezkin, formerly of KPRF. 1999

35 *United Russia* (Edinaya Rossiya, ER). Formed in 2001 by the merger of Unity

(Edinstvo) with Fatherland–All Russia (Otechestvo–Vsya Rossiya, OVR). In 2003 Vladimir Putin endorsed United Russia and in 2007 he headed its Duma list. Dmitry Medvedev was its presidential candidate in 2008. Putin was elected party chairman in April 2008, and then became prime minister. 2003–

36 *Motherland–People's Patriotic Union* (Rodina–Narodno-patrioticheskii Soyuz, R–NPS). Bloc formed in 2003 by Party of Russian Regions (later re-named Motherland (Rodina)), Socialist United Party Spiritual Heritage, and Party of National Rebirth People's Will. Split in 2004 into factions led by presidential candidate Sergei Glazyev and Dmitry Rogozin, formerly of KRO, who supported Putin in the election. In 2005, People's Will faction, led by Sergei Baburin, formed its own splinter inside Duma, but Glazyev and Rogozin were reconciled. In 2006 Motherland/R–NPS merged into Fair Russia. 2003

37 *Party of the Rebirth of Russia–Russian Party of Life* (Partiya Vozrozhdeniya Rossii–Rossiiskaya Partiya Zhizni, PVR–RPZh). Bloc of parties led respectively by KPRF Duma speaker (1996–2003) Gennady Seleznev and Federation Council chair (2001–) Sergei Mironov. In October 2006, Party of Life joined Fair Russia. In 2007, Seleznev joined list of Patriots of Russia. 2003

38 *People's Party of the Russian Federation* (Narodnaya Partiya Rossiiskoi Federatsii, NPRF). Formed on basis of People's Deputy Duma faction (1999–2003). Its deputies sat with United Russia in 2003–07 Duma. 2003

39 *Conceptual Party Unity* (Kontseptualnaya Partiya Edinenie, KPE). Oriented towards mysticism. 2003

40 *New Course: Automobile Russia* (Novy Kurs–Avtomobilnaya Rossiya, NK–AR). Bloc including anti-Berezovsky wing of Liberal Russia (Liberalnaya Rossiya), Republican Party of Russia (Respublikanskaya Partiya Rossii), and Motorists' Movement of Russia (Dvizhenie Avtomobilistov Rossii). 2003

41 *Development of Enterprise* (Razvitie Predprinimatelstva, RP). Formed by a pro-business group. 2003

42 *Great Russia–Eurasia Union* (Velikaya Rossiya–Evraziiskii Soyuz, VR–ES). Bloc of six minor parties favouring re-integration of Soviet republics. 2003

43 *Fair Russia* (Spravedlivaya Rossiya, SR). Formed 2006 by merger of Motherland–People's Patriotic Union with Party of Pensioners and Party of Life. Led by Sergei Mironov, Speaker of Federation Council (2001–). In December 2007 endorsed United Russia's presidential candidate, Dmitry Medvedev. 2007–

44 *Civic Strength* (Grazhdanskaya Sila, GS). Pro-market party that endorsed Dmitry Medvedev's candidacy in 2008. 2007–

Table 17.4a PRESIDENTIAL VOTE: 16 June, 3 July 1996

	1st Round	%	2nd Round	%
Electorate	108,495,023		108,600,730	
Valid Votes	74,515,019	68.7	73,926,240	68.1
Invalid Votes	1,072,120	1.0	780,405	0.7
Total Votes	75,587,139	69.7	74,706,645	68.8
Boris Yeltsin, Independent	26,665,495	35.3	40,208,384	53.8
Gennady Zyuganov, KPRF	24,211,686	32.0	30,113,306	40.3
Aleksandr Lebed, KRO	10,974,736	14.5	—	—
Grigory Yavlinsky, Yabloko	5,550,752	7.3	—	—
Vladimir Zhirinovsky, LDPR	4,311,479	5.7	—	—
Svyatoslav Fedorov, PST	699,158	0.9	—	—
Mikhail Gorbachev, Independent	386,069	0.5	—	—
Martin Shakkum, Independent	277,068	0.4	—	—
Yuri Vlasov, Independent	151,282	0.2	—	—
Vladimir Bryntsalov, RSP	123,065	0.2	—	—
Aman-Geldy Tuleev, KPRF[1]	308	0	—	—
Against all candidates	1,163,921	1.5	3,604,550	4.8

Sources: CEC, 1996a: 127; 1996b; 1996c.

[1] Withdrew in favour of Zyuganov. Votes reported were cast early.

Table 17.4b PRESIDENTIAL VOTE: 26 March 2000

		%
Electorate	109,372,046	
Valid Votes	74,369,773	68.0
Invalid Votes	701,003	0.6
Total Votes	75,070,776	68.6
Vladimir Putin, Independent	39,740,434	52.9
Gennady Zyuganov, KPRF	21,928,471	29.2
Grigory Yavlinsky, Yabloko	4,351,452	5.8
Aman-Geldy Tuleev, Independent	2,217,361	3.0
Vladimir Zhirinovsky, LDPR	2,026,513	2.7
Konstantin Titov, Independent	1,107,269	1.5
Ella Pamfilova, ZGD	758,966	1.0
Stanislav Govorukhin, Independent	328,723	0.4
Yuri Skuratov, Independent	319,263	0.4
Aleksei Podberezkin, DN	98,175	0.1
Umar Dzhabrailov, Independent	78,498	0.1
Against all candidates	1,414,648	1.9

Source: CEC, 2000.

Table 17.4c PRESIDENTIAL VOTE: 14 March 2004

		%
Electorate	108,064,281	
Valid Votes	68,925,785	63.8
Invalid Votes	578,824	0.5
Total Votes	69,504,609	64.3
Vladimir Putin, Independent	49,565,238	71.3
Nikolai Kharitonov, KPRF	9,513,313	13.7
Sergei Glazyev, Independent	2,850,063	4.1
Irina Khakamada, Independent	2,671,313	3.8
Oleg Malyshkin, LDPR	1,405,315	2.0
Sergei Mironov, Party of Life	524,324	0.7
Against all candidates	2,396,219	3.4

Source: CEC, 2004.

Table 17.4d PRESIDENTIAL VOTE: 2 March 2008

		%
Electorate	107,222,016	
Valid Votes	73,731,116	68.8
Invalid Votes	1,015,533	0.9
Total Votes	74,746,649	69.7
Dmitry Medvedev, United Russia	52,530,712	70.3
Gennady Zyuganov, KPRF	13,243,550	17.7
Vladimir Zhirinovsky, LDPR	6,988,510	9.3
Andrei Bogdanov, Independent	968,344	1.3

Source: CEC, 2008a.

Table 17.5a RUSSIA: List Votes for the Duma

	1993		1995		1999		2003		2007	
	List	%	List	%	List	%	List	%		%
Electorate	106,170,835		107,496,558		108,072,348		108,906,244		109,145,517	
Valid Votes	53,751,696	50.6	67,884,200	63.2	65,370,655	60.5	59,684,768	54.8	68,777,136	63.0
Invalid Votes	3,946,002	3.7	1,320,619	1.2	1,296,992	1.2	948,411	0.9	759,929	0.7
Total Votes	57,697,698	54.3	69,204,819	64.4	66,667,647	61.7	60,633,179	55.7	69,537,065	63.7
1 Liberal Democratic Party	12,318,562	21.4	7,737,431	11.2	3,989,932	6.0	6,943,885	11.5	5,660,823	8.1
2 Russia's Choice	8,339,345	14.5	2,674,084	3.9	—	—	—	—	—	—
3 Communist Party	6,666,402	11.6	15,432,963	22.3	16,195,569	24.3	7,647,820	12.6	8,046,886	11.6
4 Women of Russia	4,369,918	7.6	3,188,813	4.6	1,359,042	2.0	—	—	—	—
5 Agrarian Party of Russia	4,292,518	7.4	2,613,127	3.8	—	—	2,205,704	3.6	1,600,234	2.3
6 Yabloko	4,223,219	7.3	4,767,384	6.9	3,955,457	5.9	2,609,823	4.3	1,108,985	1.6
7 Russian Unity and Concord	3,620,035	6.3	245,977	0.4	—	—	—	—	—	—
8 Democratic Party of Russia	2,969,533	5.1	—	—	—	—	136,294	0.2	89,780	0.1
9 Movement for Dem. Reforms	2,191,505	3.8	—	—	—	—	—	—	—	—
10 Civic Union	1,038,193	1.8	—	—	—	—	—	—	—	—
11 Future of Russia	672,283	1.2	—	—	—	—	—	—	—	—
12 Greens	406,789	0.7	962,195	1.4	—	—	253,983	0.4	—	—
13 Dignity and Charity	375,431	0.7	—	—	—	—	—	—	—	—
14 Our Home Is Russia	—	—	7,009,291	10.1	791,160	1.2	—	—	—	—
15 Communists of the USSR	—	—	3,137,406	4.5	1,482,018	2.2	—	—	—	—
16 Congress Rus. Communities: KRO	—	—	2,980,137	4.3	405,295	0.6	—	—	—	—
17 Workers' Self-Government	—	—	2,756,954	4.0	—	—	—	—	—	—
18 Great Power	—	—	1,781,233	2.6	—	—	—	—	—	—
19 Forward Russia!	—	—	1,343,428	1.9	—	—	—	—	—	—
20 Power to the People!	—	—	1,112,873	1.6	—	—	—	—	—	—
21 Union of Labour	—	—	1,076,072	1.6	—	—	—	—	—	—
22 Pamfilova–Gurov–Lysenko	—	—	1,106,812	1.6	—	—	—	—	—	—
23 Ivan Rybkin Bloc	—	—	769,259	1.1	—	—	—	—	—	—

24 Stanislav Govorukhin Bloc	—	—	688,496	1.0	—	—	—	—	—	—
25 Unity	—	—	—	—	15,548,707	23.3	—	—	—	—
35 United Russia	—	—	—	—	—	—	22,779,279	37.6	44,714,241	64.3
26 Fatherland–All Russia	—	—	—	—	8,886,697	13.3	—	—	—	—
27 Union of Right Forces	—	—	—	—	5,676,982	8.5	2,408,356	4.0	669,444	1.0
28 Party of Pensioners	—	—	—	—	1,298,948	1.9	1,874,739	3.1	—	—
29 For Citizens' Dignity	—	—	—	—	402,856	0.6	—	—	—	—
30 Movement for the Army	—	—	—	—	384,392	0.6	—	—	—	—
31 Nikolaev–Fedorov Bloc	—	—	—	—	371,959	0.6	—	—	—	—
32 Russian People's Union	—	—	—	—	245,266	0.4	—	—	—	—
33 Russian Socialist Party	—	—	—	—	156,735	0.2	—	—	—	—
34 Spiritual Heritage	—	—	—	—	67,417	0.1	—	—	—	—
36 Motherland	—	—	—	—	—	—	5,469,556	9.0	—	—
37 Rebirth of Russia–Life	—	—	—	—	—	—	1,140,333	1.9	—	—
38 People's Party–NPRF	—	—	—	—	—	—	714,652	1.2	—	—
39 Conceptual Party Unity	—	—	—	—	—	—	710,538	1.2	—	—
40 New Course: Automobiles	—	—	—	—	—	—	509,241	0.8	—	—
41 Development of Enterprise	—	—	—	—	—	—	212,825	0.4	—	—
42 Great Russia-Eurasia Union	—	—	—	—	—	—	170,786	0.3	—	—
43 Fair Russia	—	—	—	—	—	—	—	—	5,383,639	7.7
44 Civic Strength	—	—	—	—	—	—	—	—	733,604	1.1
Others[1]	—	—	4,582,114	6.6	1,953,556	2.9	1,045,354	1.7	769,500	1.1
Against all	2,267,963[2]	3.9	1,918,151[2]	2.8	2,198,667	3.3	2,851,600	4.7	—[3]	—
Invalid ballots	3,946,002	6.8	1,320,619	1.9	1,296,992	1.9	948,411	1.6	759,929	1.1

Sources: CEC, 1994, 1995, 1999, 2003, 2008.

[1] Includes: 1995: 24 parties winning less than 1.0 per cent of the list vote or fewer than 2 SMD seats; 1999: 7 parties winning less than 1.0 per cent of the list vote or no SMD seats; 2003: 7 parties winning less than 1.0 per cent of the vote or no SMD seats; 2007: 2 parties winning less than 1.0 per cent of the list vote. [2] Votes against all for 1993 and 1995 are calculated by subtraction. [3] The option to vote 'against all' was abolished before the 2007 election.

Table 17.5b RUSSIA: Votes in Single-Member Districts for the Duma

	1993		1995		1999		2003	
	SMD	%	SMD	%	SMD	%	SMD	%
Electorate	105,209,671		107,496,856		107,633,708		108,626,485	
Valid Votes	53,246,321	50.6	67,585,707	62.9	64,865,922	60.3	58,975,063	54.3
Invalid Votes	4,248,927	4.0	1,582,227	1.4	1,429,779	1.3	1,247,491	1.1
Total Votes	57,495,248	54.6	69,167,934	64.3	66,295,701	61.6	60,222,554	55.4
1 Liberal Democratic Party	1,577,400	2.7	3,729,091	5.4	1,026,690	1.5	1,849,645	3.1
2 Russia's Choice	3,630,799	6.3	1,819,330	2.6	—	—	—	—
3 Communist Party	1,848,888	3.2	8,682,989	12.6	8,893,547	13.4	6,522,158	10.8
4 Women of Russia	309,378	0.5	712,072	1.0	326,884	0.5	—	—
5 Agrarian Party of Russia	2,877,610	5.0	4,066,214	5.9	—	—	1,044,735	1.7
6 Yabloko	1,849,120	3.2	2,209,945	3.2	3,289,760	5.0	1,593,618	2.6
7 Russian Unity and Concord	1,443,454	2.5	285,654	0.4	—	—	—	—
8 Democratic Party of Russia	1,094,066	1.9	—	—	—	—	94,810	0.2
9 Movement for Dem. Reforms	1,083,063	1.9	—	—	—	—	—	—
10 Civic Union	1,526,115	2.7	—	—	—	—	—	—
11 Future of Russia	411,426	0.7	—	—	—	—	—	—
12 Greens	301,266	0.5	304,896	0.4	112,167	0.2	69,585	0.1
13 Dignity and Charity	445,168	0.8	—	—	—	—	—	—
14 Our Home Is Russia	—	—	3,781,450	5.5	1,733,257	2.6	—	—
15 Communists of the USSR	—	—	1,248,577	1.8	439,770	0.7	85,999	0.1
16 Congress Rus. Communities	—	—	1,987,665	2.9	461,069	0.7	—	—
17 Workers' Self-Government	—	—	475,007	0.7	—	—	—	—
18 Great Power	—	—	420,860	0.6	—	—	—	—
19 Forward Russia!	—	—	1,054,577	1.5	—	—	—	—
20 Power to the People!	—	—	1,345,905	1.9	—	—	—	—
21 Union of Labour	—	—	619,347	0.9	—	—	—	—
22 Pamfilova–Gurov–Lysenko	—	—	476,721	0.7	—	—	—	—

23 Ivan Rybkin Bloc	—	—	1,067,477	1.5	—	—	—	—
24 Stanislav Govorukhin Bloc	—	—	483,281	0.7	—	—	—	—
25 Unity	—	—	—	—	1,408,801	2.1	—	—
35 United Russia	—	—	—	—	—	—	13,997,286	23.2
26 Fatherland–All Russia	—	—	—	—	5,670,169	8.6	—	—
27 Union of Right Forces	—	—	—	—	2,016,294	3.0	1,764,290	2.9
28 Party of Pensioners	—	—	—	—	480,087	0.7	295,098	0.5
29 For Citizens' Dignity	—	—	—	—	147,611	0.2	—	—
30 Movement for the Army	—	—	—	—	466,176	0.7	—	—
31 Nikolaev–Fedorov Bloc	—	—	—	—	676,437	1.0	—	—
32 Russian People's Union	—	—	—	—	700,976	1.1	—	—
33 Russian Socialist Party	—	—	—	—	662,030	1.0	—	—
34 Spiritual Heritage	—	—	—	—	609,349	0.9	—	—
36 Motherland	—	—	—	—	—	—	1,719,147	2.9
37 Rebirth of Russia–Life	—	—	—	—	—	—	1,584,904	2.6
38 People's Party–NPRF	—	—	—	—	—	—	2,677,889	4.4
39 Conceptual Party Unity	—	—	—	—	—	—	9,334	0.0
40 New Course: Automobiles	—	—	—	—	—	—	222,090	0.4
41 Development of Enterprise	—	—	—	—	—	—	237,527	0.4
42 Great Russia-Eurasian Union	—	—	—	—	—	—	464,602	0.8
Others[1]	377,863[2]	0.7	4,572,334	6.6	388,285	0.6	874,148	1.5
Independents	25,961,405	45.2	21,580,876	31.2	27,661,392	41.7	16,123,200	26.8
Against all	8,509,300[3]	14.8	6,661,439[2]	9.6	7,695,171	11.6	7,744,998	12.9
Invalid ballots	4,248,927	7.4	1,582,227	2.3	1,429,779	2.2	1,247,491	2.1

Sources: CEC, 1996: 157–98; 1999a; 2003a; SMD votes in 1993 aggregated from machine-readable file based on data supplied by the Central Electoral Commission. Party affiliations as listed in CEC, 1993.

[1] Includes: 1995: 24 parties winning less than 1 per cent of the list vote or fewer than 2 SMD seats; 1999: 8 parties winning less than 1 per cent of the list vote or no SMD seats; 2003: 8 parties winning less than 1 per cent of the list vote or no SMD seats.

[2] Calculated by subtraction. [3] Estimated from the percentage of the total vote reported by McFaul and Petrov, 1998: 393.

Table 17.5c RUSSIA: Number of Seats in the Duma

	1993			1995			1999			2003			2007
	List	SMD seats: cands	All	List	SMD seats: cands	All	List	SMD seats: cands	All	List	SMD seats: cands	All	
1 Liberal Democratic Party	59	5:51	64	50	1:184	51	17	0:95	17	36	1:171	37	40
2 Russia's Choice	40	30:88	70	0	9:72	9	—	—	—	—	—	—	—
3 Communist Party	32	16:98	48	99	58:130	157	67	46:129	113	40	12:169	52	57
4 Women of Russia	21	2:6	23	0	3:20	3	0	0:11	0	—	—	—	—
5 Agrarian Party of Russia	21	12:47	33	0	20:87	20	—	—	—	0	2:59	2	0
6 Yabloko	20	3:88	23	31	14:69	45	16	4:114	20	0	4:89	4	0
7 Russian Unity and Concord	18	1:71	19	0	1:23	1	—	—	—	—	—	—	—
8 Democratic Party of Russia	14	1:63	15	—	—	—	—	—	—	0	0:8	0	0
9 Movement for Dem. Reforms	0	4:59	4	—	—	—	—	—	—	—	—	—	—
10 Civic Union–GSSSP	0	1:74	1	—	—	—	—	—	—	—	—	—	—
11 Future of Russia	0	1:36	1	—	—	—	—	—	—	—	—	—	—
12 Greens	0	0:23	0	0	0:19	0	—	0:14	0	0	0:7	0	—
13 Dignity and Charity	0	2:15	2	—	—	—	—	—	—	—	—	—	—
14 Our Home Is Russia	—	—	—	45	10:103	55	0	7:90	7	—	—	—	—
15 Communists of the USSR	—	—	—	0	1:64	1	0	0:20	0	—	0:9	0	—
16 Congress Rus. Communities	—	—	—	0	5:90	5	0	1:45	1	—	—	—	—
17 Workers' Self-Government	—	—	—	0	1:27	1	—	—	—	—	—	—	—
18 Great Power	—	—	—	0	0:25	0	—	—	—	—	—	—	—
19 Forward Russia!	—	—	—	0	3:67	3	—	—	—	—	—	—	—
20 Power to the People!	—	—	—	0	9:41	9	—	—	—	—	—	—	—
21 Union of Labour	—	—	—	0	1:40	1	—	—	—	—	—	—	—
22 Pamfilova–Gurov–Lysenko	—	—	—	0	2:33	2	—	—	—	—	—	—	—
23 Ivan Rybkin Bloc	—	—	—	0	3:64	3	—	—	—	—	—	—	—
24 Stanislav Govorukhin Bloc	—	—	—	0	1:25	1	—	—	—	—	—	—	—

25 Unity	—	—	—	—	—	—	64	9:31	73	—	—	—	—
35 United Russia	—	—	—	—	—	—	—	—	—	120	103:136	223	315
26 Fatherland–All Russia	—	—	—	—	—	—	37	31:90	68	—	—	—	—
27 Union of Right Forces	—	—	—	—	—	—	24	5:66	29	0	3:90	3	0
28 Party of Pensioners	—	—	—	—	—	—	0	1:28	1	0	0:24	0	—
29 For Citizens' Dignity	—	—	—	—	—	—	0	0:13	0	—	—	—	—
30 Movement for the Army	—	—	—	—	—	—	0	2:19	2	—	—	—	—
31 Nikolaev–Fedorov Bloc	—	—	—	—	—	—	0	1:67	1	—	—	—	—
32 Russian People's Union	—	—	—	—	—	—	0	2:27	2	—	—	—	—
33 Russian Socialist Party	—	—	—	—	—	—	0	1:62	1	—	—	—	—
34 Spiritual Heritage	—	—	—	—	—	—	0	1:107	1	—	—	—	—
36 Motherland	—	—	—	—	—	—	—	—	—	29	9:49	38	—
37 Rebirth of Russia–Life	—	—	—	—	—	—	—	—	—	0	3:98	3	—
38 People's Party–NPRF	—	—	—	—	—	—	—	—	—	0	17:45	17	—
39 Conceptual Party Unity	—	—	—	—	—	—	—	—	—	0	0:4	0	—
40 New Course: Automobiles	—	—	—	—	—	—	—	—	—	0	1:10	1	—
41 Development of Enterprise	—	—	—	—	—	—	—	—	—	0	1:14	1	—
42 Great Russia-Eurasian Union	—	—	—	—	—	—	—	—	—	0	1:60	1	—
43 Fair Russia	—	—	—	—	—	—	—	—	—	—	—	—	38
44 Civic Strength	—	—	—	—	—	—	—	—	—	—	—	—	0
Others	0	0	0	0	6[1]:389	6	0	0:56	0	0	0:172	0	0
Independents	—	146: 873	146	—	77: 1055	77	—	114: 1149	114	—	68: 681	68	0
Total[2]	225	224[3]: 1,592	449	225	225: 2,627	450	225	225: 2,233	450	225	225: 1,895	450	450

Sources: CEC, 1994; 1996: 90–91, 154; 1999; 1999a; 2003; 2003a; 2008.

[1] Six parties winning 1 single-member seat each. [2] Totals include results of repeat ballots held in 8 districts after the 1999 election and 3 after 2003. [3] No SMD deputy elected in the Chechen Republic owing to the political situation.

Table 17.5d RUSSIA: Percentage of Seats in the Duma

	1993			1995			1999			2003			2007
	List	SMD	Total	List	SMD	Total	List	SMD	Total	List	SMD	Total	
1 Liberal Democratic Party	26.2	2.2	14.3	22.2	0.4	11.3	7.6	0	3.8	16.0	0.4	8.2	8.9
2 Russia's Choice	17.8	13.4	15.6	0	4.0	2.0	—	—	—	—	—	—	—
3 Communist Party	14.2	7.1	10.7	44.0	25.8	34.9	29.8	20.4	25.1	17.8	5.3	11.6	12.7
4 Women of Russia	9.3	0.9	5.1	0	1.3	0.7	0	0	0	—	—	—	—
5 Agrarian Party of Russia	9.3	5.4	7.3	0	8.9	4.4	—	—	—	0	0.9	0.4	0
6 Yabloko	8.9	1.3	5.1	13.8	6.2	10.0	7.1	1.8	4.4	0	1.8	0.9	0
7 Russian Unity and Concord	8.0	0.4	4.2	0	0.4	0.2	—	—	—	—	—	—	—
8 Democratic Party of Russia	6.2	0.4	3.3	—	—	—	—	—	—	0	0	0	0
9 Movement for Dem. Reforms	0	1.8	0.9	—	—	—	—	—	—	—	—	—	—
10 Civic Union–GSSSP	0	0.4	0.2	—	—	—	—	—	—	—	—	—	—
11 Future of Russia	0	0.4	0.2	—	—	—	—	—	—	—	—	—	—
12 Greens	0	0	0	0	0	0	—	0	0	0	0	0	—
13 Dignity and Charity	0	0.9	0.4	—	—	—	—	—	—	—	—	—	—
14 Our Home Is Russia	—	—	—	20.0	4.4	12.2	0	3.1	1.6	—	—	—	—
15 Communists of the USSR	—	—	—	0	0.4	0.2	0	0	0	—	0	0	—
16 Congress R. Communities	—	—	—	0	2.2	1.1	0	0.4	0.2	—	—	—	—
17 Workers' Self-Government	—	—	—	0	0.4	0.2	—	—	—	—	—	—	—
18 Great Power	—	—	—	0	0	0	—	—	—	—	—	—	—
19 Forward Russia!	—	—	—	0	1.3	0.7	—	—	—	—	—	—	—
20 Power to the People!	—	—	—	0	4.0	2.0	—	—	—	—	—	—	—
21 Union of Labour	—	—	—	0	0.4	0.2	—	—	—	—	—	—	—
22 Pamfilova–Gurov–Lysenko	—	—	—	0	0.9	0.4	—	—	—	—	—	—	—
23 Ivan Rybkin Bloc	—	—	—	0	1.3	0.7	—	—	—	—	—	—	—
24 Stanislav Govorukhin Bloc	—	—	—	0	0.4	0.2	—	—	—	—	—	—	—

25 Unity	—	—	—	—	—	—	28.4	4.0	16.2	—	—	—	—
35 United Russia	—	—	—	—	—	—	—	—	—	53.3	45.8	49.6	70.0
26 Fatherland–All Russia	—	—	—	—	—	—	16.4	13.8	15.1	—	—	—	—
27 Union of Right Forces	—	—	—	—	—	—	10.7	2.2	6.4	0	1.3	0.7	0
28 Party of Pensioners	—	—	—	—	—	—	0	0.4	0.2	0	0	0	—
29 For Citizens' Dignity	—	—	—	—	—	—	0	0	0	—	—	—	—
30 Movement for the Army	—	—	—	—	—	—	0	0.9	0.4	—	—	—	—
31 Nikolaev–Fedorov Bloc	—	—	—	—	—	—	0	0.4	0.2	—	—	—	—
32 Russian People's Union	—	—	—	—	—	—	0	0.9	0.4	—	—	—	—
33 Russian Socialist Party	—	—	—	—	—	—	0	0.4	0.2	—	—	—	—
34 Spiritual Heritage	—	—	—	—	—	—	0	0.4	0.2	—	—	—	—
36 Motherland	—	—	—	—	—	—	—	—	—	12.9	4.0	8.4	—
37 Rebirth of Russia–Life	—	—	—	—	—	—	—	—	—	0	1.3	0.7	—
38 People's Party–NPRF	—	—	—	—	—	—	—	—	—	0	7.6	3.8	—
39 Conceptual Party Unity	—	—	—	—	—	—	—	—	—	0	0	0	—
40 New Course: Automobiles	—	—	—	—	—	—	—	—	—	0	0.4	0.2	—
41 Development of Enterprise	—	—	—	—	—	—	—	—	—	0	0.4	0.2	—
42 Great Russia-Eurasian Union	—	—	—	—	—	—	—	—	—	0	0.4	0.2	—
43 Fair Russia	—	—	—	—	—	—	—	—	—	—	—	—	8.4
44 Civic Strength	—	—	—	—	—	—	—	—	—	—	—	—	0
Others	0	0	0	0	2.7	1.3	0	0	0	0	0	0	0
Independents	—	65.2	32.5	—	34.2	17.1	—	50.7	25.3	—	30.2	15.1	—

www.ingramcontent.com/pod-product-compliance
Lightning Source LLC
Chambersburg PA
CBHW072056020426
42334CB00017B/1534

* 9 7 8 0 9 5 5 8 2 0 3 2 8 *